REVELATION

BE INFORMED. BE PREPARED.
BE BLESSED.

A. G. Lieb

For my children,
and my children's children.
Proverbs 13:22a

Table of Contents

Author's Preface

After the initial two to three readings of the book of Revelation, I understood the narrative message of the Revelation. The question was, what to do with it. I started asking some question of those who were in my sphere of study and conversation. Wow! Anything from overflowing interest to abject indifference, with mostly controversy in the middle. This study is my contribution to the debate. It is part of my legacy of many years of enjoyable and rewarding personal Bible study. I can testify to the blessing of reading and hearing the book of Revelation. My passion is for people to be equipped, mature, prepared, and sustained. Some of the content of this commentary may end up being hay, wood, and stubble. My hope is that some of the content of this study book will add gold, silver, and precious stones to the understanding of others (Daniel 12:3).

A. G. Lieb

Book cover by C. C. Warrens

If any insights, observations, or questions about this book or its contents, the author can be reached or contacted at **wildbranchpublishing@gmail.com**.

Introduction

The book of Revelation was written for the benefit of the followers of Jesus Christ. Revelation contains encouragement to persevere for those who are obedient, and warning for those who have bought into the ways of the world. The book of Revelation draws a sharp contrast between the way of following Christ, which will draw persecution, and going along with the wisdom and ways of the world, which allows people to exist with little or no resistance. We in the West know little about persecution, enjoying the relative freedoms and liberties of life. We are not required to conform, to any large degree, to the demands of despots, dictators, and oppressive political-religious systems. The more we follow the ways of Christ, and the more a deceptive world-system encroaches upon our ability to do so, the more we will find the message of the book of Revelation relevant to our brief experience of life in these earthly bodies. The book of Revelation reveals Jesus Christ as He is now, and how the current wisdom of the world and what is behind it is leading the cosmic opposition to Him and the Gospel. Revelation foretells a consummation of history, when each person will be required to declare their allegiance to whom they truly worship. It may be at that point, when we are under persecution for our faith, that we will truly desire and come to know what the book of Revelation contains. God is always moving forward. The world is headed for a day of redemption for some, and judgement for others.

The Root of the Issue

When one looks across the schedule of the average church calendar, what event takes up the most effort in preparation, time, resources, and thought? It most likely is the Christmas season. A concerted effort of a particular keystone of our faith, the resurrection, is focused upon at Easter. But that season is short lived in comparison. It is not that these are unimportant. Certainly, without the resurrection our faith is meaningless. But what is the knowledge of the average Christian about Who Jesus is *now*! What is He doing *now*? Most visitors walk away knowing that there was a baby Jesus, and they know that there was a man killed and raised from the dead. Do we know that Jesus is the ascended Lord of all creation, and that He is going to return as a warrior King? Do we live as if He is going to hold each and every creature accountable for each and every thought, word, and deed?

The book of Revelation completes our revealed theology about God. The book of Revelation informs our theology about Christ and His present-tense activity. The early church did not focus on the birth of Christ in their worship. They focused on the saving work of Jesus in His death on the cross, His burial, and His resurrection. They also focused on His being raised and ascended to be the Lord of glory, His work today, and that He will return to set up an eternal kingdom. Indeed, almost every book of the New Testament contains some reference to the return of Jesus. When we pray the prayer Jesus taught, we say, "Thy kingdom come." When we celebrate communion, we are to remember what Jesus did (past), as often as we eat (present), until He comes again (future). Many Christmas hymns even have "second coming" language included in them. The New Testament context is written to provide encouragement and practical precepts for the believer to endure, overcome, and persevere. This encouragement is weak if we do not see it as a means of promoting Godly behavior in light of His return. The

Gospel itself has a future dynamic to its proclamation message. The book of Revelation has an individual, as well as corporate, dimension to its message. It gives encouragement as well as an ultimatum.

Is the Bible narrative really true?

That is the question that is asked or thought, directly or indirectly, out loud or in secret. The short answer is, "Yes!" Then what makes the Bible true? The Bible declares its' veracity. There are many elements that could be brought to bear to answer that question. Just one of those elements is predictive prophecy. It has been stated by different scholars that the Bible contains anywhere from twenty-seven to thirty-one percent of its content as predictive prophecy. Predictive prophecy is a message or an event, given by God, that will come to pass. Many of the prophecies that are contained in the Bible have come to pass and have been fulfilled. There are many prophecies that have yet to be fulfilled. Much of the current debate centers on which prophecies are yet to be fulfilled. Some of them involved particular, individual people, while others concerned nations or people groups. Some prophecies had short term timelines, while others stretch into the distant future. If all of the prophecies concerning the past have been fulfilled, then we can conclude that all the prophecies concerning the future will also be fulfilled. The more you understand what the Bible reveals and declares, the more you will see how God is moving, and the more you will discern the opposition against His message and plan.

Is the return of Jesus certain and definite?

How many of the prophecies of Jesus' first coming have been fulfilled? All of them! There were many convincing truths (Luke 1:1-4; John 21:24-25). How many, then, of the prophecies concerning His second coming will be fulfilled? All of them!! This is an important place to begin with a book like this. If, as many in our culture and associations maintain, the Bible is not applicable to our place and time, then the prophecies contained in the Bible will be viewed as irrelevant in how we should then live, act, and make our decisions. There *will* be a return of Jesus. He *will* issue a complete and dramatic reversal of that which has been fallen. We have a sober responsibility to live and proclaim these truths. Jesus' first coming was historical and real. His second coming will be the same. Our expectations

must be based on good, reliable truth, not on superstition or sensationalism.

What is our responsibility?

The return of Jesus is mentioned many places in Scripture. There are many characteristics and details given as the signs of His coming. We are to recognize the signs appropriately. There are many, many books written over the course of time that have addressed Jesus' return in various ways, with a wide range of emphasis. There are those who have been faithful to the text and have been helpful in encouraging further reading and study. But there have also been those, many as of late, who have fostered a disdain and neglect for the subject of the return of Christ. Some have fostered division, unhealthy debate, and have caused separation. There are many who have used a pick-and-choose approach to the book of Revelation to support their interpretation in a very limited historical context. They have neglected the big picture. Speculation and sensationalism abound. Information, speculation, and details that Scripture is silent about must be handled carefully. Conclusions that are in contradiction with other parts of Scripture must be rejected. Cynicism and sarcasm are dangerous attitudes we can fall into concerning the plethora of information about the second coming of Jesus and the book of Revelation. These attitudes can invade our thinking and keep us from being open to receive the truths of the book.

All of the characteristics of our times and the plethora of information that is available is not without design. But it is not God's design in most cases. The enemy plants error, half-truths, and misplaced additions to distract us from the main emphasis. It is the "boy who cried wolf' syndrome in many ways. So many false claims, unsubstantiated from Scripture, have caused a "so what" attitude even within the believing community. Evangelism and the confidence in our mission as a church is watered down for a comfortable orthodoxy. A correct view of Jesus is the only remedy for our complacency and mediocrity. The book of Revelation gives us just what is needed.

We will be held accountable for the information that the Bible contains concerning the return of Jesus. Jesus held the people of His day accountable for times and events of His first coming (Matthew 2:1-6; Luke 19:41-44; 24:25-27). We are told to look for the second coming of Jesus.

Paul, in 1 and 2 Thessalonians, tells his readers to comfort and encourage one another with the words he writes about Jesus' coming again (1 Thessalonians 4:18; 5:11; 2 Thessalonians 2:17). Jesus said to be alert and be watchful, to lift up our head when the redemption is near. God wants us to know what is in the book of Revelation (Amos 3:7). The book of Revelation declares a blessing to those who read and hear the prophecy of the book. It was written to the churches. He who has an ear, must hear it. It models and reinforces our own testimony. Revelation was written to encourage those believers who are, or would be, going through trials and tribulation. John writes as a fellow servant in his current tribulation. Revelation provides hope and expectation for all of these situations and contexts.

In our day, there is an over emphasis on the Nativity, while the Resurrection and Ascension take a back seat. It is true that God came into our world, Immanuel, God with us. But He came to die and restore the relationship that was lost. Many, if not most, find comfort in the Baby, and not in the returning King who will reverse the curse. The book of Revelation is also part of God's word. It cannot be neglected. The enemy does not want us to know Jesus as the Warrior-King who sovereignly controls the days we live in and has defeated Satan once and for all. Satan does not want us to be able to live victoriously in the face of sacrifice, and for the testimony of Jesus and the commandments of God. Satan does not want us to be prepared or hopeful. Satan does not want us to endure, persevere, and overcome. There is plenty of truth in the Bible concerning Jesus' second coming to encourage us towards a responsible life. Dates are not what the Scriptures maintain or promote. Setting dates only allows for misinformation and excuses for neglecting our responsibilities to faithful witness.

So, the immediate place to start is to decide if it is worthwhile to invest time in reading and studying Revelation. Each of us are responsible for the content of the Bible to the extent that we have been given opportunity. If the starting place is to dismiss or reject the Bible or prophecy outright, then at least know what you are rejecting. There are many other books, fiction and non-fiction, that will move your emotions, stir your thoughts, and draw you into the story. There are many non-fiction books that will inspire and motivate. If, however,

there is an interest or curiosity at what will be presented in this book, then continue and be challenged.

It is the goal of this work to draw the extremes of the "hardened view" and the "nominally curious" together. This is not for idle curiosity. The book of Revelation tends to polarize some and discourage others, with a small minority in the middle. We need to have a safe place for the community of faith, and those who will observe, watch, and search for the truth. We need to have a starting point for dialogue and discussion. This does not mean that we find the lowest common denominator and declare that that is where find agreement. Rather, we need to elevate the discussion to the level that maintains the veracity and authenticity of the whole Bible in a coherent, logical, and non-contradictory manner. We must practice the law of non-contradiction.[1] Anything that does not build consistency with the rest of the Bible must be abandoned.

Why another treatise on the book of Revelation? There are so many already! Maybe that is the reason. There *are* so many!! The culture around us is searching for answers in this time of apocalyptic movies and novels. Many people are fearful that history is going nowhere. There will always be error birthed by Satan, trying to pre-empt and counterfeit the truth. There are relevant answers that the book of Revelation contains to correct those errors. There needs to be some fresh thoughts to help bring the dialogue back to the table. There are many perspectives. They can all be wrong, but they cannot all be right. The community of faith cannot afford confusion and polarization any longer. The community of faith cannot afford the political correctness that allows any argument to be included just because it is given. The community of faith cannot afford disunity any longer. Disunity has caused division for too many decades. At the root of this confusion, disunity, and division, is the spirit of the age that has as its' goal the rendering of the truth of the Bible to appear as unclear, ineffective, or just another opinion. The move towards spiritualism and synchronization has infected the church. The wrong views are promoted to keep the people of God from being prepared and effective. There is a kind of division that the Bible maintains (Luke 12:51-53), but not within the body of faith. Likewise, there cannot be a unity, or a community, based on anything less than the Gospel in all of its dynamics.

While unity is what God requires, there is another reason that comes very near to the surface. Purity! If the Bible is the inspired word of God, and if it claims to transform lives, if it is true in its description of the human condition, and if God has provided a solution to that condition and the consummation of time as we know it, then there must be an attempt by the called and faithful people to contribute their input for the edification of all. All must humble themselves for this goal to be achieved.

This exposition on the book of Revelation is my contribution. I am not a Greek or Hebrew scholar (only in my wildest aspirations). Does one need to be a Greek scholar? No. I will leave that to fine authors like Mounce, Swete, Robertson, Bauckham, Aune, et al. A new believer does not need to be a scholar to understand the book of Genesis or the Gospel of John. One does not need to be able to spell every word in the English language if there is a good dictionary, thesaurus, and "spell check." It is hoped that all who read and study, and all who search for truth, would be willing to take the time necessary to make their own contributions. The ground is level for all in this format. We are told in

Scripture to see the Bereans as an example, and to test the spirits to see if they are of the truth. Physical exercise is of some value, but exercising ourselves in sound doctrinal knowledge is even more important. Each of us have the right and the responsibility to challenge and confirm what we hear and read. This book will answer some tough questions. I want to show people *how* to think, not *what* to think. I am looking for other studies that will test my conclusions. I am not arrogant enough to assume that I am the only one to have certain conclusions. My hope is to encourage all others who are quietly faithful, unknown to many, to study, teach, and proclaim their conclusions as well.

I open my study and insights to challenges, critics, and the insights of others. All of these challenges and insights must be backed with Scripture. I will also offer challenges and insights that will test others. John Lennox has stated that, "Exposing our faith to questioning, confirms it."[2] (The vast majority of my bibliography is reading that I did to test my own conclusions.) It is also true that without resistance, there will not be strengthening. I want to know the truth so passionately that I invite the testing. Together, we can truly sharpen and encourage one another. We have an event to prepare for. We cannot let the confusion, indifference, and division of the current times weaken our discipline and devotion to our preparation. We will need to look up the Scripture references included. We will need to think with our minds, and pray for the Holy Spirit to help us understand, believe, and keep the words of the book of Revelation.

The first four chapters of this book deal with the use of the apocalyptic symbolism that Revelation employs, Jesus' use of the phrase "this age and the age to come," the structure of the book of Revelation, and the literary flow of the book of Revelation. All of these are vital to a correct interpretation.

How does the book of revelation portray Jesus as He is now? Setting apart Jesus as Lord, we need to be ready to give a reason for the hope that is within us (1 Peter 3:15). The book of Revelation does both.

1

The Symbols of Revelation

The book of Revelation makes extensive use of symbolism. The very first verse describes *how* the book will be communicated. Symbols are ways of communication that we use all the time. When you think of an eight-sided road sign that is red, you do not have to really look at the words "STOP" that are printed in the middle (unless you are a foreigner or a newer driver). When you see a road sign that communicates the distance to a particular city, you do not stop at the road sign and declare that you "have arrived." The road sign communicates information about where you are headed and how far you need to continue. They are placed to allow you to plan as you move forward. The road sign is real, but not the reality to which it points. The road sign has a reality of its own, for the level that it was intended. The "reality" for which you are seeking is the city to which you are traveling. I know that the analogy may break down in so many ways, but it does help us as we move forward in this study. The first verse in the book of the Revelation declares that the content of the revelation has been sent, has been *signified*, to John (Revelation 1:1, NKJV). We will discuss signified later in this chapter. A symbol points to something greater and more significant than itself. A national flag is a symbol for a nation. To symbolize does not mean to spiritualize everything, as some claim. But you can symbolize that which is spiritual, IE: The Holy Spirit as a dove. Names can represent a people group or type (Galatians 4:21-27; Revelation 11:8).

The book of Revelation is the revealing of Jesus Christ. The word *apokalypto* is the Greek word from which our English word apocalypse comes. Apokalypto has as it root meaning, to uncover or reveal. The message of the book of Revelation was sent and signified, or signed, to the one writing it down for others to read and hear. From the beginning verses, we have been given the purpose and the method of the communication that will be used. Part of the challenge then is to remember the method of communication used, that is, symbolism and imagery, and then keep in mind Whom the book was meant to reveal. Then we can use those criteria as we read, interpret, and understand what John is writing about.

There are a few times that the symbols are interpreted for us within the text. The reader must be careful not to miss these. Most of the time we are challenged to discover the reality to which the symbols or imagery point. Part of the problem is in this nature of apocalyptic writing. This kind of writing sometimes is used to conceal the message to most readers. There can be many reasons for this. First, it is written only for an intended audience. In many ways, it could be related to parables (see Matthew 13:10-17). Second, apocalyptic writing always tends to point to some consummation of a measure of time or of judgement. One of the important dynamics of the book of Revelation is that it has almost endless allusions to previous situations and writings. Almost all of the allusions can be found in the Old Testament of the Bible. Therefore, it is true that the one who studies the book of Revelation must, or will develop, a thorough knowledge of the Old Testament.

We can read many interpretations and commentaries on the book of Revelation. At times, these commentaries jump from a literalistic approach to a symbolic approach, and sometimes a combination of the two. It is always interesting to hear or read a staunch view that something must be interpreted in a literal way, but then the same author will switch to a symbolic interpretation because the obvious picture that is being portrayed must be so understood. Then they will use contemporary examples to explain an element that the original readers would never have had a clue about, and many times is too unrealistic for even the current reader to imagine as well. One perspective that must be remembered when reading the book of Revelation is that the original readers would have indeed understood all that was presented. How else would they have been blessed and encouraged? The recipients of the book of Revelation in the first century did not have to speculate about what the symbols meant. This may sound like a bold statement. But they knew the Old Testament and the allusions and inferences to it. Whatever John actually saw, the details build up an impression which is not visual so much as auditory and dynamic. To the Greeks, beauty was visual (harmonious order), and the Hebrews were interested in the dynamic impression which the descriptions conveyed, through ear rather than eye.[1]

The book claims, both at the beginning and at the end, to bless the one who reads and hears the words of the book (Revelation 1:3; 22:17). How could the original readers receive a blessing if the understanding were not present? The church today, in general practice, does not invest enough time in knowing the types and interlocking meta-narratives of the Old Testament to understand the book of Revelation. This takes some hard work and thought.

The book of Revelation was *signified,* and that fact is important to the interpretation and understanding of its' message. The English word signified has the related Greek word "*semeion,*" which is many times translated as "sign." (S*emaino,* the Greek word used in the book of Revelation means to give a sign, that is, signify). Jesus did signs, not only for the signs themselves, but to point to something greater, who He was, and why He did them. Many of the people who followed Him did so because of the signs and miracles He performed. The signs and miracles, very real in themselves, were not the goal. When the people did not acknowledge what, or Who was behind the signs and miracles, He chastised them for missing the point. When He refused to

do them, many turned away. The book of Revelation uses many symbols, or signs, that have a reality in themselves. But we are to understand the reality behind the use of the signs. The reality that they signify or indicate. We are told "he who has ears let him hear." That is, there is a truth to understand and grasp as well. There is an outward reality and a deeper theological truth. That is true of the book of Revelation as well as many of the parables that are used in the Bible.

In his commentary on the book of Revelation, G. K. Beale has a very insightful section (pp. 50-64) on symbolic communication where he writes: "a number of authors of both popular and scholarly contend that one should interpret literally except where one is forced to interpret symbolically by clear indications of context. But the results of the analysis of (Revelation) 1:1 indicate that this rule should be turned on its head: we are told in the book's introduction that the majority of the material in it is revelatory symbolism (1:12-20 and 4:1-22:5 at the least). Hence, the predominant manner by which to approach the material will be according to a nonliteral interpretive method. Of course, some parts are not symbolic, but the essence of the book is figurative. Where there is lack of clarity about whether a thing is symbolic, the scales of judgement should be tilted in the direction of a nonliteral analysis."[2] Beale also makes note that the words and meaning in question in Revelation 1:1 are an allusion to Daniel 2:28-30, 45. The use of *semeion* (LXX) in Daniel 2 defines the use in Revelation 1:1 as referring to symbolic communication and not to mere conveyance of information.[3]

It is a criticism of many that a symbolic, metaphorical, or figurative approach to interpretation is to spiritualize the book of Revelation. The claim is that this approach takes the impact and reality away from the text. But many places in the Scriptures use many figures of speech. R. H. Mounce, in his commentary on Revelation states, "symbolism is not a denial of historicity, but a figurative method of communicating reality."[4] It is when we mix these methods that confusion and an incoherent conclusion can result. Joseph and Daniel interpreted dreams. The dreams that they interpreted were of realistic literal images that most of us relate to in our minds. But the dream had a different reality than what the dream visually contained. They

represented a future reality at a different level. In the book of Revelation, we must try our best to maintain consistency.

One can state that if "there are four living creatures with eyes all around, front and back," then that is what is literally existent. Then by principle we must accept a "lamb that has seven eyes and seven horns." But the same interpreter will say the Lamb is Jesus Christ. How do you know? Because the seven eyes *represent*, symbolically, complete omniscience and the seven horns *represent*, symbolically, complete power. Then maybe the four living beings are being described by their characteristics as well (see Ezekiel).

Studying the book of Revelation, as with any book of the Bible, has rewards that are at least equal to the effort that is put into the study itself. Michael Card, an author and composer, has stated that any true study of any book of the Bible will take you into almost every other book of the Bible to some degree. With the Book of Revelation, this is a necessity. There are so many references to the Old Testament. The book of Revelation will not contradict what Jesus Himself taught in His Olivet Discourse concerning last things. In the Olivet discourse Jesus did not contradict anything that the Prophet Daniel was given. On the contrary, He affirmed Daniel and his message.

If I were marooned someplace, and was given the choice of only two books, my two books would be a Bible and an exhaustive concordance. With those two books, you have the equivalent of the most powerful commentary of the Scriptures imaginable. Most of the symbols and imagery used in the book of Revelation are found in the Old Testament. The other needed dynamic of good Bible study is a humble spirit concerning your own limitations. There is no one who has a corner on the truth. Everyone's theology is incomplete at best. We must balance our convictions with a teachable spirit. My own conclusions have at times only come after days,

weeks, months, and even years of study on a topic or item. We will not know all until we get to paradise, where we will know as we are fully known. God does not tell us everything we want to know, but He has given us what we need to know (Deuteronomy 29:29). We are responsible for that. We need to leave room for further understanding from our studies, and from the further studies of others. The book of Daniel informs us that knowledge will increase (Daniel 12:4). Maybe that means that clarity will be given when it is time to know it. We must always be consistent and humble with our interpretation of the book of Revelation.

Be encouraged! When you read the book of Revelation, you do not need to know all about the symbols and imagery to know Who wins!!

2

This Age and the Age to Come

Believers in God the Father, and in His Son Jesus Christ, live in a tension between this age and the age to come. There are many New Testament verses that make a distinction between "this age, and the age to come." Jesus Himself used the terms, and the phrase (Matthew 12:32; 13:39-49; 28:20). How Jesus made the distinction must be a part of any interpretation of the book of Revelation. Jesus only spoke if *this age* and the *age to come.*

A similar concept, "the now, and not yet," can elicit a myriad of similar methods of interpretation. Some things have been inaugurated; others are still yet. There is a level of natural tension that is created between the concept of the 'now," and the "not yet." We may be planning a needed academic path for ourselves or someone else. We may be planning a retirement, or a major change in vocation. We may be positioning our minds and thoughts for some kind of spiritual, physical, or emotional confrontation that we know will inevitably occur. Anything that is known to be in our future but must be waited upon for a season. Most

people of faith, any faith for that matter, live in the tension of the things that are of the "now," in anticipation and hope of the things that are assumed sure, but "not yet."

The wording that we find in the Bible is "this age, and the age to come" (some translations of the Bible use the word world instead of age). There are many elements of existence that must occur until this age is completed. Jesus said He would be with us until the end of the age. Then, there are events like the harvest, that are directly associated with the end of this age. Likewise, there are elements of existence and experience that are associated with the age to come. This tension between the two ages is rarely visited when most Bible studies are conducted. Indeed, our hope in the age to come should give us courage, endurance, and perseverance in this age. How we conduct ourselves in this age, then, will have an impact on our experience in the age to come.

What elements of the book of Revelation are past, or present, or future? How do they fit into this age or the age to come? If we include this concept in our study of the book of Revelation, where should we begin? Any interpretation must address what is included in this age, and what is included in the age to come. Jesus Himself stated that He would be with us *until* the end of the age (Matthew 28:20).

First, we need to remember that we as Christians believe that we have a revealed faith. We believe that God has spoken. We would know nothing of God had not God given us general revelation. We know and read this in the first verses of Genesis chapter one (see also Romans 1:20). We would not know special revelation about ourselves and of our condition and the remedy for it, had not God spoken through the prophets, His Word, and finally in His Son (Hebrews 1:1).

Many people read the Bible to prove the existence of God. The Bible asserts His existence and proceeds from there. We are not given everything we want to know, but we are given everything we need to know (Deuteronomy 30:11-14). We are told in the Old Testament that we are to have a reverent shuddering at His word (Isaiah 66:2b). So many times, we can be guilty of "staunchly" assuming or asserting ideas and conclusions before it is time. A healthy, humble, and systematic exposition of the Scriptures is what is needed to remedy this. This author continually has this in his mind.

This healthy, humble, and systematic approach has at its root the idea that knowledge is not completely known, but is given by God sovereignly, and as His will unfolds. Daniel the prophet was given some of the most comprehensive information on the future, and the plan of God. Even at that he is not given everything. Daniel is told to go his way at the end of his life, rest with his fathers, and that knowledge will increase (Daniel 12:4,9). That Hebrew word for knowledge is the same word that is used most often in the book of Proverbs (Proverbs 1:7; 9:10; see also Hosea 6:6). The Hebrew word used has the idea of discerning, being aware, and of recognizing. We are told to watch for signs. We are told that some who have will be given more, and some who have little, that which they have will be taken away (Matthew 13:12). We are told to ask. There is an element of our responsibility to continually be on the hunt for knowledge, along with understanding God's sovereignty in dispensing it.

How we come to the book of Revelation will determine our blessing when we read and hear it, and our measure of understanding the message of the book. If we are teaching, we should be careful to not adamantly assert insights and conclusion until we have thoroughly exhausted the work of exposition. If we are the learners, and we are all exhorted to be both teachers and learners in some measure, we cannot give up because of the obstacles that are placed in our path. We should all be able to approach those who teach us with Scripture that either confirms their teaching or opposes their teaching. True teachers will always be learners and will always have a desire to edify those who choose to learn.

There are major principles in Scripture, and there are minor principles in Scripture. Though all are important as the inspired Word of God. This age, and the age to come (what is now, and not yet) is a major principle. We are told that all of creation waits for the redemption of the sons of God (Romans 8:19-22). There is something going on "now," that waits for the "not yet" of full redemption. Believers are told that we who have heard, believed, and are in Christ, are given the Holy Spirit as a guarantee of what is to come (Ephesians 1:13-14). We have been given a down payment, the indwelling Spirit, for the purchase to be redeemed in the future. It is the

tension between promise and reality. The author writing to the Hebrews tells his readers that Jesus is sitting at the right hand of God *until* His enemies are made a footstool (Hebrews 1:13). Jesus is reigning now *until* the time of final judgement (John 5:25-28; Acts 2:34-35; 3:20-21; 1 Corinthians 15:25; Hebrews 2:8). We are told that we are partakers in the divine nature, but that one day we will see Him as He is, for we will be like Him (1 John 3:2-3). Paul exhorts believers to live lives of purity, using examples from the experiences of the Old Testament people. He calls his audience, the ones living at his time, of whom the ends of the ages have come (1 Corinthians 10:11). There will be no more ends. Believers are justified, are being sanctified, and will be glorified. We as believers are (always) saved from the penalty of sin, are being (currently) saved from the power of sin, and *will be (but not yet)* saved from the presence of sin. The heavenly Jerusalem exists now, and will descend from heaven in the future (Hebrews 11:10; 12:22; 13:14; Revelation 21-22).

The book of Revelation shows activity and elements of our experience that have been inaugurated at the first coming of Jesus. It also gives the recipients a view of what is happening in this world presently, and what will be our relationship with the next. The book of Revelation gives us (in this age), a glimpse into the mysteries of what God is doing now. This glimpse encourages us with the need to be faithful in our knowledge of our vindication in the future (the age to come). The book of Revelation needs to be studied in light of this major principle: this (present) age of what has already been realized since Jesus' first coming, and the age to come.

There is a plethora of views on the book of Revelation. What is past, and what is still future? The responses to the views are many. Many are aware of the four major ways to interpret the book of Revelation. Then there are overlapping views of these. The Historicist view sees Revelation as surveying church history. The Preterist view sees the book of Revelation as completely fulfilled in the past (AD. 70 and the destruction of Jerusalem is a big part of the view, and there are partial preterists as well). The Futurist view primarily sees everything after chapter three as being fulfilled sometime in the future. The spiritual view (sometimes called the Idealist view), holds that there are no specific fulfillments in the book of Revelation, but rather a theme of the triumph of good over evil, without specific historical events. There are many resources that give explanation and comparisons of these views.

There is also a difference of interpretation for the 1,000 years mentioned in Chapter 20 of the book of Revelation: Premillennial, Postmillennial, and Millennial. Again, there are many resources that can define these. This author has been labeled as one or the other. When reading the definitions given to this point, I cannot find myself comfortable with any of the strictly defined positions.

Then there is the inviting debate about the Rapture. There are the three basic views: Pre-tribulation, Mid-tribulation, and Post-tribulation, with a few modifications within each of these. The position taken in this book will be as follows. First, that Jesus said that heaven and earth will pass away, but the Word of God will *never* pass away. Second, the Word of God must be true for *all believers*, of *all times*, until the earth passes away. Third, there could never be *any believers* who would read the Word of God and not find it true for them (Compare Daniel 12:2-3; Matthew 13:36-43; 25:31-46; 28:20).

When it comes to the four major views on interpreting the book of Revelation, I believe there have been some principles abandoned for the sake of holding a position. This is not across the board, of course. There are a few authors who comment on the Scriptures with an objective and balanced approach. There seems to be an increase of commenting and teaching about the book of Revelation that starts with a specific view being held, and then forcing that view upon the Scriptures. Some pick and choose the verses that hold up their particular view to the neglect of the verses that might force them to modify their teaching. I do not want to address the motivations for this dilemma. It is far better to start with the Scriptures and let the texts develop the view that is correct. Again, they can all be wrong, but they cannot all be right. One important fact often overlooked or forgotten is the view that the book of Revelation was written to encourage current faithfulness and prepare believers for what is in their present context (this age), and to show those same believers their vindication and rewards (the age to come).

This authors' studies have found each view to have some element of truth contained in them. For some, the continuation of insights and understanding has been arrested in favor of a certain conclusion or system. Could it be that we as a faith community have camped out around our most favorite or most liked teacher or view, and have neglected our own study and devotions? There is a problem of Biblical illiteracy in the ranks of believers, as demographic studies have concluded. The same dynamic has happened to some degree in the past with our church membership in the mainline denominations. Godly people during the time of The Reformation brought the church membership back to the Bible. The truths contained were set free by the printing press and by the blood of the reformation martyrs. Then people rallied around their particular reformation father and started a following that resulted in some of our denominational separation. The Bible speaks against this kind of separation. Could it be the reformers would turn in their graves if they knew that the reforming has long ceased for most, and that whole groups of churches and theological thought are named after them? John Calvin did not even want his grave marked.

The same could be said of the different ways of interpreting the book of Revelation. Many times, the discussion goes into listing names and celebrated teachers. Whole denominations hold a particular view instead of referencing the Scriptures. Is there a desire for unity? Is there a desire for purity and veracity? I believe there is. But the indifference of some, and political correctness of others, is not helping.

A discussion, or study, on the book of Revelation sometimes ends with the closing comment: "Well, we will have to agree to disagree." That is a good sentiment on the surface. Is it genuine, or a chance to get away? Some people are emotionally attached to a particular view. Some, do not want to do the work to agree or even risk understanding the opposing study. Most people have acquired their view from some outside source and have not studied it for themselves. All of these dynamics keep maintenance on division within the church, even as the Day approaches. The return of Christ is a conclusion that every believer must hold. The results of His return will issue a reversal of sin, and the end of suffering and death that we can only imagine. The resurrection, reunion,

and eternity that is in store for us, no mind can conceive.

Other discussions in which I have been involved often include the rationale that: the reason for the divisions in interpretation are that: "all of the differing views of the book of Revelation can be defended by Scripture." That perspective is a very dangerous position to hold. Is God the author of division and confusion? There is a difference between exegesis, drawing meaning out of, and eisegeses, reading meaning into. We should be aware of how Satan uses incorrect conclusions.

We believe that the Bible is the Word of God, and therefore, inspired. We are given testimony of that truth in 2 Timothy 3:16, among other references. Concerning the topics at hand, the Apostle Paul writing to the Thessalonians about the end times, gives many of the characteristics and details of the resurrection and the Coming of Jesus. In both letters Paul emphasizes to his readers to "encourage each other with these words." The book of Revelation states at the beginning, and at the end, that those who read and hear the words of the book will be blessed (the only book of the Bible that does so). The question needs to be asked, "If all the views can be defended with the Bible," how do we end up divided and indifferent, instead of encouraged and blessed by a book that is inspired and meant for our instruction? Then there is the bigger issue of the person and nature of God. If all the views can be defended by God's Word, there is an indirect, and overlooked, inference being made that God could be the author of this division and confusion. On the contrary, God is a God of order, not confusion. It is not the Bible that causes confusion, but our misunderstanding and incomplete application of the whole counsel of God that causes confusion. All of us must remember the warning and caution given in James 3:1.

We are told to always be ready to give a defense to everyone who asks you the reason for the hope that is in us (1 Peter 3:15-17). That defense must be given with good conduct. Some of the language I have used may sound harsh to some. In the church, some are called to be in the leadership of others, while all are called to be in submission to Jesus Christ. Those in leadership are also called to encourage with sound doctrine and oppose those who contradict (Titus 1:9). In this age where opposing another's view is labeled negative, we have found ourselves being told to be tolerant. There are areas where tolerance is a virtue. Not with untruth. Truth is exclusive and excluding. Humility before the Word of God is where we need to begin. This has bearing on this age, *and* the age to come.

Be encouraged! Jesus promised to be with us until the end of the age!!

3

The Structure of Revelation

Many are familiar with the web tools and application that allow you to see the earth from different perspectives and altitudes. One that is particularly interesting is the one that starts someplace in space, moves closer and closer, gets more focused and more focused, until you are seeing details as if you are standing on the ground. This is all done in a matter of seconds. Many times, this scenario is used during a spy movie, or a scene where satellite surveillance is necessary to the plot.

Flying or hovering thousands of feet above the earth, we are not able to see enough details to make an educated decision about what activity is happening. Likewise, at ground level the characteristics and details of a location may seem the same or irrelevant if we are not familiar with those details. The bigger picture is needed to get our bearing. We might be lost in the woods and see nothing but trees. A little altitude could help us see our location in the woods, the shortest route out of the woods, and avoid dangers. A little more altitude could even tell us which forest we are in and in what country the forest is located.

Good Bible study has many of the same characteristics as the illustration given above. The three main starting principles of good Bible study are context, context, and context. We can start by picking a book in the Bible to study, and then get its context from where it is placed in the cannon of Scripture. Next, where does it fit within the chronological context of the whole of Scripture, and what kind of literature is it and why it was written. We could then discover who the author is, to whom it was written, and what issues it addresses. Then, when we read the text we would have a better idea of the narrative, principles, and truths that are contained.

In the same reversed way, if we start by picking a verse of Scripture, it is important to know the context. What is the verse before and after? Are we familiar with the context of the paragraph of which the verse is a part? How does the paragraph fit into the chapter? What does the chapter add to the book's message? What does the book add to the testament of which it is a part? How is the book addressing the main emphasis of the Bible as a whole? Where are similar ideas and concepts presented within other parts of the Bible? What does the book contribute to our understanding of the Bible, and our understanding of the author? What is the application to, and for, us? Not all of these questions are conscious paths we need to take each and every time, but all of them are important to be aware of as we humbly pursue our goals of understanding.

The author, date of writing, and critics (good and bad) of the book of Revelation will not be a large part of this book. They are very important for tempering our need for context. Many a fine scholar has done a huge service for us in these areas. Some of these are listed at the end of this book. While these resources are invaluable to the few who wish to have them added to their understanding, the message of the book is little changed by debating the dates of writing and higher criticism issues. However, the date discussion given by John Walvoord based on the internal evidence is convincing.[1]

The message of the book of Revelation is validated and verified by its references to the rest of Scripture. The internal contexts will be the focus of this chapter and the next. The book of Revelation is part of the inspired works included in the cannon of Scripture. That has been settled. Revelation declares, at the beginning, and at the end, that the reader and hearer will receive a blessing. It is the only book that makes such a declaration. If we do not come with that anticipation, the blessing will evade us.

In my study, there has been a principle, or proposition, that I have maintained for some time. I have used it over and over in my Bible study groups. It is this: How we see the book of Revelation unfold as we read will help us to interpret and understand the symbols and the message in its entirety. Therefore, the context of where it is in the cannon, its references and allusions to other parts of Scripture, and the use of symbolic communication contribute greatly in seeing this unfolding occur. The structure of the book is vital. When we are at "10,000 feet," what do we see when looking at the text? Are there patterns and designs (not to be confused with "hidden" codes or messages)? When we are at "30,000 feet," what do we find similar in other books of the Bible?

It must be remembered that the book of Revelation was given to be *read and heard* (Revelation 1:3). It contains three main genres or types of literature. It is a letter, a prophecy, and an apocalypse. When looking at the text as a whole, from an "elevated" perspective there are interesting similarities and often repeated characteristics. There are seven churches, seven seals, seven trumpets, and seven bowls. Revelation has an heptadic structure. It has been suggested that the use of the number seven in Revelation cannot be exhausted. But the churches, seals, trumpets, and bowls seem to be the major content of the book of Revelation. That being said, is the rest of the book narrative historical revelation of these four sets of sevens? Historical revelation of past, present, and future prophecy? What ties these four groups of seven together? How are they related, or interrelated?

Keeping in mind the exhortation to read and to hear the book, there are, as we might surmise, verbal cues that the hearers would be alerted to as the book was read out loud. John states that he was *in the spirit* four times (Revelation 1:10; 4:2; 17:3; 21:10). Each of these instances introduces the major visions that he is given to see. There are three places where there are mentioned the combination of noises, thunderings, lightnings, and an earthquake (Revelation 8:5; 11:16; 16:18). There are three great signs that John beholds (Revelation 12:1; 12:3; and 15:1). These set out the verbal and auditory markers that give a structure to the book. (See below: Diagram #2, Page 31.) The book of Revelation was to be read, so these were important to the listeners as well.

Another element that gives structure to the narrative of the book of Revelation is the use of angels as messengers (See below: Diagram 3A, Page 31). The first verse of the book gives an indication of the way in which this revelation of Jesus Christ is passed along or communicated. There are activities involving angels throughout the book. The angel mentioned at the beginning of the book may be the most significant of the angels in that he seems to be the angel that gives John most of the explanations (compare Revelation 1:1; 5:2; 10:1; 10:9; 19:9-10; 22:6-10). In the book of Revelation, as in other parts of Scripture, messengers often represented the same importance and authority as the ones who sent them. Believers have the same responsibility as being ambassadors for Christ.

Numbers are used throughout the book of Revelation. We use numbers and symbols for counting, and for describing things that cannot be seen with the eye, such as in quantum physics. This is not to be confused with numerology. Numbers in the book of Revelation give us relationships and describe spiritual truths that are important to grasp.

At the top of these is the number seven. The book of Revelation is replete with sevens, or groups of seven. The number seven is most often referred to as the number of completion, or of completeness. God's use of seven may be His fingerprint for His program. On the seventh day God rested. Joseph's dreams are filled with sevens. The year of Jubilee is a culmination of seven sevens. Seven is a pattern in the fall of Jericho. Seven cycles of turning are found in the book of Judges. Daniel is given a prophecy that is based on sevens. In the Gospel of John, Jesus uses seven "I am" statements of Himself. There are seven lamps of the candlestick in the tabernacle. Seven is used to describe complete worship, or complete purification (Psalm 119:164; Daniel 4:16-32). Seven is used as a description of various characteristics being "complete" throughout the book of Revelation.

It is important to study the relationships between the different chapters of the book of Revelation. The first of these is the seven churches. The seven churches represent the complete church in all of its characteristics, existing from the time of the writing of Revelation until the end of the age. Most commentaries and teachings, written or spoken, will separate Chapter 1 from Chapter 2 through 3. We need to remember that the chapter and verse numbers came long after the initial manuscripts. While they are very helpful in locating texts in the Bible, they are not inspired and at times are not placed well and do not aid in understanding the thoughts of some connected passages. It is important to observe that the descriptions of the risen Christ given in Chapter 1:12-17 are then interspersed among the seven churches of Chapters 2 and 3. Each church gets the description appropriate to their need and exhortation. But the Spirit then exhorts, "He who has an ear, let him hear what the Spirit says to the "churches"."

Other items are also part of the passage connecting chapter 1 with chapters 2 and 3. The command to write, the mention of the seven churches (in unity and as a separate churches), the stars in the hand of Christ, and the risen Christ in the midst of the lampstands (His intimate knowledge of their condition). *So, it is possible to read Chapter 1:4 to the end of Chapter 3 as one complete section.* It may be suggested that the reason the seven churches are given first, is because in many cases we need to know that Jesus is concerned about us personally before we are ready and able to see the big picture. We often get so caught up in the details of our experiences that we forget Jesus is in our midst, personally and corporately. One phrase common to each church is the statement that "I know." The churches are either encouraged to continue or exhorted to repent and change.

In this endeavor, it is important to address the interpretation of Revelation 1:19. Many commentators insist that this verse is an outline for the book of Revelation. The command is to write the things which you have seen, and the things which are, and the things that will take place after this (NKJV). I would like to strongly suggest that to see this command as writing about past, present, and future, does not capture the sense of what John is told to communicate. While the English translation surely gives us the impression of the above tripartite impression, the Greek word meanings within the text need to be studied for a thorough understanding. For this apologetic, I will use a passage found in John 20:1-10.

John 20:1-10 is the account of Peter and John being told of the empty tomb, and their resulting race to go and see it. In verse 5, John (the other disciple), is already there first. He stoops down and looking in, saw the linen cloths lying there. In verses 6-7 Simon Peter went into the tomb; and saw the linen cloths lying there, and the face cloth folded and lying separate from the rest. Then, in verse 8, the other disciple, that came into the tomb first, went in, saw, and believed.

Verse 5 – John, *looking into* - (Greek word *parakupto)* - to stoop to look into.

Verse 5 – John *saw* the linen – (Greek word *blepo)* - to look at, have sight, to regard.

Verse 6 – Peter *saw* the linen - (Greek word *theoreo)* - careful perusal of details, to behold, to contemplate.

Verse 8 – John, going in also, _saw_ and believed – (Greek word _eido)_ - to know in fulness, recognize, to grasp as reality, to understand, (personally-that is, he believed).

We might hear or use the phrase, "Do you see what this means?" What we are really asking is, "Do you grasp, or understand, the full implications of the situation?"

It is interesting that the Greek words bring distinction and progression to the narrative of John 20:5-8 that the English translation does not. The same Greek word found in John 20:8, _eido_, is used in Revelation 1:19. Thus, the intention of the command in verse 19, which is an expansion of the command in verse 11 (see from the visions given), may be understood as; "Therefore, write the things which you have grasped as reality and understood in their fullness, even _the things_ which are, and (also) _the things_ which shall be hereafter in the last days. John is told to write about two items, the things which are and the things that will be. The English "the things," is not in the Greek text. If there is a tripartite pattern to the book of Revelation, it is not found from this verse.

The evidence for present and future things is also in chapters 2-3. The evidence for past, present, and future events is also part of everything depicted beyond Chapter 4:1 (see Revelation 12). Said another way, some parts of chapters 2 and 3 deal with the future, and some events of chapters 4 through 22 deal with the past.[2] Coming to a study with a preconception, as with this verse, will keep us from seeing some of the important conclusions we need to understand. We must let the book unfold properly on its own.

Chapter 4 begins the vision of the next set of seven, the seals. It is a change in panorama, not chronology.[3] Chapter 4:1 introduces again what John first experienced by hearing the voice like a trumpet (chapter 1:10). He is told to "come up here" to be shown what must take place after this, in the last days. If this is correct, it is coherent with other passages of an inaugurated (already begun) flavor concerning the time of Christ's first coming until the end of the age, as _being_ the last days (see Matthew 28:20; 2 Timothy 3:1; Hebrews 1:2, 9:26).

Is the last part of chapter 4:1 telling us that the beginning of the last things is going to be described in chapters 4 and 5? Here again, the chapter and verse heading can get in the way of the continuing context. It should be obvious that Chapters 4 and 5 are a continuous picture. But there is a direct connection to Chapter 6. First, to see Chapters 4 and 5 as yet future violates many other portions of Scripture as to the exaltation of Jesus Christ. There is no event yet to occur that gives, or can give, any more authority and reign to Jesus beyond His resurrection and ascension at the time of His first coming (see Matthew 28:18; John 17:5; Acts 2:34-36; 7:54-56; Philippians 2:5-11; Colossians 1:13-18; Hebrews 1:1-3; and Revelation 3:21). What chapters 4 and 5 represent is exactly that event, His exaltation.

Secondly, the connection to chapter 6 is apparent because it is the same Lamb (notice the seven horns and seven eyes, chapter 5:6), who was worthy to take the scroll and open it. The Lamb is opening the seals in chapters 6-8:5. The living creatures, among other elements, are also a connection to chapter 6. Chapters 4-5 are describing an event of inauguration: the exaltation and authority of Jesus Christ. It is past tense for John on Patmos, and certainly for the readers of the book of Revelation. This second set of seven,

the seals, ends with noises, lightnings, thunderings, and an earthquake. So, this section, the scroll and the seals, begins at chapter 4:1 and concludes at chapter 8:5.

The third set of sevens, the trumpets, begins at chapter 8:6 and ends in chapter 11:19, and is connected from within the seventh seal. The trumpets are in themselves a revelation that ends the same way the seals end, but with a little more detail. The magnitude, intensity, and scope increases. While the seals end with the altar and noises, lightnings, thunderings, and an earthquake, the seventh trumpet ends a little farther into the tabernacle setting with a view of the Ark of His Covenant. We then read about lightnings, noises, thunderings, an earthquake, and great hail. The scope, intensity, and magnitude are increased.

The fourth set of sevens, the bowls, is not textually next in the reading. It is important, however, to note that there are connections to the trumpets that cannot be missed. The fifth trumpet is called the first woe. The resurrection of the two witnesses is associated with the second woe. The bowls end in the same manner as the seals and the trumpets. Are the bowls the third woe? We are not given a text within the book that specifically tells us the identity of the third woe. We are told in chapters 15 and 16 that with the bowls the wrath of God is complete. In chapter 15:5 the Ark is open, and the seven angels holding the bowls are bid to act. When the seventh bowl is poured out (chapter 16:18), there are noises, lightnings, thunderings, an earthquake, and great hail. The details again are increased and intensified. And they are final.

With the activity at the end of the seals, the trumpets, and the bowls being relatively consistent, the question must be asked: Are there three separate endings in these series of sevens, or is it the same ending given three times? Are the endings related in a somewhat concurrent design? This author maintains a view that the endings are the same single ending, with more detail as the narrative unfolds and the focus and magnitude and intensity is increased.

It is the design of the text to have the seven bowls unfold within the seventh trumpet, and the seven trumpets as activity of the seventh seal (as is seen in reverse order). We can see this same pattern in action with Joshua and the Israelites marching around

the city of Jericho for seven days. On the seventh day, they marched around the city seven times (Joshua 6). The prophet Ezekiel is given the same pattern of judgement when he sees the wheel within a wheel (Ezekiel 1:16). (A similar pattern of sevens is seen when understanding the Sabbath day in relation to the Sabbath years and the year of Jubilee.) (See below: Diagram #1 - relationship of seals to trumpets to bowls, Page 30.) It could almost be associated with a computer program where we see the platform of a window, within a window, within a window.

This is the most obvious observation of the events that unfold within the book of Revelation. There are 4 major series of seven. The rest of the text is narrative that gives encouragement and explanation to these 4 sets of seven. There are also 4 significant times that John is in the spirit, and there are 3 great signs that John beholds (See below: Diagrams 3B and 3C, Page 32). Why so much text between the seventh trumpet and the seven bowls? That is the discussion of the next chapter.

Be encouraged! The Holy Spirit will help us see the story of Revelation!!

Diagram #1

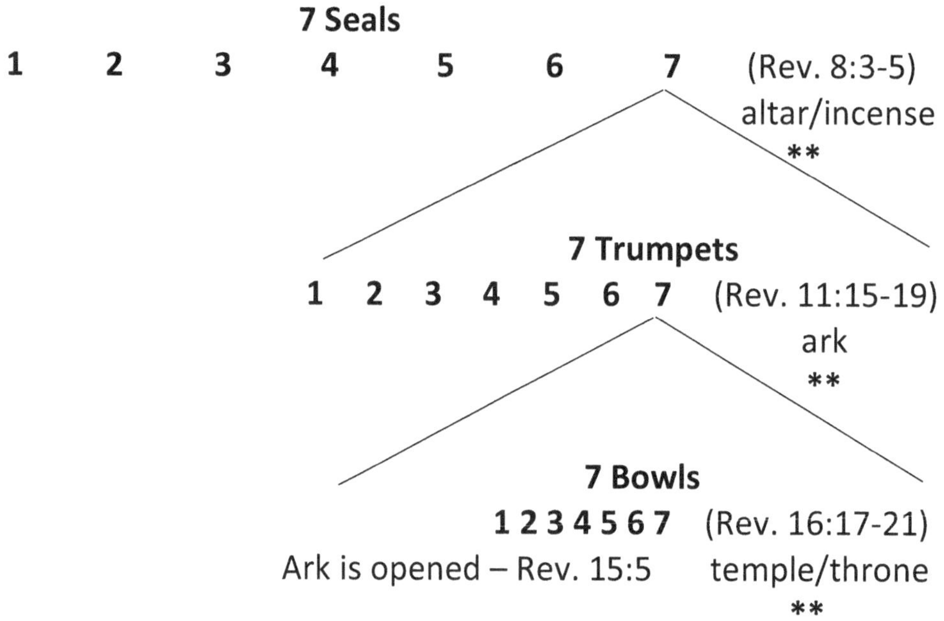

7 Seals

1   2   3   4   5   6   7   (Rev. 8:3-5)
altar/incense
**

7 Trumpets

1 2 3 4 5 6 7 (Rev. 11:15-19)
ark
**

7 Bowls

1 2 3 4 5 6 7 (Rev. 16:17-21)
Ark is opened – Rev. 15:5   temple/throne
**

(**) = Noises, Lightnings, Thunderings, Earthquake.
Hail is associated with 7th trumpet and 7th bowl.

Within the literary structure of the book there are seven churches, seven seals, seven trumpets, and seven bowls. The seventh seal consists of the seven trumpets, and seventh trumpet consists of the seven bowls. (In reverse order, the seven bowls are part of the seventh trumpet, and the seven trumpets are part of the seventh seal.) This could be called a form of recapitulation. Each series of seven occurs within a shorter time-span. The seventh of each series represents the end of this age. Also, the seventh of each series contains similar characteristics and descriptions that increase in scope, magnitude, and intensity. There is a successive movement from a position outside the holy of holies (7th seal), to in front of the altar of incense (7th trumpet), into the Holy of Holies where the Ark of the Covenant is seen (7th bowl).

Diagram #2

The Literary Structure of the Book of Revelation

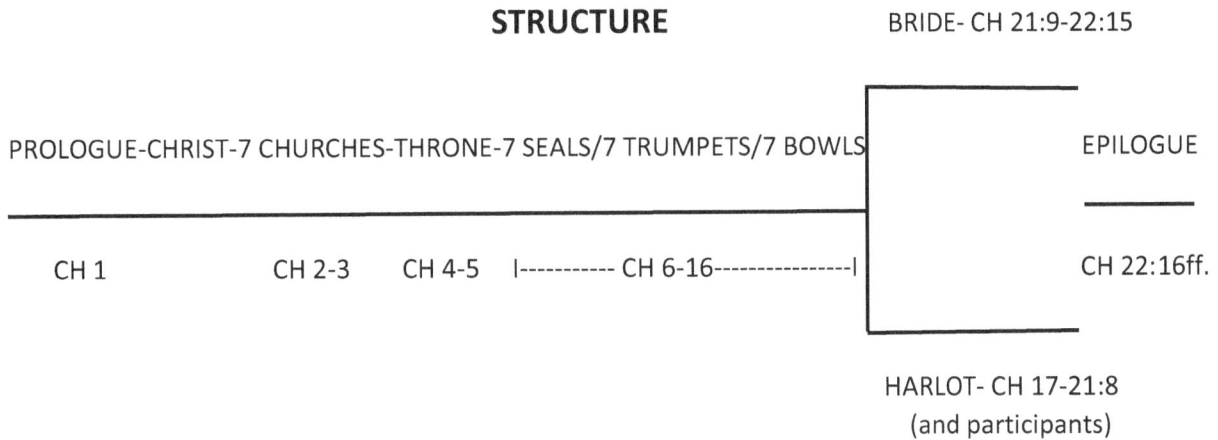

STRUCTURE

BRIDE- CH 21:9-22:15

PROLOGUE-CHRIST-7 CHURCHES-THRONE-7 SEALS/7 TRUMPETS/7 BOWLS

EPILOGUE

CH 1   CH 2-3   CH 4-5   I----------- CH 6-16----------------I

CH 22:16ff.

HARLOT- CH 17-21:8
(and participants)

VERBAL and AUDITORY CUES

Diagram #3A

FOUR SIGNIFICANT ANGELS

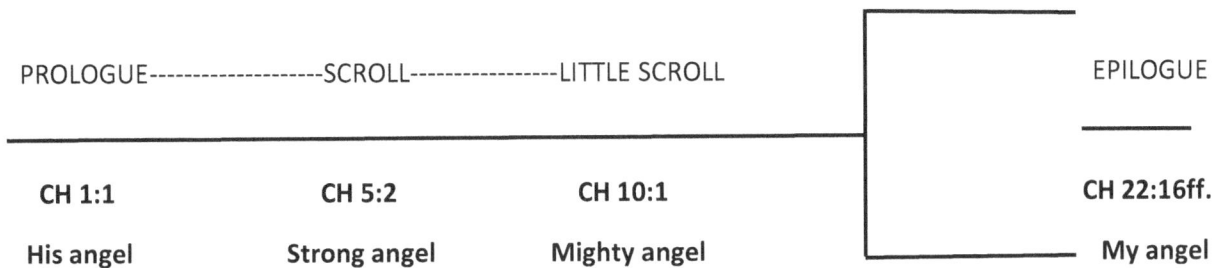

PROLOGUE-------------------SCROLL-----------------LITTLE SCROLL

EPILOGUE

CH 1:1   **CH 5:2**   **CH 10:1**

CH 22:16ff.

His angel   Strong angel   Mighty angel

My angel

Diagram #3B

JOHN – IN THE SPIRIT (4X)

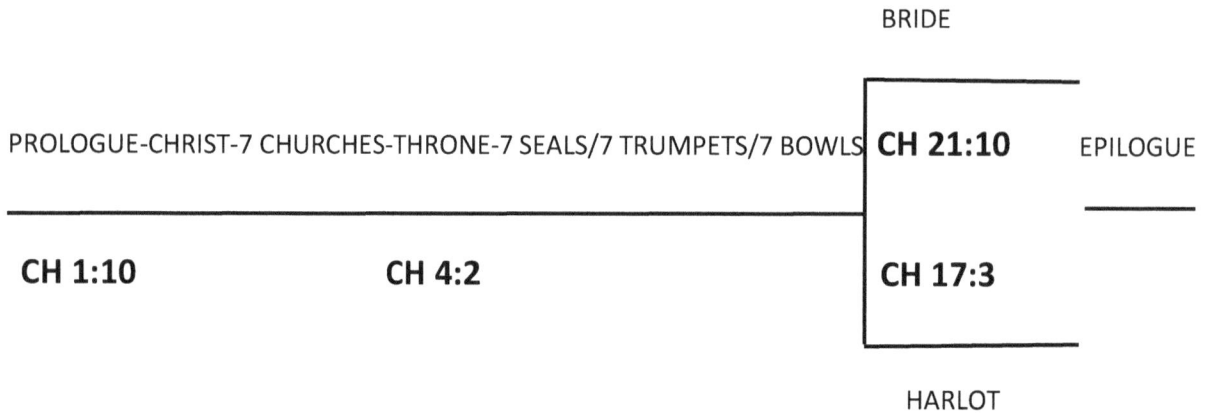

BRIDE

PROLOGUE-CHRIST-7 CHURCHES-THRONE-7 SEALS/7 TRUMPETS/7 BOWLS **CH 21:10** EPILOGUE

CH 1:10   **CH 4:2**   **CH 17:3**

HARLOT

Diagram #3C

THREE SIGNS IN HEAVEN

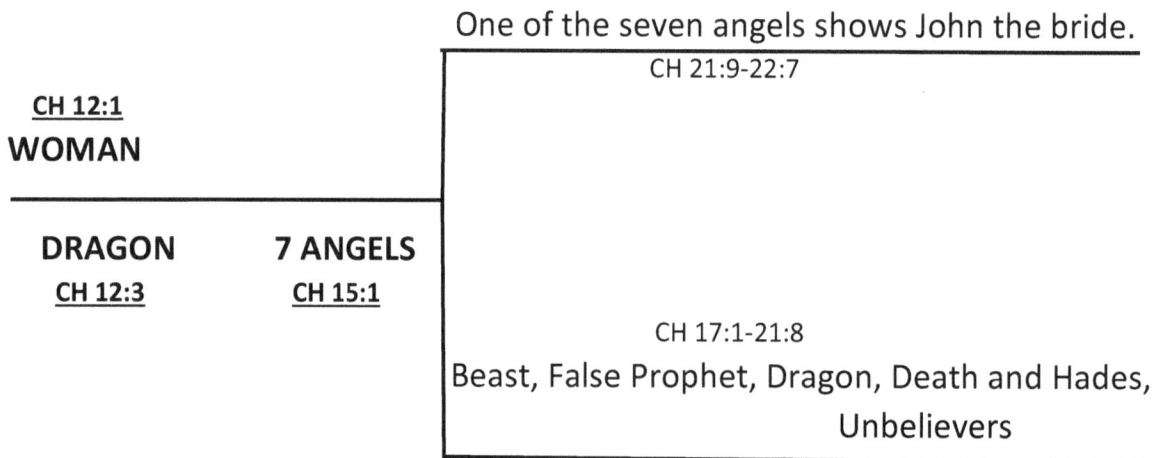

One of the seven angels shows John the bride.

CH 21:9-22:7

CH 12:1
WOMAN

DRAGON   **7 ANGELS**
CH 12:3   **CH 15:1**

CH 17:1-21:8
Beast, False Prophet, Dragon, Death and Hades, Unbelievers

One of the seven angels shows John the judgement of the harlot and her participants. All participants are cast into the lake of fire.

4

The Flow of Revelation

The last chapter covered the 4 major sets of seven that the book of Revelation contains. Three are presented to the reader of the book of Revelation primarily in the first half of the book, Chapters 1 through 11. The fourth set of seven, the bowls, are in chapters 15-16 (see diagram at the end of the last chapter). This leaves most of the second half of the book of Revelation portraying final judgement elements.

At this point it will be important to address the literary insertions, or parenthetical portions, that appear before the seventh seal, before the seventh trumpet, and before the seven bowls. Before the seventh seal we read about the sealing of the 144,000, and the multitude in heaven (Revelation 7). Before the seventh trumpet we read about the two witnesses and a great earthquake (Revelation 10:1-11:14). Before the seven bowls, the insertion is chapters 12 through 14. What are these literary insertions meant to communicate? Just this: the particular consecration, vocation, preservation, and final liberation (deliverance or exodus) of

the covenant people of God (See below: Diagram #4).

The second half of the Revelation begins in chapter 12 and goes to chapter 22:15, closing with an epilogue. The focus of the second half of the book of Revelation deals with a narrative that informs the reader of the separation between true worship and false worship. Chapters 12-14 give us the characters and their origins (historical identity) that will be dealt with in the final separation during the bowls, finalized by the results narratives of chapters 17-22. The seven bowls of wrath are then the final act that forever makes permanent the rewards for true worship, and the punishment for false worship.

There is somewhat of an overlap in the narrative, format, and design of this prophecy. This should not be foreign to the reader of prophetic passages. The book of Daniel has a division of primarily personal historical narrative in Daniel chapters 1-6, and future historical prophecy in chapters 7-12. The reader needs to know that Daniel's visions given in chapters 7-12 then dovetail back into chapters 1-6 at various points as the historical chronology unfolds in the life of Daniel. There is some prophecy in both divisions, as well as historical narrative. The same holds true for the book of Revelation. There are three items that frame chapters 12-22, with the focus of the narrative driving us to the culmination and results of the seven bowls. These three items are the wonders (or signs) in heaven mentioned at chapter 12:1; 12:3; and 15:1. Some interpreters see seven significant visions in the last half of the book of Revelation. This author focuses on the book of Revelation as having four sets of seven, and three wonders in heaven, thus giving seven major elements (completeness) to the book.

These three wonders in heaven: the woman, the dragon, and the seven angels with seven bowls, are the symbols of the final seven. These wonders describe, in symbolism, a spiritual reality inclusive within the physical reality of which the readers of Revelation are always a part. They reveal what we cannot know on our own, and could not know apart from God's help and revelation. The three wonders show the "behind the scenes" conflict between truth and error, good and evil, true worship and deception. They reveal the elements of division between true worship and false worship (deception). In these

three wonders, and their conclusions, the saints are informed and encouraged to overcome, endure, and persevere. The emphasis of this part of the book gives the "last days" detail and fulfillment that Daniel was told to seal up (Daniel 12:4, 9). Daniel was given part of the story for his days, and then told that knowledge will increase (Daniel 12:4). We are given the details, the increase of knowledge, for our days. And finally, we are given knowledge of the sovereign plan of God in its fulfillment being played out and worked to its consummation in the rule, reign, and physical presence of Christ with His people in a new heaven and new earth.

In this fulfillment narrative, we can then look for, and see, the design and structure of the book of Revelation after the seven bowls. This would be from chapter 17 to the end of the book of Revelation. Indeed, the bowls are called the *completed* wrath of God. With the final bowl, the voice out of the temple of heaven, from the throne, says, "It is done!" In chapter 15:1 we are told that the third wonder in heaven is the seven angels with the seven bowls. In chapter 17:1ff, we have one of the angels who had the seven bowls, showing John the judgement of the great harlot. In chapter 21:9ff, we have one of the angels who had the seven bowls showing John the bride, the Lamb's wife. In one scene John is shown the harlot and all the parts and participants who make up the false system of worship. In the second scene John is shown the bride, the true worshippers and their eternal fellowship with God. At this point in the narrative the division of judgements and rewards are described and final for all of eternity. Included is the historical identity that defines and gives clarity to each of the parts and participants.

This view of how the book of Revelation unfolds presents challenges for some. The contexts deliver the meanings. My desire is to be true to the book and its intent, and to the nature and person of God. If this view seems too simplistic, do not dismiss or reject it outright. This view is open for challenge and critiquing. There are complicated interpretations that are forced to add more than one coming of Christ because of the exegesis that is held. Is there a secret coming of Christ, and then a visual coming of Christ? There are interpretations that need to add multiple times of judgement to handle separate groups of unbelievers. Is there more than one bride? There are interpretations that have several separate and distinct groups of saints introduced throughout. Are there believers who experience the wrath of God? We must not force added narratives that are not revealed in the texts. There is a warning about adding to the prophecy. Let us allow the book to speak for itself.

Study Diagram #4 that is included on page 36. If you are visual, let the diagram assist you in seeing the structure of the book, but always go back to the Scriptures. The structure of the book will help in understanding how the book unfolds. The chapter and verse headings, while helpful for indexing where to find sections, at times hinder our observation of what thoughts go together. We can now begin to allow the book of Revelation to bless our minds with the truth contained in it.

Be encouraged! God is always caring for His people in the midst of their experiences!!

Diagram #4

PARENTHETICAL SECTIONS IN BOLD TYPE

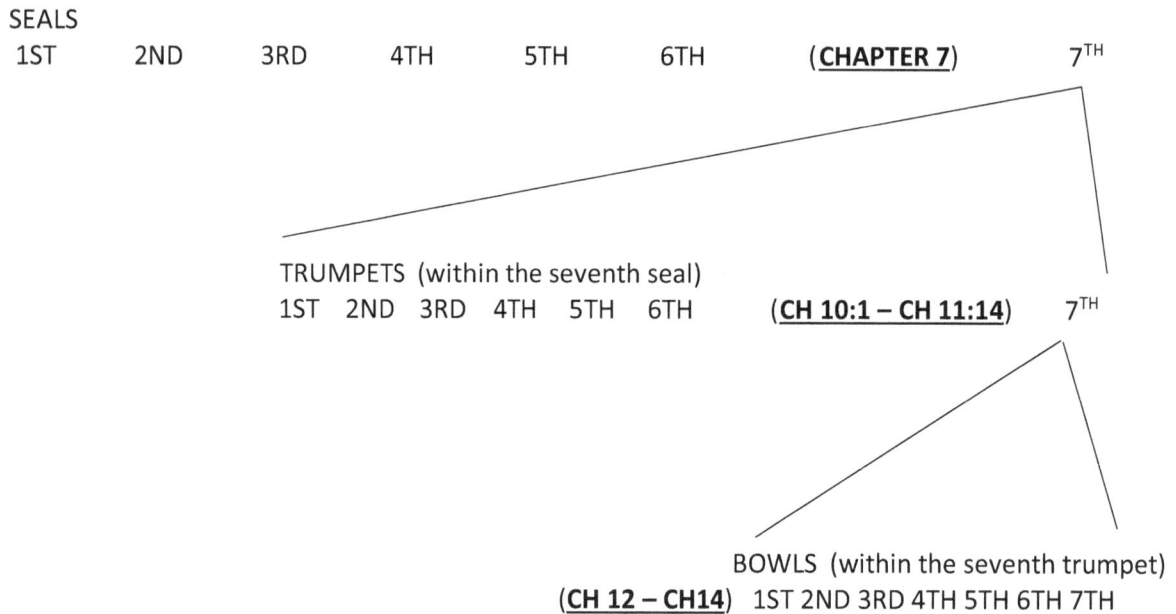

SEALS

| 1ST | 2ND | 3RD | 4TH | 5TH | 6TH | (**CHAPTER 7**) | 7TH |

TRUMPETS (within the seventh seal)

1ST 2ND 3RD 4TH 5TH 6TH   (**CH 10:1 – CH 11:14**)   7TH

BOWLS (within the seventh trumpet)
(**CH 12 – CH14**) 1ST 2ND 3RD 4TH 5TH 6TH 7TH

The parenthetical sections (in bold type) reveal to the readers, the consecration, vocation, preservation, and the liberation (rescue and exodus) of the covenant community of God. Because the bowls occur so swiftly during the seventh trumpet, chapters 12- 14 contain, or are, the parenthetical section. These chapters set the stage for the bowls. They also contain elements of the historical origins of the conflict. Remember that the seventh seal contains the seven trumpets, and the seventh trumpet contains the seven bowls (see Diagram #1, page 30).

5

The Seven Churches
(Part 1)

As this chapter begins it must be reiterated that it is not the scope of this book to specifically address the position of who the author may or may not be. There are many good arguments for the Apostle John. There is no conclusive evidence that this John is not the same as the author of the Gospel of John (i.e., the use of Hebraisms) and the Epistles of 1, 2, and 3 John. In addition, the date for the writing will not be addressed directly. These and other issues are found in a multitude of very good works. The insights that many good academic teachers and their commentaries do give is invaluable to those who would like to read further on these issues. The list of resources that this author has used and read are at the end of this book. It is enough to know that the Word of God is inspired, and that He has superintended what He desired to be included in the Bible. The author and date of Revelation, and the debates that ensue, are ancillary issues to the message of the book when read and interpreted according to the whole council of God. Any Scripture, or references to other books of the Bible, used within the text of this commentary will be from the New King James Version, unless noted otherwise.

The Introduction and Prologue
Revelation 1:1-3

In the very first verse we read the purpose and method of the book of Revelation. The book, or epistle, is a revealing of Jesus Christ. The book of Revelation, given in the form of letter to the churches, is from God, to Jesus, sent by His angel, to John, to His servants. This is not the initial revealing that we received that the Gospels and the book of Hebrews includes. It is a continued revealing of Jesus, as the One who is now portrayed as sovereignly in control until the consummation of this age and into the age to come. John, bearing witness to the word of God, and the testimony of Jesus, writes down all that he saw. The Greek word "*eido* (or *oida*)," for saw, means to know in fullness and grasp as reality, is used here and in 1:19. What is going to be portrayed is soon, and is very quickly to come to pass.

This verse also informs the reader that the method of communication will be signified, in the form of symbols and with signs. These two characteristics of the book of Revelation must be in the forefront of our focus and interpretation. That the book will include the phrase, "He who has ears let him hear" at different points, gives a clue that much of what is given is similarly understood as one would understand the parables given in the Gospels. There are many references to angels used throughout the book. The book of Revelation is declared to be given through the mediation of His angel, or messenger, to His servant, John (see also Revelation 22:6). Prophecy gives the condition and future of its subjects. Their understanding will be aided and proved by a knowledge of the Old Testament. John is told that the time is at hand, or near. The integrity of the book of Revelation is declared as being a prophecy.

This is the only book in the Bible that declares a blessing, at the beginning and end of the book (see also Revelation 22:7). The one who reads, and the one who hears, will be blessed by keeping (guard, preserve, observe) the things written in it. This is the first indication that those who originally received the book were meant to, and did, understand the message.

The Salutation
Revelation 1:4-8

Grace and peace from the originator of the book, God the Father, and the Holy Spirit and His sevenfold ministry, and from the resurrected, exalted, and enthroned Jesus Christ. Jesus, who has died for the sins of those He loves, makes them a kingdom of priests to God the Father. He is forever exalted. Jesus is surely coming again. That Jesus comes in the clouds is a statement of His deity and Oneness with the Godhead. Clouds are reserved for the presence of deity. No one will miss His coming, even those who rejected Him will be grieved when He actually comes, and all will see His coming. The validation and veracity of the message comes from the One who sent it: I am Alpha and Omega, First and the Last, Who is, was, and is to come (see Isaiah 41:4; 44:6; and 48:12). This phrase will be used of God, and of Jesus the Lamb.

John and His First Vision.
Revelation 1:9-20

John is the one who receives the visions and the command to write them down. It is evident from the text that he is no longer on the island of

Patmos, and that the actual writing of the Revelation was some time later. He associates with those who will receive the book as one who also is suffering tribulation, (the Greek word *thlipsis*). The persecution was because of his personal testimony of faith in Jesus Christ (see Rev. 12:17). Tribulation is that which believers suffer and endure from the world and Satan because of who they are in Christ. Tribulation is used to persecute believers. We are called to endure and persevere, and God uses it to purify and refine his people (John 16:33; 1 Thessalonians 3:4). The island of Patmos was a place of banishment, located in the Aegean Sea. He was most likely exiled there because of his testimony, or rejection of Emperor worship.

John testifies that he was in worship, in the Spirit (see Ezekiel 3:14; 5:9) on the Lord's Day, the first day of the week. There are three other occasions of John being in the spirit (Revelation 4:1; 17:3; 21:10). John was called to attention by an undeniably loud and significant voice. The voice identifies Itself as descriptive of God. John is told to write in a book what he sees, and to send it to seven churches in Asia. The churches listed here are also the same listed in Chapters 2-3. These were not the only churches in the province, but they seem to be the ones that are central to a circular mail route used at that time in history. The messages would have conceivably been distributed to other groups of believers via this route. There is a reason only seven were given the message. That is important when the number seven is seen to represent completeness, a greater reality than just for these seven churches. We will discuss these ideas later in the book.

These verses describe the vision of the exalted Christ. John turns to the voice that spoke (Jesus Christ). There are seven golden lampstands. Later we are given the key to the symbolism of the lampstands (see 1:20). In the midst of, or among the lampstands is "One like the Son of Man." This is a Messianic term for the Messiah, the Hebrew term for Christ taken from Daniel 7:13. That Jesus is in the midst of the churches portrays His intimacy with them. Jesus works in and through them. Many churches will never know the error in which they are involved without the insights of the book of Revelation. The sash around the chest signifies service, as opposed to a sash around the waist, meaning prepared for conflict (Daniel 10:5). He is clothed in the garb of priestly function. The whiteness of His head and hair represent His purity, righteousness, and holiness, in which He rules and guides all that He does (Daniel 7:9) In His eyes, He has the nature to see completely, know fully, and has perfect judgement on all that His gaze falls upon. His feet being of the finest brass represent His authority and position that is sure and firm. His voice is the source, a representation of the combined testimony and witness of all the prophets, teachers, and people who have held up His word (see Revelation 14:2; 17:1; 19:6). In His right hand, the place of honor and privilege, He holds seven stars. The stars represent the messengers of the seven churches (see 1:20). Stars are light bearers of guidance. Out of His mouth goes a sharp two-edged sword, which is the Word of God, of which He is the source. His whole countenance, who He is and what He is, is a full revelation of God. All of this is to declare that He is God. If you have seen Him, you have seen the Father (John 14:7-9). Jesus and the Father are one (John 10:30).

John falls at His feet as though dead (see Daniel 10:7-12). He is revived and lifted up, encouraged, and told not to fear. John hears a title of deity, the Old Testament name for God (Isaiah 44:6).

He then is given the words that harken back to the crucifixion, that the one who died is alive, and alive forevermore. Because of Jesus' triumph over death and the grave, He now has authority and dominion over the place of the dead, and of death itself.

John was told (he is no longer on Patmos, see verse 9): "Therefore write!" Write the things you have seen, the things that you have come to fully know understand (eida – see verse 2), that is, even the things which are, and the things that will take place after this (review discussion in chapter 3 of this book).

John is given the explanation for the symbolism that is used for stars and lampstands. They represent the angels of the churches, and the churches. These were first introduced in 1:12 and 1:16. They are said to be a mystery revealed for John. A mystery in the Bible is that which we would not know unless God gives us the answer. (It is not a mystery in the Sherlock Holmes sense, where we can deductively discover the truth.) Angels are representatives, messengers, or agents of the one sending them. The symbolism of stars and the lampstands are together used to represent the churches. In the description of the woman clothed with the sun in chapter 12, the crown of twelve starts represent the twelve tribes of Israel (Revelation 12:1). The stars in that vision stand for the individual brothers, and collectively for the people that each represent. In the same way, the seven stars represent the church collectively, the messenger, angel, and representative of Christ. The Greek text does not limit the messenger to being a single, individual person. The vision of the exalted Christ is directly connected to the messages for the seven churches.

As we move ahead to the messages to the individual churches, we will find that Christ is present, knowing, and intimately involved in the life, ministry, and issues of each church.

Be encouraged! The book of Revelation was given to His church so that believers would know what will take place!!

6

The Seven Churches
(Part 2)

This will be the first major explanation in a defense of understanding how the book of Revelation is in its design and format. Is there a past tense to present tense shown between chapter 1 and chapters 2 through 3? Again, the chapter and verse headings were given later in the history of Bible translations and are not inspired. So, I want to make the argument that: **chapters 1:4 through 3 are read as a section**. Indeed, the whole book is written to the churches, but there are connections that bind chapters 1 through 3 into a unit.

John is told to write to the churches by name (1:11). Jesus is seen as being in the midst of the lampstands. When you read the letters to each church, there is a present tense intimacy that He has with their internal conditions and their history. The mention of the churches as lampstands, and the messengers as stars being held in His right hand are all in the present tense. These images are carried into the next two chapters. John is given the credentials of the One who dictates, and then is told to write the

dictations. Of great import to the connection is the description of the risen Christ. Some element of the description is given or presented to each of the churches individually. Each church is given exactly the characteristic that they need. It is also noticeable that Jesus addresses the past, present, and future within each letter unique to that church. One of the main emphases of these letters was to encourage a sound theology as well as a high Christology. This would, in turn, issue into the correct behavior in light of their situations.

Why these seven churches? These are churches that actually, historically, and geographically did exist. It is suggestive from the writings of the early church fathers that the Apostle John would have been close to this area geographically, and that he spent his last years in, or near Ephesus. This list of churches represents a postal route that would have been used at that time. The other churches in the area would have benefitted as a result of this postal route. We know from other Scripture that churches shared letters written to them (Colossians 4:15-16). That the text of Revelation uses numbers, which is part of the symbolic communication, means that these letters would have an impact and message to the church universal, and as a whole.

These churches each had a name. Each of the seven letters begins with an address to the angel of the respective church. The address seems to point to a single person, or personality. Some suggest a guardian angel for each church. The guardian angel idea can be defended for an individual, but there is no evidence for a specific angel for a specific church (although princes are mentioned in connection with kingdoms (Daniel 10:20-21)).

Is the letter being sent to the leader, or pastor, of the church? Whenever the leadership of the church is addressed in other parts of Scripture it is always in the plural (the qualifications are singular). The commendations and warnings are not for a specific angel or a specific person, but for the church. In other parts of Scripture, the church as a whole is called the Body of Christ. We are to be light bearers, individually, and corporately. Could it be that each church in the book of Revelation is seen and addressed as a spiritual entity on its own, and that the letter is written to the messenger or agent of Christ, that is, the church itself?[1] That

it should function as a unity, a single body, even as it consists of individual members is true (see for instance Romans 12; 1 Corinthians 12-14). The church, any church, becomes the messenger, or representative, of Christ to the world where it exists. In the book of Revelation, the angels mentioned throughout, and the message they have, are seen to appear with the same characteristics of the ones they represent. This interpretation maintains the symbolism of the book.

There is a personal aspect to each member of these churches. There is also an appeal to "all" the churches within each letter. It is easy to see the characteristics of these churches existing somewhere, in some place, in some condition of relevant similarity, from the time of the writing up to the present day. Each church is, to some degree, a product of its history. The statements to overcome have universality to all believers in their content. There is a progression of church life and history that can be observed in the list as it is given. But within the context of the letters it does not hold up. These letters are written to show the message going to all churches of all time, as a unified instruction. It is simple to create a matrix that can list the similarities and differences between the churches. The reader would find it beneficial to do this matrix.

At the end of each letter is an admonition or exhortation to overcome (John 16:33; 1 John 5:4-5; Revelation 21:7). To overcome is to have a continuing attitude and behavior of one who *is* conquering. With each admonition is a reward to the one who overcomes. The endings of each letter also are similar in that they all have the statement, "He who has an ear, let him hear." The order throughout the seven churches is not the same. The first three have a different order than the last four. It is as if in the first three churches one has to do, that is to hear, in order to overcome. In the last four churches one has to overcome, to be able to do. The first three rewards to the overcomers are present realities in this life. The last four rewards are realities of the life to come for those who overcome. It is also true that all the rewards are possessions of all the overcomers: "Hear what the Spirit says to the *churches,*" is at the end of each individual letter.

Practically, there are many churches today who are engaged in activities or traditions that have lost, or never had, any Biblical connection. Therefore, the people within those churches have a false sense of security about what the church truly is and should be. There is a false sense of security because their trust is, in reality, in membership to a man-made model or institution. True conversion has not been established. The Biblical mandates have been replaced by worldly conventions. The same is true in church leadership. Only God can call a person to church leadership. Anything else that we can use to standardize the requirements can only affirm the call. Generally, Biblical knowledge is at a minimum and waning, and leaders do not admonish the church to correction.

Revelation 2:1-7   Ephesus

The church at Ephesus might be the most referenced body of believers in the New Testament (next to Jerusalem). It is mentioned by Luke in Acts 19-20 and has an epistle from the Apostle Paul written to them. Along with being the first in the list, Ephesus was considered the entry point into Asia Minor. The church at Ephesus is given one of the descriptive characteristics of Jesus that John had seen (see 1:12, 16). He has them in His hand and walks in their midst. Jesus states right at the beginning His authority and knowledge of their condition (I know!). He is also informing them of their privileged position and of His care. This church was considered by Jesus to be strong in doctrine, and they were tenacious in testing for wolves in sheep clothing, that is, false teachers (Acts 20:29-31).

Ephesus was a bulldog when it came to the doctrines. But they had abandoned their first love. This is the love and devotion of greatest importance. Including love for one another. They were out of balance. They had the rules without the relationship. They have lost their way, and have fallen from a position of their testimony and witness being a light that others might see. In the epistle to the Ephesians, Paul exhorts them about their being seated in the heavenly places in Christ, and to continue according to the Spirit that indwells them (Ephesians 1:3-14). They are told to repent and turn back to the proper order of priorities. They may lose their ability to be a light bearer, a lampstand, if the light is not placed where it is intended. Lampstands lift the light. They would lose their corporate witness, not the light.

They are commended for not choosing the path and practice of the Nicolaitans. Jesus hates the deeds of the Nicolaitans (see also Revelation 2:15). The etymology of the title Nicolaitan means victory over, or, overcomer of the people. Nicodemus, of John chapter 3 has this kind of meaning in his name. I believe that what is being rejected is any form of prideful hierarchy within the church. It is true that some are called to be in the leadership of others, but we are all called to be in submission to Christ as the head. Church leaders are to follow Christ as their example (1 Peter 5:1-4). Many times, this is violated by individuals and cliques within Christianity. We are to have a different attitude of leadership, fellowship, and submission than the world (Matthew 20:25-28; John 13:1-17; Romans 16; 1 Corinthians 13; Philippians 2; 1 Peter 5:1-4). We are not to be lords over one-another as are the Gentiles (Matthew 24:24-28).

There are many who see in the Nicolaitans a group started by one of the individuals, Nicolas, who was a servant of the early church. Nicolas was one of the seven who served in the role of a deacon (Acts 6:5). This group, supposedly started by Nicolas, was leading the people to take advantage of grace, and permitted all kinds of behavioral compromise with sin. This could be true of overbearing and controlling leaders. Many in the church give their allegiance and trust to leadership without being discerning and wise in the Word of God. It could be that all the characteristics above could be true. Using leadership positions to suppose license or freedom, by declaring a spiritual advantage, to engage in sinful activity will garner a greater condemnation (James 3:1). Any leadership that guides the church into any communion with worldly wisdom, using their "exceptionally spiritual status," so-called, will be found guilty of compromising or marginalizing the devotion to Christ alone, which they are to model (1 Corinthians 11:1; Revelation 14:4). These compromises can begin as subtle distractions from the mandates given by Jesus for the church.

Some know all too well, the controlling rule of certain types of leaders. Leaders put there by value of their degree, family or community status, or even money. In many cases the deacons, or trustees, rule the church, without consideration of calling and giftedness. They are often at odds with the pastor that is present,

and the pastor has a restricted leadership role. Most leadership boards are focused on the maintenance of attendance, buildings, and cash. They operate more like a civic organization than a church, and, perform badly at both. There is a propensity in the human condition to have control. Deacons have a temporary role, while the calling for elders is for life, unless gross moral behavior occurs. Rotation of deacons does not solve the control issues. To be fair, there are popes, priests, and pastors, who hold legitimate positions of Biblical leadership, who are only there to fleece and lead away the flocks under their authority. These are false shepherds who bring intentional harm (Matthew 7:15-20; Acts 20:29-30). Rejection of God's principles for church polity, for the preservation of man-made forms of religious expression and forms, is idolatry.

The church members, as individuals are challenged to hear. To hear, according to this Greek word definition, means to understand, accept, and obey. We are to be: *not hearers only.* The churches are to continually fight the battle against compromise in any form by following and keeping the commands of Christ.

To those who are overcoming, will be given to eat of the Tree of Life (John 5:24-25). Eating equals intimacy. This is a present reality restored to the believer and reversed from the Fall.

Revelation 2:8-11   **Smyrna**

The name Smyrna comes from the same root word from which the word myrrh comes. Myrrh was used in anointing for burial. Myrrh has a sweet smell, used for incense and perfume (see Song of Solomon). The substance was only able to be smelled when the hardened plant gum was crushed. This association is important to the church of Smyrna, as they are experiencing persecution. Jesus identifies Himself to the church as the "the First and the Last, who was dead, and came to life," (Revelation 1:11, 17). This would have been a great encouragement to them.

Jesus informs them of His knowledge of their works, that is, their tribulation and poverty. He tells them that they have true riches. He identifies the source of their troubles as those who say they are Jews and are not. They should have been the first to make the transition from the Ceremonial Law to the One who fulfilled the Law. These are ones who have been challenged to move from the shadow to the reality

(see the book of Hebrews). In their rejection of Jesus, and in their unwillingness to accept Him as their Messiah, they now persecute the followers of Jesus. (see Matthew 21:33-42; 23:15, 29-35; John 8:12-59; 15:18-25; Acts 7:51-52). The Jews have a record of rejecting the Word of God (1 Kings 19:14; Jeremiah 25:3-4; Ezra 9:11; Nehemiah 9:26), killing the Prophets (Matthew 23:34-35; Acts 7:51-53), and persecuting the Apostles (Acts 9:1-9; 13:44-52; 2 Corinthians 11:24). He calls them a synagogue of Satan. Some of the greatest persecutions inflicted on the followers of Christ, have been perpetrated by institutional religions. This message is for all those who are trapped in legalism and would deny, or marginalize, the work of Christ to the point of being a persecutor. This situation has an example from recent history. We know of reformers who were persecuted, and even martyred by being burned at the stake for saying the world was round, for translating the Scriptures into common languages, and printing Bibles and distributing them. Institutional religion has been a large participant in this kind of persecution.

Jesus encourages them to not fear. He knows the future for some of the members of the church. The devil, who is behind all tribulation and persecution, will throw some of them into prison to test their faith. They then would be martyred. This test of their faith has a dual purpose. It also has the idea of assaying a character. What the devil uses to tempt, God uses to refine. It is the same word used in the church at Ephesus when they are commended in their testing the doctrine of teachers. They are encouraged to be faithful unto death. It is also a sober fact that Jesus, by informing them of the facts, at times will sanction persecution and tribulation for His purposes.

The book of Revelation is more about not being deceived, than it is about preserving our physical life. This physical, fallen life, was never meant to be all there is about our existence. The church at Smyrna is promised a crown of life. This is better understood as a crown "that consists of life." The Greek word used here for crown, *stephanos*, is not the crown or diadem of authority or rule, a *diadema*. The crown, *stephanos*, is for the triumph of an athlete. It is the crown that consists of all the surroundings of position, either negatively, or in advantages and benefits of being a winner in the games. If they overcome

they will not be hurt by the second death. The second death represents eternal punishment and separation (see Revelation 20:6, 14; 21:8).

Revelation 2:12-17   Pergamos

Jesus addresses the church at Pergamos (Pergamum) as from: The One who has the sharp two-edged sword (Revelation 1:16). He knows their works and where they dwell. They dwell where Satan's throne is. They are keeping Jesus' name even though there was already the martyrdom of at least one of their members. There were temple cults of worship to Zeus, Aesculapius, and Caesar. Zeus is the highest god of the Greek pantheon of gods. Aesculapius represented healing, as seen even today as the symbol on many medically related signs and emblems. Aesculapius worship has its roots in the Babylonian mystery religion as far back as Nimrod. Pergamos may have had the oldest temple for Caesar worship. Satan, the devil, is behind all forms of idolatry and false worship.

Some of the ploys that Satan uses are right up front and can be easily seen. Other times Satan will go through the back door using our most basic needs or base desires. The story of Balaam from the book of Numbers, chapters

22-25, is used as a teaching example and warning to this church. This is a compromise into disobedience that was used to deceive the people, from outside the camp, and from the bottom up. Any compromise in the physical realm has a spiritual aspect to it. The use of Old Testament narratives is one of the characteristics of a number of the churches in this set of seven. This characteristic opposes the view that these chapters are dealing with a "church age."

The church at Pergamos is also admonished about the members who hold to the doctrine of the Nicolaitans (see above, Revelation 1:6; 2:4). They are warned to repent or He will come and deal with them personally, by the power of His word. That Jesus would be quick to respond is close to the idea that was given in Revelation 1:1 about what must immediately begin to take place.

To the ones that overcome will be given some of the hidden manna to eat. Manna was the supernatural means of sustenance that God provided during the wilderness wanderings of the Israelites (Exodus 13). The manna was memorialized by storing it in a gold pot and placing it inside the ark of the covenant (Exodus

16:33; Hebrews 9:4). Jesus declares that He was, and is, the bread that comes down from heaven (John 6:46-51). Jesus is our sustenance while we are in this time of waiting for the promise.

The overcomer will be given a stone of acquittal, or justification. In the world of John's day, the adjudication of a court decision was made by judges who decided a case by casting a white stone or black stone into a container. The white stone was a judicial decision of being free from guilt. The new name was a sign of a new identity and status. The identity is as being adopted, being a new creation, being of and in Christ, being a child of God, and being a possessor of a new kind of life. It is noteworthy to observe Who is doing the giving. Who the son sets free, is free indeed (John 8:36). That the one having the new name is the only one who knows it, speaks of being personal and significant to that person (see Revelation 19:12).

As we continue with the list of churches, we should be able to begin identifying dynamics of our own experiences that we are encouraged to correct or take encouragement from. Be encouraged! The Lord of love desires it!!

7

The Seven Churches
(Part 3)

Revelation 2:18-29   Thyatira

Thyatira is sent their greeting from the One who is the Son of God. This title that the risen Christ uses for Himself leaves no question as to His deity. The religious leaders of Jesus' day crucified Him for His identification with God the Father. This is also a title which harkens back to the temptations of Jesus in the wilderness (Luke 4:1-13). He has eyes that see all and righteously judges. His feet are positioned in a firm and immovable stance with the authority of His message (see Revelation 1:14-15). He knows the works of this church. Jesus commends the church at Thyatira for their love, faith, service, and perseverance, and that these dynamics have increased and grown.

Christ chastises the church for their toleration of a woman named Jezebel. In the Old Testament, Jezebel was the wife of King Ahab. Ahab was a terrible king in the Northern Kingdom during the times of the divided nation of Israel (1 Kings 21-26). Jezebel's influence was not a small issue in the narrative of the times and included the conflict and persecution of Elijah. Jezebel's influence was inside the camp, from the top down (Balaam was outside the camp, see church at Pergamos). Her teachings and seductions led the people into the worship of idols, which often included sexual immorality. These two characteristics were often combined as worship to a patron god in the trade guilds of the day. Prophets had a significant position in the life of a people, and Jezebel was as a foreign prophetess. Her seduction was never challenged or checked by king Ahab. Ahab had made an alliance with the nation from which she came. She and king Ahab are given many warning messages, but they were too entrenched in their control. Jezebel was very good at appealing to King Ahab's selfish nature (1 Kings 21). Even after her demise, her influences were felt for many years through her daughter, Athalia (2 Kings 11).

The church at Thyatira was being warned about making any alliances outside of the commands and precepts of God. These alliances were with agents of false worship. The results of these alliances are far reaching and will have far reaching affects. The ones who are responsible for these initial dealings will be placed into suffering that has no hope for recovery, along with those who take part in them. The judgement will be thorough in its scope, and reach as far as necessary to eradicate any trace of the idolatry and false worship. The judgement will be personal and individual.

To those members of the church who have not fallen prey to the temptations and seductions that come from Satan, the father of lies, comes the encouragement to hold fast to the truth that they firmly have. They are commended for not buying into the lie that there is a better and easier way to get what is promised (Luke 4:7). They are aware of the extent to which Satan will go to deceive them, even twisting Scripture to get them to doubt and mistrust the very word of God (Genesis 3:1-4). To these members will be added no other requirements for perseverance.

To those who overcome, by keeping and guarding the commands given by Jesus Christ, will be given the authority of rule. This authoritative rule is a co-reigning with Christ, who has gone ahead and now rules (Psalm 2:8-9; Revelation 12:5, 19:15). Christ is the last Adam, who has won back the dominion and stewardship of the earth that the first Adam lost in the Fall. The overcomer will also be confirmed in the giving of the morning star. Where He is ruling, we will also be ruling (2 Peter 1:19; Revelation 3:21; 22:16). This first light of a new day is confirmed by the promises of God (2 Peter 1:19). This promise is of a new creation, existence, and new life which is promised to the redeemed. It is given in Scripture, and first revealed in the believer's heart at the time of believing in Christ as Messiah. These promises to the overcomers are written to all the churches.

Revelation 3:1-6 **Sardis**

Sardis was thought to be the oldest city of the region. The city's founding goes back to at least the Lydian empire. It was considered practically impregnable by the citizens because of its geographical position on a cliff. In spite of that, the city was conquered and taken over several times by its enemies, during the night, because its citizens and watchmen were not keeping watch. These historical characteristics will be important as the address is made known. The church at Sardis is addressed by Jesus, as the One who has the seven spirits of God and the seven stars. The seven spirits of God represent the work of the Holy Spirit (Revelation 1:4; 4:5; 5:6), and the seven stars are a reminder that the church in its complete totality are in the care of Jesus (see Revelation 1:16, 20).

Jesus knows their works. They have a name that is alive, but the church is dead. There is also a Sardis stone that was known. The Sardis stone was once considered precious, but became common. That the church is dead and in need of the Spirit of God to revive them is the utmost need. The Apostle Paul had exhorted Timothy that in the last days there would be groups of people who will have a form of godliness but will deny its power (2Timothy 3:5). Paul uses the metaphors of sleep and night to describe unbelievers who will not keep watch (1 Thessalonians 5:1-8).

The church at Sardis is commanded to be watchful, and to stabilize the things that are left and about to die. God can make much from the very little. Before God, they are not moving on to maturity, and their works have yet to be complete and fulfilled. They are neglectful. The church is to remember the basics of the faith. They need to remember what they had heard and believed and were to re-establish

their priorities. They needed to turn away from their path of dying. If they do not become watchful, they will not see the "thief in the night" that will take them by surprise. The thief in the night, and the hour of coming, are both used in the context of the second coming of Jesus. Sardis, and any group of people who are not living for God and are caught up in the ways of the world, will not be ready and expectant of the Day of the Lord (Matthew 24:36-44; 1 Thessalonians 5:2; 2 Peter 3:10; Revelation 16:15).

The church is commended for having a remnant. God always will have a remnant of His people who remain faithful (1 Kings 19:18). The Lord knows who are His, and, He knows where they are. Unfortunately, the remnant will always be a minority (Matthew 7:13-14). Those who have remained faithful and are not participating in idolatry or any other form of false worship, will walk in righteousness.

The one who overcomes, endures, and perseveres to the end, is promised to be clothed in white garments. White garments represent salvation and moral purity (Revelation 4:4; 6:11; 7:9-13; 19:8, 14). There is a promise that their name will remain in the Book of Life. The Book of Life is the register that God keeps in heaven of all who are promised eternal life (Exodus 32:32-33; Daniel 12:1; Luke 10:20; Romans 9:1-3; Revelation 13:8; 17:8; 20:12, 15; 21:27; 22:19). It is most interesting that the Scriptures speak of names being in, found written in, or being found in, the Book of Life. There is no mention of a name now being written (present tense writing) or will be written (future tense) in the context of the Biblical narrative. Are we written in at the moment of justification, or are we eternally confirmed in the Book of Life at that time? Is a person who rejects the call of God blotted out because of not responding to His Gospel (Luke 19:44; John 3:15-17; Romans 5:19; 11:5-28, 32; 1 Peter 2:12; 2 Peter 3:9)? We do not earn being in the Book of Life, but we can forfeit membership. Jesus Himself will confess to the Father all those who confess Him to the world around them (Matthew 10:32; Mark 8:38; Luke 9:26, 12:8; Romans 10:8-10; Revelation 17:14). What is said to the one who hears at Sardis, is meant for all the faithful in all the churches.

Revelation 3:7-13   Philadelphia

Philadelphia was a city that was used as an entry point to promote Greek culture in that region and beyond. It was a city that suffered many earthquakes, and the ensuing tremors, for many years. These two characteristics of their past history would be informative for the message that the risen Christ had for them. Their message should remind churches today that Jesus is very intimate with their condition and their needs. Jesus has passionate desires for their future. Jesus, who is set apart, One of a kind, and the embodiment of truth, is the one who encourages this church. He is the One who has the keys of David, the One who opens doors and closes doors (2 Samuel 7:1-16; Isaiah 22:15-25). Jesus, as the promised Messiah King, was the father and a descendent of David, whose rule and reign will never end. There is no one who has more authority (Psalm 110:1; Revelation 1:18).

The church at Philadelphia had kept His word and not denied His name (John 14-17). Because of this, they had an open door of opportunity (as in Acts 14:27). If this is related directly to what the Greeks were doing,

Philadelphia was given a green light to be the church to promote the Gospel to that area, and beyond.

Similar to the church at Smyrna, this church was experiencing persecution and opposition from "those who say they are Jews and are not" (Revelation 2:9). There is an additional item: that those who antagonize the church will be required to worship before the feet of the church at Philadelphia. This Old´ Testament phrase was used of the nations who would one day come to the covenant people of God in the same way (Isaiah 60:14; see Romans 10:19; 11:11). The Jews would confess that Jesus loves the church. This dynamic of love is placed on the ones that are chosen (John 13:1; Galatians 2:20; Ephesians 5:2). (For the idea of choosing and loving, see Revelation 12:11.) This was a characteristic given to Israel of the Old Testament (Isaiah 43:4) The Israelites of the Old Testament were to be the peculiar people of God. He had set His love on them (Deuteronomy 7:6-7). Because the church at Philadelphia had kept His word and His name, what they were doing would increase.

The church at Philadelphia, like the church at Smyrna, does not receive any critical exhortation. Because of this, they are told that they will be kept through, or kept out of, the coming hour of testing that will come upon the whole world. The whole world is mentioned in relation to the testing. This verse must be taken within the complete context given to the churches. In any event of Biblical history, God always protects, provides for, and preserves His remnant of people. This protection may, or may not, include protection from death (see Smyrna). It is God's prerogative to restrain evil from any person, or group of people, He sees fit. The believer can be in the world and kept from the evil one (John 17:15). Believers can pray to be kept from the attacks of the evil one (Matthew 6:13). Believers are preserved from certain judgements (Revelation 7:1-8; 9:4). Being preserved from the hour of testing means not that they will be physically absent, but rather that they will not be touched by that which touches others.[1]

This church is busy about spreading the Gospel. Their condition of faithfulness and condition of ministry may be why God has chosen to protect, sustain, and preserve them during the worst of times. His supernatural provision, keeping them from the persecution by the evil one, is not a principle for all, but is a selective sovereign grace that He, and He alone, gives for a season and a purpose. The church at Philadelphia is encouraged to hold fast to the things they have, and not to lose their crown. The mention of a crown is another relationship that this church has in common with Smyrna. They are reminded that when He comes, it will be quickly, so they are always to be aware and prepared.

The overcomer is promised to be a pillar in the temple of My God (used 4 times here) and will go out no more. They are eternally united with God. Historical records maintain that the city of Philadelphia suffered the tremors of earthquakes. Many residents of the city lived outside the city for fear of falling structures and possible destruction. A pillar in God's temple would be a supporting column that is immoveable and sturdy and could never be moved. Overcomers will have the Name of God written on them. The overcomers are to have this new name written on them by Jesus Himself. The name represented the identity, possession, and nature of the one who gives it. The very Name of God denotes adoption, blessings, and eternal security. The name of the city of God represents that which God is

now creating and will be finalized when Jesus returns (Hebrews 11:10; Revelation 7:3). The word city, used in the Old and New Testaments, has the meaning of: the inhabitants, community, and population. It is not restricted to only the static geographical location or the physical brick and mortar structures (Luke 13:34; Galatians 4:25-26; Hebrews 11:10, 12;22-24, 13:14; Revelation 21:1-27). It is a new, eternal, community. It is interesting that the first mention of the city of Jerusalem in the book of Revelation is in connection with those who say they are Jews and are not. A new, and eternal name brings new status and association. The overcomers are promised to have the Name of Jesus written on them. Jesus' name represents all that the Scriptures declare about His reputation, character, and His work. The overcomer belongs to Him. These promises are addressed to all the churches.

Revelation 3:14-22   Laodicea

Jesus addresses the church at Laodicea. He is the Amen, the Faithful and True Witness (Revelation 1:5). Jesus is the final acknowledgement, agreement, and fulfillment of the plan and purposes of God, the Yes and Amen (2 Corinthians 1:20). He is the one who is a perfectly accurate and trustworthy testimony to the truth. He is the beginning of the creation of God. The Greek word translated beginning has the idea of originator, ruler, and initiator of creation (Colossians 1:15-20). The Colossian church was close by. (Paul, in his epistle to the Colossians, asked them to trade letters with the Laodicean church (Colossians 4:13-16)).

Jesus knows the truth about the Laodicean church, that they are neither hot nor cold. He wishes they were one or the other. At issue here, is not hot *for* Him, or cold *against* Him, as in passion or rejection. The issue here is usefulness. The city needed fresh water. There was an aqueduct built to supply cool water from a nearby city. There were also hot springs in another nearby city that were used for recreation and medicinal purposes. Tepid water is relatively useless, and often will make a person feel ill if they drink it. The "tepidness" of the church forces Christ to say the he will "vomit" them out of His mouth. He cannot, and will not, be able to use them.

The city of Laodicea was a wealthy city that included merchants, bankers, and physicians. They had a successful commerce of black wool, finance, and eye salve. It is documented that whenever the city had an earthquake, the inhabitants refused help from Rome in rebuilding, rather choosing to be independent and financing their own recovery. The church in Laodicea had taken on this same characteristic and had an attitude of independence from the provisions of Christ.

He says of the church that they are miserable, wretched, poor, blind, and naked. This was a direct chastisement of their reliance on themselves and their wealth. The risen Christ gives them counsel to obtain from Him true riches, refined and tested and of eternal value. The church is to receive from Him white garments to cover their nakedness. White garments represent righteous acts, and nakedness is symbolic of sin that is exposed and uncovered. Our sin is taken away by Christ's work on the cross, and we are covered by the righteousness given to us in Christ. The church at Laodicea needed to have spiritual sight restored to them so that they can see. These chastisements are because Jesus has a great love for this church (Hebrews

12:3-11). Because of this love, they need to be, and should be eager to repent. If any members of this church would hear these words and be willing to open the door to the risen Christ, He is willing to enter and continue life and fellowship with them. He is currently outside the church and will not force His way into it.

To the overcomer is a promise to sit with Christ on His throne. This throne is a position of authority and rule as co-reigning, co-heirs, with Him over the new creation (Romans 8:16-17; 15:20; 2 Timothy 2:12; Revelation 2:26; 5:10; 22:4-5). This is a restoration of the dominion that the first Adam lost at the Fall. Jesus is our example of overcoming. As through His victory on the cross and the joyful completion of His work to the end, He now is restored to the glory He once shared fully with the Father (John 16:33; 17:1-5; Philippians 2:5-11). This promise is for all the overcomers of all the churches.

This ends the letters to the seven churches. Having been assured of the presence of Christ in the midst of His church, we now turn to the event of the Ascension of Jesus, and the part of the Revelation that begins the narrative of His Person, work, and judgements associated with His present rule, and His second advent.

Be encouraged! Jesus in in the midst of His church. Listen for His voice!!

8

The Throne of God
Revelation 4:1-11

As we begin chapter 4 it must be reiterated that: how we read, see, and hear the book of Revelation unfolding is crucial in interpreting the signs and images, and understanding the message in its entirety. Chapter 4 starts the next section. This next section concludes at Revelation 8:5. Chapters 4 and 5 in themselves are a picture of the exaltation of the Lamb. The characteristics and activities of chapter 6 will include elements that are initiated in chapters 4 and 5. These characteristics include the Lamb, the scroll, the seals, and the living creatures.

There are many interpretations that assert that chapter 4 is future and that the elements that will happen from that point on are only for the very last days. This is part of the futurist view of Revelation. An alternate futurist view maintains that everything written after the beginning of chapter 6 is describing the very last days. The first element that must be discussed is what is being described in chapters 4 and 5.

Did John see an event that is past tense or future tense for him? Is it past or future tense for us? Did Jesus receive all of His authority at His resurrection and ascension, or is there more authority He was yet to receive? To suggest that these are yet to happen and are not already a past reality is to ignore the whole of Scripture.

The preponderance of Scripture declares that He *has* received all authority (Matthew 28:18; John 17:5; Acts 2:34-36; 7:54-56; 1 Corinthians 15:25; Philippians 2:5-11; Colossians 1:13-18; Hebrews 1: 1-3; Revelation 1:17-18; 3:21). Revelation 12:4-5 is considered to be the abbreviated version of the life of Christ given in the middle of Revelation, and yet is mentioned after chapters 4-5. The Greek term translated "after these things" is, in this instance, showing a change in panorama for John, not a chronological step (Revelation 4:1). This phrase is used many more times in Revelation in the same way (Revelation 7:1, 9; 15:5; 18:1; 19:1). The last part of chapter 4:1 is helpful in determining the meaning of the verse. This similar phrase is used in Daniel to give a prophecy that includes the current reign of Nebuchadnezzar as part of the last days that Daniel interprets (Daniel 2:28-29, 45).

Another interpretive issue is declaring that since the word church does not appear after chapter 4:1, the catching away of the church must have occurred. The Greek word *"ekklesia"* is the word translated church in most English translations of the Bible. This Greek word means "the called out of ones." What must be declared is that if you have a group of people with the characteristics of the church, or the characteristics of a member of the church, you then have the presence of the church. Indeed, in the book of Revelation you find those who have been sealed as with the Holy Spirit (compare Ephesians 1:13-14 and Revelation 7:3). There are saints mentioned after these chapters involved in the activity that is narrated (Revelation 7:3; 13:7-10; 14:12; 17:6; 18:24; 20:9). There are those who hold the testimony and witness of Jesus (Revelation 6:9; 11:7; 12:11, 17; 19:10; 20:4). To decide that the church is not present through the whole context of the book, is to make a distinction of a third group of people whom God is addressing. To consider the plight of this third group of people as being only Jews is borderline anti-Semitic in its outworking. That they

should be part of a persecution, the great tribulation, that the rest of the church will be spared is not Biblical. That is not coherent logic. If not having the word "church" appear in the context is proof of its absence, then finding it in other parts of Scripture must be proof that it, the church, is present therein (so Acts 7:38; 19:32-41). (The Hebrew word *edah* is translated church in the Septuagint (LXX), the translation of the Hebrew Old Testament into Greek.)

One way of limiting our understanding of the book of Revelation, is to broaden the use of certain words beyond their meaning, or to use words interchangeably that cannot be interchanged. Some suggest that believers will not experience the wrath of God, and therefore will not be present during the great tribulation. It is true that the believer is not appointed unto the wrath of God once conversion has happened. We are placed in Christ (1 Thessalonians 1:10; 5:9). We are already saved from the wrath to come. But the Greek word for wrath and the Greek word for tribulation are two distinct words in the Greek language, as well as in English. Jesus said that in this world we will have tribulation (John 16:33). There are saints and believers in the book of Revelation who go through tribulation, and, suffer persecution and death (Revelation 2:10; 3:10; 5:11; 9:4; 12:11; 13:7,15; 14:12-13). In the book of Revelation John declares that he is a companion in tribulation (Revelation 1:9). Paul spoke of tribulation as part of the life of the believer (Acts 14:22; Romans 5:3; 8:35; 12:12; 2 Corinthians 1:4; 7:4; 1 Thessalonians 3:4). Tribulation is what the believer receives for being a follower of Jesus. Wrath is the settled disposition that God has placed on the unbeliever for rejecting Him (Romans 1:18; Ephesians 2:3). We must use the whole counsel of God to give the people of God the whole truth of God.

The Landscape of Reality

4:1 John starts this section by describing his privilege of seeing a door, or portal, into heaven by which he is able to have entry and the ability to see into a spiritual reality. The voice like a trumpet that he heard previously, now is speaking again (Revelation 1:10). He is told that he will be shown all that is related to the last days. John states that he is in the Spirit as these visions are revealed to him (Acts 10:9-11; Revelation 1:10; 17:3; 21:10). The servant of God may see visions or scenes by supernatural means that are out of the normal sight and perception of our five senses. We must always be discerning as to who, or what, is initiating and allowing such opportunities. John will be given this vision by God Himself.

4:2-3 John sees a throne, a symbol of authority, positioned in heaven. He sees the One who is seated on the throne. The One who is seated on the throne is described in precious stones and colors. There is a description of something that encircles the throne, which again is seen as a color. God often reveals Himself, and the means by which He governs, as of precious stones and in the colors that light reveals. God is Light. Jesus is the Light that has come into the world. He wraps Himself in light (Psalm 104:2; Ezekiel 1:28).

The stones mentioned here are the first and last stones used on the High Priest's breastplate (Exodus 28:5-13; 39:1-14). Everything described by John is in relationship to the throne. Each participant given in chapters 4-5 has a role in the narrative of the book of Revelation. All of the prepositions, and prepositional phrases, give us a clue to the positions, functions, purposes, and the relationships of the participants to each other. This scene is heard, as well as read.

4:4 Around the throne are twenty-four thrones, and on these twenty-four thrones sat twenty-four elders. They are around the throne, but they do not have equal authority with the throne at the center. Their relationship around the throne is co-reigning authority. In the Old Testament, there were twenty-four courses of Levites who were to serve in the temple of the Lord in worship (1 Chronicles 23-24). The Levites represented all the people of God. These twenty-four elders represent the redeemed, triumphant, righteous, mature people of God. That they are seated tells us their work finished and they are at rest. Elders have rule, authority, maturity, and responsibility. Angels do not rule. And angels are never given crowns. (Angels are ministering spirits and are not, as originally created beings, given their own authority.)

4:5 From the throne proceed the governing commands and voice of God. This is a picture of His presence in majesty and power (Exodus 19:16). Before the throne were the seven Spirits of God (see Revelation 1:4). The seven Spirits of God represent the Holy Spirit in the fullness of His work.

The Holy Spirit is in the presence of God, being God, and works on behalf of God in the world (John 16:7-11). These seven lamps, or torches, are not to be confused with the lampstands of the seven churches. Lampstands are used to elevate the light. Torches are representative of being light itself.

4:6a Also before the throne was a sea of glass, like crystal. The sea is in the same positional relationship as the seven lamps, that is, on behalf of God and by His authority. The sea in no way is equal to the seven lamps, but represents that which was to serve before God on behalf of His authority. The sea is mentioned other places in the book of Revelation, and from these we can get help in interpreting what is symbolized here. In this chapter of Revelation, the sea is glass, like crystal. There will be a beast that persecutes the saints that arises out of the sea (Revelation 13:1). Later in the book of Revelation the sea is described as being mingled with fire (Revelation 15:2). Fire is most times associated with divine judgement and purification. There, the redeemed 144,000 are seen as standing *on* the sea of glass, an indication of being overcomers. Later in the narrative we are told that in the new heaven and new earth, there is no longer any sea (Revelation 21:1).

It is important to note that all of the images participating in this scene have something in common in relationship to the throne. They have personality as beings (the One on the throne, the elders, seven lamps, the sea, the four living creatures, and the Lamb). The sea represents cosmic evil, corporeal and spiritual, the seen and the unseen, and is representative of all that is in indifference, enmity, and in rejection of God and His design. (In the ancient world, the sea was always considered evil, in chaos, even though at the time it was created everything was very good.)

The sea is first represented as not being in final judgement (see Revelation 4:6). Then a beast is formed from within the sea, the beast being a kingdom which consists of people and a system in opposition to God (Daniel 7; Revelation 13:1). Just before the final bowls of wrath, the redeemed are separated from the sea, and the sea has fire (final judgement) in its midst (15:2). And in eternity, there is no sea, meaning there is no longer a cosmic evil participant that is in rejection or defiance of God's purpose and design (21:1). This interpretation that the sea is a symbol

for an evil cosmos works for the places it is mentioned.

4:6b-8 The next thing John sees in this vision of heaven opened, will try the understanding of the best of readers. What he sees defies description in a visual-only sense. Let us remember that every word in the Bible is inspired and is put just where it is for a purpose. The descriptions that are given must be understood in relationship to their position to the throne, and to the other participants. The descriptions are there to give us characteristics more than a visual reference.

There are four *living* creatures. They have life, are animated, are not of evil, and they are created. Their proximity to the thrones tells of their intimacy in design and their purpose, as does their number. The number four is generally symbolic of all that is seen and is related to creation. The four living creatures are always portrayed together, and unified in their activity. The living creatures are in the midst of the throne, and around the throne. Jesus is described as being in the midst of, among, or at the center of the seven lampstands (Rev. 1:13). These four living creatures are close to the throne. They also encircle, or surround, the throne. It brings to mind a quarterback going down on one knee to use up time at the end of a football game, with the rest of the players forming a protective huddle around him. The four living creatures are placed to represent separation. They are guardians of the divine presence.

They are full of eyes in front, *and* in back. These four living creatures appear the same from whatever side you observe. That they are full of eyes gives us an idea of their second characteristic, or function: permitting revelation. The eye is called the window to the soul (Matthew 6:22-23; Luke 11:34; Ephesians 1:18). The concept of the word used for the eye also has the idea of a portal, means, or fountain. It is used as a metaphor for something that allows passage of another element through it. The four living creatures are full to capacity in their function of allowing a "two-way" passing of information to occur. This information flows between the throne, and everything else that is, *or has been*, separated from the throne.

The four living creatures are described by four distinct characteristics. Notice, the four descriptions are not given in the same format. The first is *like* a lion. The second is *like* a calf. The third had *the face like* a man. The fourth was *like*

a flying eagle. These descriptions give us characteristics, as if in a composite, not a visual to be seen. Like a lion informs us of their powerful position and equally powerful function. The calf is the offspring of a bull, which had the distinction of being representative of majesty, strength, and superiority (Deuteronomy 33:17). This description brings in the characteristic of work, and especially of being a servant. This living creature characteristic is assuredly portraying prominent service, but because it is shown as a calf, is a derived prominence. Neither of these first two creatures can be confused with the One who is on the throne. They are created beings serving as they were created to do.

The third living creature has the *face like* a man. The face was seen as the most prominent part of the body that is presented toward, in front of, or standing before or against another individual (Psalm 34:16). The idea here is that this living creature presents an "in your face" position toward the ones it keeps at a distance. This characteristic shows the task of opposition to the unholy, that which is separated from that which it separates: sinful creation. The fourth living creature is presented as a large bird in flight, that is, the wings are spread. Whenever wings are used as a metaphor or an anthropomorphism, the idea is of the activity the wings perform or provide. Under His wings I am safely abiding (Psalm 36:7). His wings carry the Israelites out of Egypt (Exodus 19:4). Wings are a picture of safety and power. They are never portrayed as just existing and folded on the side of a bird. The wings of the fourth living creature are active in their duty. They are covering, spread out in a posture of the complete and guaranteed enclosure of the throne, as portrayed on the mercy seat of the ark of the covenant.

All of these characteristics of the four living creatures identify, and, are a testimony of their duty and purpose. They are not independent of each other. They continually declare the holiness of the One who is seated on the throne. Holy is the position of being separate and distinct. Three times holy is a statement God's absolute, complete, and replete holiness. He is without equal. There is no doubt about Who, and to Whom they are speaking.

4:9-11 A response of worship is given by the twenty-four elders. The twenty-four elders give honor to the One on the throne by casting their crowns before Him. There is also a song of praise given to exalt the creative power and purposes of God.

There is a further description of the living creatures found in Ezekiel 1:4-8, and Ezekiel 10:1-22. Using these passages, one will find similarities and variations in their descriptions. To the conclusion that the two authors, Ezekiel and John, have seen the same beings, we can get a composite picture of what they represent. One element that is present in both visions is the unity and the unified activities of the four living creatures. There is a discussion of the two author's visions (John's and Ezekiel's) in Appendix A, found at the back of this book.

As we move forward in this drama of redemption, we will now be reminded of the desperate state in which creation existed, and the solution that God has provided.

Be encouraged! God is on His throne!!

9
The Uniqueness of the Lamb
Revelation 5:1-14

5:1 Chapter 5 continues the scene that chapter 4 begins. The continuation of the narrative is sustained in verse 1. All of the participants are involved. John sees a scroll in the right hand of the One seated on the throne. This scroll contains something that has originated from the One who is seated on the throne. The contents of the scroll are of great importance, as the context will bear out. The right hand is the place of honor, privilege, and testimony. The scroll is written on the front and the back, and, sealed with seven seals. There is a precedent given for the scroll in the Old Testament (Jeremiah 32; Ezekiel 2:9-10; Zechariah 5:1-4).

In the custom of the day, a scroll of this design was made to show and record the right of redemption or inheritance for a piece of property. The scroll was written, and a sealed, or closed copy was witnessed by a declared number of people and put away for safe keeping. At some future date, the scroll was opened before the witnesses verifying the deed and the one who inherited the property. This particular scroll is sealed with seven seals, that is, completely sealed. The only one who could legally open the scroll was the inheritor. The scroll being written inside and out would represent the fullness of the deed. If similar to the scroll in Ezekiel, the writing inside and out would represent lamentation and woe, characteristics indeed contained in the book of Revelation (see Ezekiel 2:9-10).

5:2-6 John hears a strong angel with a loud voice ask, "Who is worthy to open the scroll and loose its seals?" This announcement ends up being a rhetorical question, because the next verse informs that there is no one in all of creation who is worthy to open the scroll, much less look at it. John is devastated and in grief. This tells us that John understood the significance of the scroll and its implications. He is comforted by an elder who encourages him that there is One who has prevailed and is worthy to open the scroll and implement it. The titles given to the One who has prevailed leaves no margin of error as to the identity of this person. These are Messianic titles coming from the prophecies of the Old Testament (Genesis 49:8-10; Isaiah 11:1ff).

John turns to see the One who is the lion, and, sees a Lamb as though it had been slain. This is one of many instances where what is heard (the inner reality) by John, is interpreted alongside what he sees. The Lamb is in the midst of the throne and the four living creatures, and, He is in the midst of the elders. Notice that in the previous chapter that the four living creatures are in the midst of the throne, and the elders are around the throne. The Lamb is in the midst of the throne, as well as, in the midst of the elders. This speaks of nothing less than the Lamb's sharing the presence of God, and sharing the presence of the elders. He has deity and He has humanity. The elders are not angels. They are representative of the triumphant people of God.

The Lamb is seen as having seven eyes and seven horns. This is one place where symbolic communication is shown at its best. We can be sure that the Lamb represents Jesus. This picture of Jesus as the Lamb, looks back to His work on the cross in the same way that John the Baptist declared Jesus as the Lamb, looking forward to His work on the cross (John 1:29-36). The seven eyes represent His complete omniscience and identity with the Spirit, and the seven horns represent His complete power and strength (Revelation 4:5). Horns are generally figurative for power and strength (2 Samuel 22:3).

5:7 The Lamb came and took the scroll out of the right hand of Him who was seated on the throne. The fact that the Lamb took the scroll bars all imposter interpretations that do not conclude that this is the risen Christ who has all authority. In so many places it is said, that "it was given" (as in Revelation 9:1-5). In this scene, there is no giving. The Lamb is completely worthy, and He is able.

At this point it is imperative to understand the authority of the Lamb in relation to what the scroll represents, and what it contains. The interpretation of this section does not allow it to be placed into the future. There are many places in Scripture that maintain the Lamb, Jesus Christ, has already received all authority because of His completed work of redemption on the cross and His subsequent ascension. The Gospel writers record that Jesus said, "All authority has been given to Me in heaven and on earth" (Matthew 28:18; see also John 3:35; Acts 1:9-11; Philippians 2:9-11; Colossians 1:15-18; Hebrews 1:3,13; Revelation 3:21). Many people neglect to consider the

Ascension of Jesus and what He received *at that time*. **This is Jesus' enthronement scene.** To consider that there is any other rule that He is to receive in the future is error and leads to misunderstanding the structure of what is occurring in Revelation 5. He has the authority to take the final decree of God and break the seals.

The seals then, represent what will, and what has been in play since the first coming of Jesus. The scroll, representing the final decree and the redeemed possession of God, cannot be separated from the prophecies that have come before. To this end, we must look at what the scroll represents in context with the rest of the Scriptures. We must look at the prophecies of Daniel, among others, to give us insight and closure to what has already been given. We know that the book of Revelation is the revealing of Jesus Christ. He is the warrior king Who has complete sovereignty over the seals and the contents of the scroll. Let us go back and pick up the history of redemption.

Soon after the Fall, God set in motion the plan of redemption that involved the seed of the woman in conflict with the seed of the serpent (Genesis 3:15). God set out to create a people for Himself from which the Messiah, the Redeemer, would ultimately come (Deuteronomy 18:15; Romans 9:4-5). He set out a plan of sanctification that included the people being set apart, and a pattern of worship and observances the would show them their responsibility and privileges. They were to follow these commands to the fulfillment of the plan of God. Through the course of their history the people failed many times. It was during the life and ministry of Daniel, while in captivity in Babylon, that the Lord gave a prophecy, among many given to Daniel, to wrap up His plan of redemption (Daniel 9:24-27). While the prophecy was not complete in its detail, it is the foundation for what we have been given in the book of Revelation.

The background for this prophecy is tied to why they were in Babylonian captivity, and to the length of time for the captivity and the desolation of Jerusalem. Daniel had been reading in Jeremiah the Prophet that the captivity they were experiencing was about come to an end (Jeremiah 25:11-12; 29:10). The length of time for this punishment was for the violation of the Sabbath laws concerning the Sabbath year, when the land was to be given rest (Leviticus

25:4-5; 26:32-35). The people were in captivity, and their land was desolate for the same number of Sabbath years that they did not give the land rest as they were commanded. So, if every seventh year was a year of rest, the people were to be in captivity and the land to be desolate for those seventy Sabbath years. The violations concerning the Sabbath years started 490 years before the desolation of Jerusalem began, which occurred in 586 B.C. That puts the first violation at about the time of Eli and his two sons (1 Samuel 1-4).

The specific prophecy that Daniel was given involved another 490 years, or 70 weeks of years, to "finish transgression, make an end of sin, make reconciliation for iniquity, bring in everlasting righteousness, seal up vision and prophecy, and anoint the Most Holy" (Daniel 9:24). Daniel is then given a timeline of events, not dates, of significant points in the plan of redemption. The 70 weeks of years are broken into three sections (See below). The first is 7 weeks of years, or 49 years. The second is 62 weeks, or 434 years. The third and last is of 1 week, or 7 years, often referred to as the Seventieth week of Daniel.

DANIEL 9:24-27 DIAGRAM

70 WEEKS
Seventy sevens

Finish transgression, End of sins, Reconciliation for iniquity, Everlasting righteousness, Seal vision and prophecy, Anoint most holy.

Seven sevens (49 Years)	Sixty-two sevens (434 Years)		One seven (7 Years)
Street	Messiah cut off	War	He
Wall	Prince to come	Desolations decreed	Confirms a covenant
Troubled times	Destroy City		One week
	Flood		Middle of week
			End of sacrifice
			Abomination
			Consummation
			Poured on desolator

It is interesting that the first section is 49 years and is consistent with an ordinance of a Jubilee cycle (Leviticus 25:9-54). Did the land revert to the possession of the Israelites in the fiftieth year after their release? We know that the first Passover after the release from captivity is noted in Ezra 6:19.

From the issuing of a decree to restore and rebuild Jerusalem until Messiah, there will be 7 and 62 weeks, or 483 years (Daniel 9:25). The timeline begins with the decree of Artaxerxes Longimanus in the year 454 B.C. (Nehemiah 1-2).[1] This ruler of Persia served as Co-rex with his father for 9 years, and he gave the decree and the supplies to Nehemiah to rebuild the city of Jerusalem. After the 62 weeks of years, the Messiah will be cut off, or killed (Daniel 9:26). The Messiah, or Anointed One, understood to be Jesus, is crucified for His people in the year A.D. 30.

There follows then, desolations of different kinds until a prince comes to make a covenant with a group of people for the last week of seven years, breaking the covenant in the middle, ending with this prince being destroyed (Daniel 9:27). This week of seven years has yet to be fulfilled. If the prince that makes the covenant is the Man of Lawlessness, then other parts of Scripture can be consulted for this fulfillment (see 2 Thessalonians 2; Revelation 13). (Much help and insight were gleaned from the works of Floyd Jones: Chronology of the Old Testament.) If this prophecy can be understood as concluding at the beginning of eternity, then it has a foundational part to play in how we see the book of Revelation in the context of completed prophecy. Revelation gives us the details about the end of this age as we know it. It is the assertion of this author, that Daniel chapters 10-12 must be read and understood without a postponement of the 70th week. This postponement did occur because of the unbelieving people of Jesus day.

The Worship of the Lamb

5:8 The book of Revelation was meant to be read aloud and heard (Revelation 1:3; 22:14). This is most apparent in the worship passages that are placed throughout the text. Indeed, the book of Revelation, being described as a revealing of Jesus Christ, should bring forth nothing but adoration, praise, and worship. To worship is to bring worth to the object or person to which your attention is focused. The entire book of Revelation is about Jesus Christ. Jerry Flora, a seminary professor and good friend, states in his work that, "The Revelation is not to be read silently and analyzed, but to be listened to, experienced, and obeyed," and "it was to be declared in a public setting."[2] This truth comes to its zenith in the worship that is contained in the book. The Revelation focuses our worship on the person and promises of Jesus Christ.

The vision of the risen Christ in chapter 1 gives us a picture of the One who has authority and identity with, and as, the Lord of all. The worship that begins in these verses acknowledges the work of the One who has given all and has overcome to redeem His people. When the Lamb takes the scroll from the One seated on the throne there is a scene of worship that takes place in heaven. The four living creatures, who have the role of maintaining the oversight and separation of creation from the throne, and the elders who represent the triumphant saints, worship in response to the One who now can execute the contents of the scroll. They have harps to show the peace that they now have. They also have bowls that contain the prayers of petition from the saints that are on the earth.

5:9-14 Their song contains a declaration of the triumph and worthiness of the Lamb to execute the deed. The criterion for this exaltation is the redeeming work of the Lamb in being slain and providing redemption. Those being redeemed are from all peoples of the earth. This redemption issues into a status of being a royal priesthood who will reign on the earth (1 Peter 2:4-10).

John then sees the innumerable host in heaven in praise of the Lamb. The attributes of their worship numbers seven. The Lamb receives a complete and full acknowledgement of praise and merit. Then, a full representation of those redeemed in the whole of the cosmos respond in worship. The four living creatures declare it to be true, and the elders fall down again in worship.

The end of this magnificent scene involves the fourfold worship of all creatures who identify the Lamb with the One Who sits on the throne. This is a clear declaration of deity assigned to the Lamb who is Jesus Christ. The four living creatures declare it to be so, with the representatives of the victorious people of God serving in worship. Be encouraged! Let us join them!!

10

The Sovereignty of the Lamb
Revelation 6:1-17

As we begin our look at the seven seals, it is important to notice what connects these seals together with chapters 4 and 5. There is no indication in the text that there is a gap, or postponement, between the Lamb taking the scroll and opening the first seal. There is also no indication of any event that happens in the "space" between chapter 5 and chapter 6. There will be a direct application from the first six seals and what can be observed from the facts of history, from the time of Jesus' first coming until the present day. The seals will represent the general operating conditions and characteristics of the world until He returns. The seals have a direct correlation to the events that Jesus gave to the disciples on the Mount of Olives concerning things to come (Matthew 24; Mark 13; Luke 21). (See Appendix B for this comparison.)

The Lamb, the scroll, the seals, and the living creatures provide the continuity and connection of the narrative into the next chapter. The seals as a unit, and as a whole, present to the reader

and the hearer a complete picture of their own. In that interpretation, we must consider what they have in common. This is a big step towards interpreting the details contained in them. The Lamb is the One who breaks and has sovereignty over each of the seals. He is the One who has the authority and the right to do so. Jesus is the faithful and true witness. Each of the first six seals begin something that is continued until the seventh seal is opened. The seventh seal contains the same idea of finality that is present in the seventh trumpet and the seventh bowl (compare Revelation 8:5; 11:15-19; 16:17-21). The seventh bowl being the last of the wrath of God (Revelation 15:1; 16:17). There is a strong indication that all of the seals can be understood as containing results due to the effects of sin.

The scroll in the time of the first century, was in the design of a long piece of parchment, or sometimes papyrus, that was used to record written information. The long pieces were rolled onto two rods or decorative dowel like pieces. The two rods were rolled towards one another gathering the parchment into a bundle that could be easily carried or stored. Some scrolls reached several feet in length depending on the amount of writing that was needed. There is not any evidence, nor does it make any practical sense, that any of the contents of the scroll could be executed until all of the seals were broken. Once all the seals are broken, and only then, can the actions of the trumpets and bowls be in play. If the seven trumpets are actions within the seventh seal opening, then this is crucial to the design and speed of the ending. This is an important point in how the book of Revelation is interpreted. There is issue with an interpretation that allows a seal to be broken, and *part* of the scroll being read. (There is evidence that a codex type of writing began to exist at the time of the first century, but no evidence that this type of book was used by John in his description.) Again, the Old Testament is our key to understanding the symbols in this case. What the scroll actually contains is of utmost importance. This scroll contains the final decree of God.

In the book of Jeremiah, the scroll represents the deed of inheritance of the one to whom the scroll belongs. It is executed by the "faithful and true witness." In Jeremiah, the scroll represents the return of the people of God to the land of their promise. The return would happen after a designated time of seventy years (Jeremiah 25:11; 29:10; Daniel 9:2). It is Daniel that is given a prophecy that describes the wrapping up of history as we know it (Daniel 9:24-27). The Anointed is cut off after the sixty-ninth week, and the last week of sevens has yet to be fulfilled (Daniel 9:27). This author holds that the activities of the seventieth week are the contents written within the scroll.

The first four seals are often associated with the title, "the four horsemen of the apocalypse." The first four seals are similar, and, are most likely the same four horses mentioned in the Old Testament (Zechariah 1:6-11; 6:1-8). These horses are seen as a unit, being sent by the Spirit of God. They cause unrest in all of its dimensions and, are used for the sovereign purposes of God. The four horses are directly associated with the four living creatures, who are involved in allowing, and even commanding them to go forward. The symbolism of the number four informs the hearer that these two sets of four are involved with the realm of the created, that which is seen and experienced primarily on earth.

It must be noted that whenever John states that he saw, or that he looked, he is almost always using the Greek word *eido* (see chapter 3 and Revelation 1:19). This word was discussed earlier in this book. It has the meaning of grasping, understanding, and fully knowing that which he is beholding. This is different in meaning than just physically seeing the vision. The book of Revelation is to be heard *and* understood. The readers must also understand that Christ is not only aware of the transpiring horses and riders, but that He is also sovereign over their ride.

Revelation 6:1-13 The First Six Seals

6:1-2 John sees the first of the seven seals opened by the Lamb. The first living creature gives the command to come and see. The voice like thunder associates the living creatures with the One they serve, that is, God. Immediately a white horse appears. The white horse was used many times to represent the victory of the conquering leader. The use here may represent one who is, or has, some measure of victory. It is not logical that the Lamb is the one on the white horse, as He is the one who is opening the seals. Revelation chapter 19:11-16 is used many times to give definition to the rider on the white horse of the first seal. Rather, we must see the white horse as part of the whole unit, portrayed much like the unit in

Zechariah. There is no indication that Christ is riding the white horse in Zechariah. In fact, the Angel of the Lord who stood among the myrtle trees may be an Old Testament appearance of Christ Jesus (Joshua 5:13; Zechariah 1:12). The last three horses are initiated by the white horse (Revelation 6:8).

The one who sat on this white horse had a bow. Contrast Jesus, the rider with many diadems (Revelation 19:12). The bow was used in hunting and in warfare. The results of hunting and warfare was the same: inflicted death. The white horse rider has the appearance of, and is acting in, victory. His activity leads to the second horse, as each horse leads to the next successive stage that is represented. The rider on the white horse is given a crown. Anything given is for God's purpose. There is no hint in the book of Revelation that Christ is given anything. Jesus *has* the authority and sovereignty. He *receives* worship because He is worthy. He *takes* the scroll from the One who sits on the throne. This rider is *given* his authority. There are many places in the book of Revelation where the term "given," or "it was given," is used. Mostly, anything given is always to something evil, not to Christ.

Anything that happens, or happens to the saints, is sanctioned by God because He is sovereign.

The Greek word for crown is *stephanos*, which has the idea of a surrounding character and environment. This rider is sent out to serve the purposes of God. The rider's tools result in unrest and strife. The rider went out conquering and to conquer. The Greek word for conquer is also translated many times as prevail or overcome. Associated with this horse is subjugation and oppression in a negative sense. Who, or what, does this rider and conquer overcome? The references to the ones he wishes to overcome are many, if we identify him with the work of Satan. We know his time is short, and that he is angry (Revelation 12:12, 17). Scripture tells us many times that there are seasons and places in history when Satan will prevail over the Saints (Daniel 7:21, 25; Daniel 12:7; Revelation 11:7; 12:13-17; 13:7). The strife and deception of the first rider will lead to the activity of the second (James 4:1-4). Some interpret the white horse to represent the victory of the Gospel. The Gospel is never won by warfare and does not lead to the second horse. The Gospel is victorious through submission, suffering, and sacrifice. Christ is our example.

6:3-4 Christ opens the second seal and the second living creature bids a fiery red horse to come. Red speaks of death. It was granted to the one riding the horse to take peace from the earth. The peace being taken away from the earth is in contrast to the peace that the believer has with God through the work of Christ (Romans 5:1). Not only is peace taken from the earth, it is taken from between those who dwell on the earth. The result is bloodshed. The sword of this rider is used for up-close combat, assassinations, and revolt.

6:5-6 When the Lamb opened the third seal, the third living creature brings the third horse into activity. The third horse is a black horse. This horse represents famine. There are a pair of scales in the hands of the rider. The scales were a sign used to denote scarcity (Ezekiel 4:16). The Greek word for scale comes from the same root that also has a meaning of a yoke. Famine can be a great burden. Famine is a result of war. Putting the scales and the grain together was a picture of eating bread by weight. This was a judgement from God for disobedience (Leviticus 26:26; Ezekiel 4:16-17). Famine creates a longing and dissatisfaction that was meant to turn people back to God. The basic foods of people were to be affected. Wheat was a staple for all, and barley was the food of the poor. It could be that not harming oil and wine, the substance of wealth, could mean the imbalance or uneven distribution of goods and services. This famine does not go to the most extreme of affecting the oil and wine.

In the Old Testament, many times, famine was also associated with disobedience to the word of God. In addition, there was a kind of judgement that involved a famine of the word of God (Amos 8:11). In relation to that kind of famine, a limitation of the oil and wine could represent a restricted presence of the spirit and joy in the midst of the trials. Hunger, caused by a famine, was meant to instill in us a desire to turn back to God. We are to see this hunger in both physical and spiritual dimensions.

Oil and wine are both used as metaphors for the blessings of God. Wheat, barley, oil, and wine are mentioned together in various places. They were given to the Levites and Priests (2 Chronicles 2:10; Nehemiah 10:39; 13:12). The restriction of not harming the oil and the wine has a symbolic representation in this picture. Oil was used for anointing and authority, consecration, and represented God's blessing (Exodus 29:7; 40:9; Isaiah 61:3). Oil was also used for the continual light in the temple (Exodus 27:20; Leviticus 24:2). Light represents the illuminating work and testimony of the Holy Spirit.

Wine was created by Jesus in His first miracle, to represent the beginning of the new Covenant in Him (John 2:1-10). Jesus taught that it is also best to put new wine into new wineskins, a parable of the new Covenant (Luke 5:36-39). Oil and wine are used together to aid in cleansing, healing, and restoration (Luke 10:33-34). During the experiences of the famines of the black horse, there will be a continual, unharmed presence and ongoing working out of the blessings, illumination, and restoration that are of God's new Covenant in Christ. This is during the seals (Matthew 16:18).

6:7-8 When the Lamb opened the fourth seal, the fourth living creature calls the fourth horse into activity. The fourth horse was pale and had the name of Death, and Hades followed death. Hades is the Greek word that means "place of the dead." Power was given to them over all the earth to kill with the sword, hunger, death, and by wild beasts. The sword used here is not the short dagger, but the long sword. This sword is for reaching a great distance (Luke 2:35; Revelation 1:16). Death has a one to one ratio, in that it affects each and every person. Wild beast is a metaphor used many times to refer to a foreign nation that is a hostile enemy (Leviticus 26:22; Jeremiah 11:9-14). The nations of the earth will be enemies of one another, subjecting one another to death.

6:9-11 The fifth seal moves from the seen, the physical creation, to the unseen or spiritual dimension. John understands that there is a record of those who have been martyred because of their faith and testimony for the word of God. Slain, or martyred, could also represent all those who have died in the Lord. Martyrdom is being used as the extreme measure, so as to include all who have died in Christ. The altar, is the altar of sacrifice. Under the altar speaks of the agency by which their death is rendered. That they are represented as being souls would imply that their conditions are not yet glorified. Their plea for justice, or vindication, reinforces this condition. The white robes are mentioned other places in the Revelation as garments that represent a reward of

immortality to the overcomer (Revelation 3:5). The saints under the altar were told to rest a while longer until the completed number of those who would die like they did is accomplished. Martyrdom will also continue until the Day of the Lord.

6:12-13 John looks when the Lamb opens the sixth seal. There is a great earthquake. The Greek word for earthquake, *seismos* (we get the words seismology and seismograph), describes the changing of a landscape or a great shaking. The earthquake imagery is often used in Scripture and apocalyptic literature to symbolize the power and sovereignty of God, or the fall of one kingdom to the rising of the next. The landscape of the heavens is changed (Hebrews 12:25-27). The sun, moon, and stars, are affected. It must be remembered that this is a book full of symbolism. If so, what do these heavenly bodies represent? Together they are light bearers. They are creations of God to give aid, guidance, and revelation to those on the earth. The illumination given by these heavenly bodies is used for guidance. Light makes things visible.

The first place that all three light bearers are mentioned together as a group is in the creation narrative (Genesis 1:14-18). The nations were chastised for worshipping the heavenly bodies. It is of special interest to this study is the inclusion of the three heavenly bodies shown in the dreams of Joseph, and the interpretations given by his father Jacob (Genesis 37:9-11). Jacob gives part of the interpretation of the dream as symbolizing himself, Joseph's mother, and Joseph's eleven brothers. This gives us the first picture of the nation of Israel as being represented as the sun, moon, and the stars. We then have the nation of Israel symbolized as a woman clothed with the sun in chapter 12, with the moon under her feet, and a crown of twelve stars. The sun, moon, and stars are mentioned together in several other poignant places (Joel 2:31; Matthew 24:29; Mark 13:24; Luke 21:25; Acts 2:20; 3:17-26). All of these last references are in the context of the last days. All of these must be interpreted correctly and in proper context.

The author of Hebrews tells us that God: "has in these last days, spoken to us by His Son" (Hebrews 1:2). The last days started with Jesus first coming. On the day of Pentecost, Peter declared that, "In the last days the Spirit would be poured out, and the "heavenly bodies" would be changed,

before the coming of the great and awesome Day of the Lord, and it shall come to pass that all who call on the name of the Lord shall be saved" (Acts 2:17-21). All of these events shall occur, *and then*, it shall come to pass that each person shall call upon the Lord. What does the sun and moon activity represent in this context?

Light makes things visible. The sun is our major source of revelation, how we see things. We would know nothing if God had not graciously revealed Himself and our condition to us. He is our sun, our revealer (Psalm 84:11). The moon reflects the light of the sun. The cycles of the moon are also the markers to which the ceremonial law was tied. These ceremonial laws gave the pattern for approaching God. The nation of Israel, was God's agent of the ceremonial law. To them was given the stewardship, and responsibility of expressing the priestly role before God to the world (Romans 9:4-5). The stars are used to represent angels, messengers, ambassadors, and princes. The twelve brothers are the princes of Israel, the representatives of the twelve tribes. The nation of Israel was clothed with revelation from God (Romans 3:2; 9:4). She had responsibility, and, was an agent of the ceremonies that were practiced as a shadow of the heavenly temple (Hebrews 8:5). The stars were eventually to be the individual persons in the nation of Israel that were responsible to be priests of God to the nations (Exodus 19:5-6; Daniel 12:3). Stars are used for guidance and direction while it was night, or during the night.

The sun is darkened. It will lose its position of giving revelation. Jesus is the light that has now come into the world. The moon will turn to blood. The system of worship and identification with the pattern to approach God will die and pass away (Hebrews 8:13). Jesus has fulfilled the temple worship. The stars will fall from the sky. The stars will no longer be needed as the representatives for direction and guidance, as each person will be able to call upon the Lord for themselves (Hebrews 8:10-11). The natural cataclysm, as it seems to be perceived, is rather a change in the spiritual landscape of heaven in how revelation, or guidance, is to be given. This is also a symbolic way of showing how the revelation is changing from an external means to an internal means. A move from an ethnic, physical, and works covenant, to an invisible, spiritual covenant of

grace through faith alone. The church, as the Body of Christ, now fulfills the role of what the ethnic nation of Israel previously was to perform. Some are calling this replacement theology. It should be thought through as fulfillment theology (Exodus 19:6; 1 Peter 2:5-9).

6:14-16 The next phase that John is given is an observation of the sky being closed, or, the places of refuge being removed from reliability or familiarity. The same idea is given as part of the white throne judgement (Revelation 20:11). Every human being, from the greatest to the smallest, that has trusted in the known and familiar, seeks to hide themselves in the features of mountains. If we remember that this is part of the results of the earthquake mentioned in verse 12, then we can see that this is a transition from the particular ethnic nation of God's people and the temple, to the fulfillment that is found in Jesus Christ. The references found here bring forward the same judgement language portrayed in the Old Testament (Isaiah 2:12-19; Isaiah 34:4; Hosea 10:1-8). The judgement is not just from God alone, but, also from the Lamb. The image of the Lamb is always associated with the cross of

Calvary. God has now put all judgement into the hands of Jesus. The reference to the Lamb takes us back to chapter 5 where John sees a Lamb as if it had been slain. What the Old Testament people had for the covering of sin is now fulfilled in the Lamb on the cross. He takes away their sin! How can we escape if we reject so great a salvation (Hebrews 2:3)? For the Father has committed all judgement to the Son (John 5:22-23).

The religious leaders claimed they understood their rejection of Jesus, and so their sin remains unto them (John 9:41). No one comes to the Father except through Jesus (John 14:6). The Holy Spirit will convict the world of sin because they do not know Him (John 16:9). The Lamb on the cross now becomes that which saves or condemns. Judgement is now based on rejection of the Lamb and His completed work on the cross. Jesus, as He is headed to His crucifixion, states this same scenario as judgement to the people of His day concerning His rejection (see Luke 23:27-31). This also puts the fulfillment of this seal at the time of His first coming. Until the Lord returns, all the characteristics of these seals are in play. One can find the same pattern in the Creation narrative

of six days and a day of rest. All six days of creation are simultaneously existing from the beginning until the new heaven and new earth, the time of rest.

6:17 Everything that the Old Testament predicted by way of the Messiah's first coming has come to pass. The Lamb that takes away the sin of the world has declared from the cross that it is finished. They ask the question, "who can stand?" This question harkens back to the prophet Malachi who gives a picture of the work of God's messenger (Malachi 3:4ff). This Messenger will come to purify and make clean the people of God. He will come near to do the work of God. How will the people respond? The question has two answers and creates a separation. Jesus spoke of this time and occasion (Luke 12:49-53). One answer will take unbelievers straight to the seventh seal (Revelation 8:1). The answer to who can stand, is given in chapter 7!

The seals in their order represent: the spirit of conquest, war, famine, death, martyrdom, and fulfillment. They are inaugurated at the exaltation of Jesus at His ascension, and, are actively in play and leading to the Day of the Lord. The seventh seal represents the Day of the Lord.

11

The Redeemed of the Lamb
Revelation 7

After the sixth seal John is given a parenthetical section, an interlude, before the seventh seal (see Diagram #4, pg. 36). The seventh seal will be the completion of the set of seals. It should be remembered that all six seals are located before the Day of the Lord and are not part of it (Joel 2:28-32; Acts 2:20). The interlude is an explanation of the details of the redeemed (Revelation 7:1-17). The seventh seal represents the judgement of the Day of the Lord. It is important to the interpretation of the book of Revelation, that other options be considered than the ones put forth that rely heavily on the chapter and verse headings in most translations. Some of these hinder the narrative at times.

The event that occurs as a result of the seventh seal being opened at the beginning of chapter 8, portrays a picture of separation. The separation is the redeemed from the unbelievers. This separation is maintained throughout the seven trumpets, and then finalized by the seven bowls of wrath. Chapter 7 sets the parameters of the separation. There are those who will suffer the judgement and wrath of God, and there are those who have been sovereignly exempted from the wrath. The Lamb is central to the separation. He is the reason for the separation. As the book of Revelation is further unfolded in the series of trumpets, the separation is given in more details. When we read of the seven bowls, the separation has been firmly established and will be permanent.

7:1 John is given the vision of four angels standing at the four corners of the earth, that is: the whole earth. These four angels are holding back the four winds of the earth. Winds are symbolic of adversity and calamity (Job 27:21; Jeremiah 49:36; Matthew 7:25-27; Ephesians 4:14). The winds are held back from blowing on the earth, on the sea, or on any tree. The Greek word for on, *epi*, can be translated many different ways: on, over, across, at, against, into, or toward, etc. It is important to consider that the winds of adversity are held back from blowing on *the* earth, *the* sea, and *the* trees. The earth, sea, and trees are not passive spectators, they are the targets. All of these represent groups of people.

A tree, for example, is used often to represent an individual person in many passages of Scripture (Judges 9; Psalm 1:3; Isaiah 11:1; Jeremiah 17:5-8; Ezekiel 17; 31; Zechariah 4:11-14; Matthew 7:15-20; Jude 12; Revelation 9:4; 11:4). Trees are symbolic as representing individual rulers and people of stature. We have already discussed the symbolism of the sea in chapter 4, and it must be seen as a particular mass of people. The earth is also symbolic of a particular group of people in contrast to the sea. The earth is the group of people who rise above the sea and follow the precepts of God as they know them, even if it is indirectly. This is specific to the ones who govern and have principality. The earth is a creation of God, and man, who is created to worship God, is made from the dust of the earth.

7:2-3 John then sees another angel coming from the east with the seal of the living God. The angel is *from the east,* from the rising of the sun. There are two cases in the New Testament where the term, *from (of) the east*, is used. This verse, and another passage concerning the kings *from the east* (Revelation 16:12). The LXX translation of the Hebrew Old Testament translates the Hebrew word, *the Branch,* using the Greek name *Anatole* (Zechariah 6:12, LXX). The same term, *anatole,* is used in Revelation 7:2 and 16:12. *The Branch,* used in the Old Testament, is a Messianic term for the Messiah, or Anointed One. (The Branch, like Son of David, The Prophet, and Holy One, are just a few names that fall under the umbrella term of Messiah.) This, then, is an angel coming from the Messiah. When Jesus returns, He comes like lightning from the east (Matthew 24:27). There are other Scriptures that contain the same idea concerning the Messiah (Isaiah 9:2; 60:1-3; Malachi 4:2; Luke 1:78; 2 Peter 1:19; Revelation 22:16). (See discussion at Revelation 16:12, also.)

The "seal" is the same Greek word used in the New Testament to describe the security and guarantee of the Holy Spirit in the believers' life (2 Corinthians 1:22; Ephesians 1:13; 4:30). The angel cries loudly to the four angels not to harm anything *until* the seal of God is placed on the foreheads of the servants of God. At this point there is a major division in understanding what is actually happening in this sequence. One view is that the "sealing" is a beginning action that continues in the ones being sealed, then going forward as a group to be involved in the remainder of the book of Revelation. Remembering the symbolism of the seventh, and that the seventh seal will be the culmination of the seals, this does not do due justice to the context. The seventh seal, seventh trumpet, and the seventh bowl all portray the same ending event in increasing detail and intensity. The four angels who are sent to harm the elements are withheld *until* the sealing is completed. The sealed number, then, is not a beginning number, but a number of fullness, completeness, a multiplied maximum. Once that number is reached, the four angels are free to execute their duty of harm and judgement represented by the last seal (Revelation 9:4).

7:4 John hears a specific number that are sealed, and then a further detailed breakdown of that number with specific names. At this point a question must be asked of the preterist and ultra-dispensational approaches to the interpretation of the book. If the following verses are only for the church of the past to find application, or if they are for a future time in which only a select, finite number of individuals who need to be aware, what does this mean in the context of the book and its prologue declarations? To be sure, there are many prophecies that did not directly affect the ones hearing it at the time they were given. But we cannot ignore the statements that this prophecy was relevant to the original hearers and to the hearers of our contemporary times.[1,2] These verses in chapter seven hold much for our understanding and are similar in their meaning as is the description of the holy city, the new Jerusalem of chapters 21–22. The whole of Scripture begs us to know the correct interpretation. We must remember that Revelation is apocalyptic literature. As such, it uses symbolic representation which must be observed in this passage.

The total number being sealed is 144,000. The number 144 is also part of the description of the holy city (Revelation 21:12-17). This number is the square of 12, which is the number of God's administration, or how He governs. To have a number squared gives the concept of fullness. To have the number multiplied by 1,000 is to give it the meaning of entirety (Deuteronomy 1:11; 7:9; Psalm 50:10; 90:4). To be sealed means the idea of possession, security, and being set apart (see above). That which is numbered and sealed is included into a complete, united group called Israel.[3]

At this point an issue of semantics needs to come into focus. The terms Israel, Jew, and Hebrew are not the same words, and do not have the same definitions. They can have some overlap, but cannot be used interchangeably in most cases. The confusion exists when we use words that are not in the text. This is often due to our ignorance of the terms and their use in the historical, biblical narratives. The verse declares from all the tribes of Israel, not that they must be Jews alone (Revelation 2:9; 3:9). If we do not use the correct terms in their proper way, the interpretation will elude us.

Israel is the sacral term for the chosen totality of the elect of God and those united to Him. Kittle states that Israel represents the people chosen by God and revealed in them, denoting inner essence.[4] The rise and subsequent separation of the monarchy changed the use. The northern kingdom was called Israel, but were not in compliance with God's commands. The use of the title does not change its meaning and intent given by God. Israel means to struggle and strive with God, and possibly, to rule with God.

Jew is the term given to the adherents of the ceremonial law, an inhabitant of Judah, or those of a specific religious confession. Not all those given to be part of Israel fall under the name Jew. Indeed, Abraham, Isaac, and Jacob (whose name was changed to Israel) were not part of the formal ceremonial law given later through Moses. And yet they are included in the Commonwealth of Israel, along with the current church, the body of Christ (Ephesians 2:11-13). The term Jew does not appear in Scripture until late in the divided monarchy (2 Kings 18ff). To suggest that the term Israel can be interchanged for the term Jews, who were antagonistic to Jesus and the Apostles, is to confuse the term and the narratives of the Gospel of John and the book of Acts.

The etymology of the term Hebrew belongs to the name Eber, an ancestor of the Hebrew people (Genesis 10:21). It had the connotation of being a nomad with no settled property. The name Hebrew was often used in a vein of contempt, and sometimes humility. It is interesting that the New Testament book of Hebrews is addressing those who need to move on to, or come back to, the reality and rest of their faith beginnings.

It is traditional in the Old Testament, that whenever a military campaign was to be engaged, a census of the military qualified individuals was taken. This census represents the covenant people militant in distinction to the covenant people triumphant (Revelation 7:9).[5] There are other qualifications of this militant group, which are similar in scope to the Old Testament narratives (see Revelation 14:4-5).

7:5-8 So then, in these verses we are given a census of sorts. Each of the tribes listed is given the same number. There is no other place in Scripture where the tribes of Israel are even close to being equal in population. This of itself is indicative of the symbolism we must see. The second item to notice is the exclusion of two tribes, Ephraim and Dan. This is intriguing in light of verse 4 which states that this constitutes *all* the tribes of Israel. They are not *all* listed. Much has been made of the order, and that is not to be ignored. Most of the lists in Scripture do not have any set order except maybe for the tribe of Judah, moving to the first position because of a prophecy, as is the case here (Genesis 49:8-10). Likewise, there are many explanations as to why Ephraim is excluded, and that the tribe should be included in Joseph. That does not explain why Manasseh is listed. The reasons for Dan being

excluded is the closest to the correct interpretation. There are even reasons for the tribal exclusions given that include scribal errors. That explanation could be valid if it were proven by variant manuscripts. Being none, we must not assume to say God cannot superintend His word. The biblical narrative answers the questions, along with the purpose of the book of Revelation itself.

Why does it state from *all* the tribes of Israel, and yet omit two of them? We are given the names of only twelve tribes. In most cases we understand the number of tribes to be twelve (Matthew 19:28; Acts 26:7; James 1:1). The patriarch Jacob had twelve sons from his two wives and his two wives' maidservants. They are listed in the first book of the Bible (Genesis 35:23-25). Joseph, one of the sons of Jacob, is sold into slavery in Egypt and has two sons of his own, Manasseh and Ephraim (Genesis 46:20). Jacob, after moving to Egypt and meeting the two boys, blesses Joseph's two sons and adopts them as his own (48:8-20). Jacob then blesses his own sons, who still number twelve (Genesis 49).

At the beginning of Exodus, we are told of the twelve brothers and their fruitfulness in number (Exodus 1:1-4). But how many tribes left Egypt during the exodus of Moses time? We are told of the census that was taken during the beginning of the wilderness campaign (Numbers 1:1-15ff). Manasseh and Ephraim are called the people of Joseph, and, are given the distinguishing titles of tribes of Israel. The tribe of Levi is involved in a separate census (see Numbers 3-4). Together, there are *thirteen* tribes that leave Egypt during the exodus. The tribe of Levi is set apart for their zeal for the Name of the Lord (Exodus 32:25-29; Numbers 17). Notice, the tribe of Levi is then listed in chapter 7 of Revelation (7:7). (See table below.)

The 12 Tribes

Genesis 35, 49	Numbers 1	Revelation 7
REUBEN	REUBEN	JUDAH
SIMEON	SIMEON	REUBEN
LEVI	GAD	GAD
JUDAH	JUDAH	ASHER
ISSACHAR	ISSACHAR	NAPHTALI
ZEBULUN	ZEBULUN	MANASSEH
JOSEPH	EPHRAIM	SIMEON
BENJAMIN	MANASSEH	LEVI
DAN	BENJAMIN	ISSACHAR
NAPHTALI	DAN	ZEBULUN
GAD	ASHER	JOSEPH
ASHER	NAPHTALI	BENJAMIN
	LEVI - Num. 1:46-49 (a 13TH TRIBE)	OMITTED: DAN EPHRAIM

Again, there are two tribes normally included in the Scriptural narrative that are not included in the list in chapter 7. These two tribes are Ephraim and Dan. Of extra note is the inclusion of Joseph as a tribe with only one his two sons, the one named Manasseh. What must be adhered to, is the instructions in the first part of the book declaring that this prophecy is given and signified. At issue is not what is included in the list of tribes, but *what is omitted and why*. The sense of the whole book of Revelation is not the preservation of the lives of the readers, but not being deceived into idolatry, or any form of false worship.

As one follows the Biblical narrative of the Old Testament, there are two major events that trigger the explanation of the two tribes that are omitted from the list. The first is found in Judges. This occurs when the nation is first allotted land after the Exodus. After many battles and victories, each tribe is allotted a portion of land according the Word of the Lord as given to Joshua (Joshua 13-19). Dan initially takes their land, but very soon migrated to the far North of the area and conquers and settles in a different location. Not only did they migrate to a different area, but they also set up their own system of false worship (Judges 17-18). They never did follow the Lord in His direction to worship where God designated (Deuteronomy 12). At no point in the narrative of the Bible are we ever given any indication of their compliance about worship.

The second event occurs at the outset of the divided monarchy. The kingdom of Israel is separated into two parts.

The southern kingdom, being two (or three) tribes, takes on the name of the largest tribe, named Judah. The northern kingdom takes the name of Israel, but is also frequently called by the name of the largest, leading tribe, named Ephraim (Isaiah 7:1-17; Hosea 4-14). At the occasion of the separation of the tribes, Jeroboam, who takes rule of the northern kingdom, sets up two places of false worship to keep the people of the north from desiring to travel to Jerusalem to worship the Lord (1 Kings 11:26; 1 Kings 12:26-33). The northern kingdom never had a good king, and never followed the prescribed worship. This continued up to the time of the destruction and deportation of the people by the Assyrians in 722 B.C. Ephraim, and its leaders from that tribe, were responsible for taking the northern kingdom into idolatry.

Now, as we look at the passage in question, we can see the symbolism of the list. The list includes the component tribes of the covenant people of God minus the tribes that were led, or led others, into a false system or place of worship against the commands of God (Deuteronomy 12).

7:9-10 Remembering that the number seven means completeness, and that the seventh seal will then complete the set, we then need to see the narrative of the last part of chapter 7 as completing the scene before the seventh seal is broken. So as John moves from the completed number and name of the covenant people of God who are present on earth, he now sees the completed innumerable number of the redeemed from all ages assembled in heaven just before the end of the set of seals. These redeemed have come from all tribes, nations, and tongues, just as the prophets of the Old and New Testaments have foretold (Hosea 1:10; Luke 2:29-32; Romans 9:25-26). They are clothed with white robes, with palm branches in their hands. These are signs of righteousness and victory. They proclaim the salvation that belongs to God, and to the Lamb. There is no other name under heaven by which men can be saved. And certainly, no other means.

7:11-17 These verses give evidence that the event is final and cosmic. The participants of this scene are all together and of one accord. It includes all the elements of worship and the participation of all of the redeemed. The song that is sung contains a sevenfold message of complete honor and glory in its worship language. Evidence is also given in these verses that the separation is complete and that the multitude is complete for all eternity. The first verses of this chapter portray the completed number of saints on earth while, these verses continue the description of the eternal state of the completed host of saints of all time. They are not just the ones who have endured the great tribulation, but all who are included up through and including the tribulation saints. Their final state is the same that is promised in other parts of Scripture describing the eternal rest. They have robes of righteousness and serve before God. He personally dwells with them, they hunger and thirst not, and there are no effects of the Fall. They are led to the living water, as God had promised (Isaiah 55:1). They are forever in the presence of the Great Shepherd and have no more evidence of tears of grief or pain. Be encouraged! God's promises are yes and amen in Jesus!!

12

The Seventh Seal
Revelation 8:1-5

Keeping in mind the structure of the book of Revelation, we come to the seventh seal. The number seven has the meaning of completion. In the creation narrative God rested on the seventh day, ceasing His work in creation. He does not cease all work, but ceases His specific work of creation. The seventh seal represents the end of the scenario given in the seals. It is not until the seventh seal is broken that the contents of the scroll, the final decrees of God, can be operative. The structure of the book maintains that the seventh seal contains the seven trumpets, and that the seventh trumpet contains the seven bowls. What then are we to conclude about the seventh seal? Mainly, it is one picture given of the end. The contents of the seventh seal will give evidence to this, both in the few verses that will be discussed and explained, and in what can be added from other references from Scripture. Looking at just the verses that are associated directly with the seventh seal, we can draw some inferences and conclusions.

When He, the Lamb, opens the seventh seal there is silence in heaven for about half an hour. The silence is as a result of the seventh seal being opened. The silence is pregnant with meaning as related to the structure of the book. The opening of the seventh seal brings mention of the seven angels who stand before God and are given seven trumpets. There is an angel associated with the opening of the seventh seal in relation to the prayers of the saints and the golden altar. The golden altar was the part of the worship ceremony that represented atonement, or the taking away of sin. The activity of this angel gives the impression of something judgmental and final. And finally, the noises, lightnings, thunderings, and earthquake, will be similar to the last trumpet and the last bowl (Revelation 11:19; 16:19).

8:1 He, the Lamb, opened the seventh seal. What is about to unfold as a result of the breaking all seven seals is by no means unknown or unpermitted by the Lord Jesus Christ. The implications of this are great and grave. There are some who find it very hard to reconcile the suffering, evil, and martyrdom of this life as having little or no purposeful explanation. The response, in part, is that Jesus is our example. The whole world lies under the sway of the wicked one (1 John 5:19). Jesus stated that the world hated Him, therefore, the world will hate us (John 15:18-19). It is through suffering that Jesus won our redemption. It is through suffering that we overcome the evil system, and the one who orchestrates that system. Add to this the truth that, for the believer who hopes for a better existence, this life is not all there is. Nor do we want it to be. In addition, the book of Revelation is more about not being deceived than it is about preserving our physical life. The opening of the seventh seal issues the world into the final, future, and cosmic culmination of what God, and God alone has planned for the redemption of all that is His. The now opened scroll is the final decree of God. The authority has been given to the Lamb who was slain.

There is silence in heaven for about a half an hour. What does this silence represent? Some, if not most, suggest that this is a time of reverent worship and awe at what is about to happen. This does not suffice to answer the reference of silence. Worship and awe may involve silence at times, but the indications of what is associated with this silence is more than a provoking of worship. Nowhere else in the book of Revelation does silence issue from, or into, worship. No, the silence represents something much more intensive. The seven trumpets are associated with the silence that comes with the seventh seal. The language of atonement and judgement are associated with the seventh seal. And, the noises, lightnings, thunderings, and the earthquake, as part of the context, do not give an impression of silence in the auditory sense.

This silence is the posture that heaven will take to allow "all Hell" to break loose, to use a common metaphor. Edmund Burke has been quoted: "All that is necessary for evil to triumph is for good men to do nothing." The association is in no way equal, for evil will never ultimately triumph. But it does have the same idea. In order for the final, future, and cosmic unfolding of the Day of the Lord to be complete, the world, evil, and its current steward the devil, must be permitted to run their final course. Then God's final judgement will be meted out in its fullness. This silence is permission, or the allowance for that to occur.

There are many times in the Psalms where the enemies of God seem to have free reign to prevail over His people. The Psalmist passionately asks

God why He is silent, or states "be not silent" (as in Psalm 35:21-25; 83:1-3). In these cases, the Psalmist is persuaded by his faith, even in the midst of the appearance of God's silence, that he will be vindicated. This kind of faith will be needed when the cosmic time of testing begins. Many places in the narrative of Revelation it is stated that it "was given" in relation to the forces of evil. This will be in order that evil can run rampant and headlong into judgement (Revelation 6:2,4,8; 9:1,3,5; 13:5,7). It is also stated in Revelation that the Dragon is full of wrath because his time is short (Revelation 12:12). Is this the same brief time?

Why is it *about* a half an hour? This is obviously a short amount of time. Many a time Jesus was noted as saying: "it is not my hour," or, "it is his hour" (John 2:4; 4:23; 5:28; 12:23; 17:1). This phrase was to intend that it was "not the time," or "it was the time," for a certain event or season to occur. It this author's view that this half an hour is a reference to a specific event to occur in a relatively brief amount of time in relation to the rest of the narrative. It is also of great encouragement and hope for the readers to know that: 1) the event is not yet in play, and 2) when it does issue forth, that the endurance needed will not be extended, and 3) it will have a definite end.

There are associated passages of prophecy that concur with this interpretation. Daniel is one reference that is often not used fully to explain or interpret the book of Revelation. It must always be remembered that the whole counsel of God will never contradict itself. You cannot use the book of Revelation to promote a view that does not hold consistent with the rest of Scripture. Jesus Himself quoted Daniel and stated that Daniel was a prophet (Matthew 24:15). Daniel was given some of the most detailed, forward looking, prophecies in the Old Testament. The unfolding of events as we know them, and revealed in Scripture, are the foundations on which we build our interpretations of the times.

Daniel chapters 7-12 are the chapters that dovetail into the historical narrative of Daniel's life. In chapter 12 Daniel is given some end time details and order of events. The details and events are not complete, as he is told to "seal up the book" (Daniel 12:4). We note in Revelation that we have the completion of these details because John is told to "not seal the book" (Revelation 22:10).

In Daniel 12:1, Daniel is given the words of prophecy that pertain to the end. In this prophecy, there is an event that occurs that shows the posture of Michael, "the great prince who stands watch over the sons of your people." A Jewish commentary on Daniel suggests, that Michael "will be silent," at that time.[1] At that time, Michael, "shall stand up." The result of that "standing up" will be a time of trouble for the people. Michael is one of the two Archangels mentioned in scripture, Gabriel being the other. Michael is always mentioned as being the warrior and protecting angel. Gabriel is always present with the announcements of deity. Now, if Michael is the protector of God's people, why does his "standing up" issue a time of trouble? The answer is in what the Hebrew word used in the phrase implies.

The Hebrew word for "stand" has the same various connotations that our English word stand has in its definition. One can take a stand, make a stand, be in a posture of standing before a dignitary, be still, or to be motionless. The same Hebrew root word for "stand," is used to describe a pillar. In the context of Daniel 12:1 Michael is said to be the protector of the people and that he will at some point "stand." This same Hebrew word is used in Nehemiah 8:5 to describe what the people did when the book of the Lord was brought before them for reciting. The people stopped, or ceased, from what they were doing to listen to the words. Is it possible that the people all rose to their feet? In verse 3 it states that Ezra read from morning until midday. More likely the people were silent, still, and were in a posture of inactivity.

In Joshua 10:12-13, Joshua speaking of a battle makes mention of the sun and moon standing still, or ceasing their motion during the defeat of the Hebrew's enemies. The same Hebrew word is used here, as in Daniel 12. In Acts 21:40 the Apostle Paul motions for a crowd to listen to him, and they were silent, that is, stopped their activity to listen.

This whole discussion hinges on what must happen in order for evil to run its course. How many have criticized God for His apparent silence in the face of trial and tribulation? Many feel the world and its' ways are going to improve as we move along. That is a relative perception, relative to what is considered meant by the notion of improving. The book of Revelation was an overwhelming encouragement to the readers of its day, and to those readers today who are, or will face the ultimate decision-making moments. Certainly, it will be for the ones who will experience the future calamity that will come upon the world.

This view of what the silence in chapter 8 represents brings into sharper focus the discussion Paul puts forth in 2 Thessalonians 2:1ff. Of the three things that must occur before our being gathered together with the Lord, the first is the removing of the restrainer. This removing of the restrainer allows the man of sin, or lawless one, to be revealed. It is clear in Daniel 10:21 that Michael has been a restrainer of sorts in other contexts. It is interesting that the Septuagint translates the passage with the Greek word *"anastasatai,"* which means: one who is removed, or one who allows to pass through.

From our perspective God appears silent at times? But our trust in His sovereignty must overrule what we see and feel. The Psalmist gives testimony to this truth many times. When He rested after creation He did not cease working. Indeed, Jesus says that He is always working (John 5:17). We must remember that the book of Revelation is primarily a book of symbolism. The symbolism of the silence in chapter 8 is full of meaning. Where it is placed in the structure of the book is poignant.

8:2 There are seven angels who stand before God who are given seven trumpets. Being before God speaks of the position of their authority, and the source of the message and activity that they will bring. The use of trumpets is most significant. Trumpets were used as a way to gather the people for various events and to inform them of significant activity. A trumpet blast was used in the year of Jubilee on the first day of Atonement (Leviticus 25:9). This is key to what occurs in chapter 8, verses 3-5. Trumpets were used to denote the arrival of royalty, for calling to battle (Joshua 6:4-20), impending disaster (Ezekiel 33:1-6), and the approach of enemies (Hosea 5:8). A trumpet is used at the return of the Lord Jesus to gather His people from the four corners of the earth (Matthew 24:31; 1 Corinthians 15:52; 1 Thessalonians 4:16). It could very well be, that all of these uses for trumpets could coalesce in their use here. This is intensified even further by Jesus' and Paul's use of the trumpet at Jesus' return at the end of the age.[2]

It is of great importance to be reminded of the Feast of Trumpets,

Day of Atonement, and the Feast of Tabernacles (Leviticus 23). These three feasts play a prominent role in the book of Revelation. That they are represented, by inference and allusion, is not to be overlooked.

There are seven feasts that were part of the calendar year for the Hebrews. When Jesus came the first time He fulfilled, in His earthly ministry, the first three feasts required in the ceremonial year: Passover, Unleavened bread, and Firstfruits. (These three were appointed feasts in the spring.) The Day of Pentecost fulfilled the Feast of Weeks (Acts 2:1). We would be amiss to not see some relation between Jesus' second coming and the fulfillment of the final three feasts that were appointed in the Fall. These were the Feast of Trumpets, the Day of Atonement, and Tabernacles (dwelling with God, and God dwelling with them). All are alluded to in the book of Revelation.

8:3-5 Everything about the activity of this angel suggests something final. The angel was given a censor used for offering incense. The incense is almost always associated with the prayers of God's people. This incense, with the prayers of the saints, is offered on the golden altar. There were two altars in the tabernacle and temple building.

The bronze altar was just inside the court and was used for the daily offerings for sin. The golden altar was positioned inside the Holy Place and just outside the Most Holy Place. The altar mentioned here in this verse is important in its placement before the throne. Is this the heavenly reality of which the earthly tabernacle was only a shadow? In the earthly tabernacle, the golden altar was before the Holy of Holies. The Holy of Holies contained the Ark of the Covenant, the place where God met with Moses, and where the Hight Priest ventured once each year on the Day of Atonement. Here it is before the throne, which is much more significant in relation to chapter 4 of Revelation. Also, the prayers of the saints and the incense, and what happens as a result of their subsequent offering, may be a response to the plea of the souls under the altar (see Revelation 6:9-11). Are their prayers being answered?

If this is representative of atonement, then the activity of the angel taking fire from the altar and throwing it to the earth is an extreme act of judgement, in light of the context. Sin is being removed, forever. That this is final, being the seventh seal, has the same meaning as the seventh trumpet and the seventh bowl. Each successive set of seven is more intense and has a greater magnitude in its effect. The events of the seventh seal, seventh trumpet, and seventh bowl, each in their own degree, represents the acts of final judgement.

Excursus

At this point it is already obvious to ask the question: Where are we on the eschatological timeline? Looking at the first two series of sevens, the churches and the seals, where are we as these events unfold? Remember that the seven churches represent the complete church until the time that Jesus returns. Jesus said that He would be with us until the end of the age (Matthew 28:20). Jesus also gave the event of His coming as a harvest, with angels, at the end of the age (Matthew 13:39-40). He will separate the evil from the righteous at the end of the age (Matthew 13:49). The disciples asked about "the end of the age" (Matthew 24:3). Jesus stated that the Gospel will be proclaimed until the end, and that those that endure to the end will be saved (Matthew 24:13-15).

Are there believers that will be present until the end of the age? Is the church present until the end of the age? We must conclude from the Scriptures that the church will be (Revelation 3:3). Do all believers have the same promises given to them? Yes! Then there cannot be some who are removed from the earth and some who are left to endure tribulation. Some will endure great tribulation, while all will experience some tribulation (John 16:33). Currently, there are only pockets of persecution and tribulation. At the end of the age there will be tribulation on a global scale.

The seals represent conquest, war, famine, death, martyrdom, and judgement. Jesus listed these as characteristics of the world that would occur before His return (Matthew 24:5-30). These have been, and are occurring in the world since the church first began. The perpetrators have changed, but not the results.

It will be like the days of Noah. There will be nothing that the ungodly will heed that warns them of impending doom (Matthew 25:39). The believers are informed that Jesus *will not* come as a thief in the night (1 Thessalonians 5:1-11). Be encouraged! God will keep us through the worst of times!!

13

Trumpets 1-6
Revelation 8:6 – 9:21

Introduction. It is important as we understand and interpret the Trumpets, that we remember and consider the structure of the book of Revelation. This is the third major set of sevens. This set of seven, runs from chapter 8, verse 6, and concludes with chapter 11, verse 19. (The first set being the seven churches, and the second set being the seven seals.) In reading and hearing the book, it is also important to grasp that the seven trumpets are part of, and contained within, the seventh seal. The seven seals are operative in and during this present dispensation. The seven seals were broken, that is, sovereignly initiated by the exalted Christ. The seven trumpets represent a shorter, more intense time period than the seals. Their intensity, and magnitude will be greater. In our present experience, they are yet future. The trumpets have the same pattern as the seals, in that they initiate their own time period and conclude with the seventh being the final action. Just like the seals, the first four affect that which is seen and earthly, with the last three operating in the spiritual realm.

What do the trumpets represent? In keeping with the whole of Scripture, these trumpets represent the final week of Daniel. In previous discussions, it can be noted that all the uses of trumpets in the Old Testament can all be brought to focus in their use at this point in the reading. The final week of Daniel has yet to be fulfilled. The use of trumpets gives announcement, warning, gathering, and calls attention to what God is doing. The order of what the trumpets affect, seem to have a direct relationship to the order of what the bowls affect. The order is: the earth, the sea, the waters, the sun, a kingdom, an event.

8:6-7 The seven angels with the seven trumpets are seen as a group. The first angel sounds. At the sounding of the first trumpet hail and fire, both of which are associated with acts of judgement, are thrown to the earth. The results of these acts of judgement will be death. Blood is most always associated with death, or the results that lead to a death.

Much can be said, and much has been interpreted, of the quantitative nature concerning the use of "a third" mentioned all throughout the trumpets. It is at first, inviting to attach a quantitative aspect to the acts of these trumpets. The nature of what is occurring here is a season, or a state of testing, rather than of a quantitative amount. In the Old Testament, the prophet Zechariah gives a prophecy concerning the time after the Messiah comes, but before the Day of the Lord (Zechariah 13:7-14:15). During this time, there will be a division of the people into two-thirds and one-third. The one-third, not using specific numbers, are appointed to a time of testing which is used to refine them. If the trumpets are a call to attention, warning, and gathering before the ultimate end, then this timeframe will also be of the same nature. This is also a time of testing that results in separation.

Knowing that the testing and separation in Zechariah involves human beings gives us the interpretation of what the grass and trees symbolize and represent. This is nothing new or foreign to the reader of the Bible. There are many times that people, or mankind, or flesh, is represented as grass in a simile or metaphor (2 Kings 19:26; Job 5:25; Psalm 103:15-16; 129:6; Isaiah 40:6-8; 51:12). Prominent people are represented as trees (Judges 9; Psalm 1:3; Isaiah 11; Jeremiah 17:5-8; Ezekiel 17 and 31; Daniel 4; Zechariah 3-4;

Matthew 7:15-20; Jude 12; Revelation 11:40). These human beings, in whatever status, grass or trees, are burned up. To be burned up means to be consumed, or immersed, in the testing for the purpose of refinement or judgement. God allowing testing will always have one of two affects, a confirming for judgement or a refining of faith. It confirms the judgement of unbelievers and refines the believer (James 1:2-3; 1 Peter 1:6-7). When we pray, lead us not into temptation, but deliver us from the evil one, we are asking God to not allow the testing, by the deceptions of Satan, to result in a failure on our part (Matthew 6:13). When we confess our failures, He is faithful to forgive us because of what Christ has done on our behalf (1 John 1:9).

8:8-9 The second angel sounded, and something *like* a great mountain was cast into the sea. Mountains are used in prophetic means to represent kingdoms (Daniel 2:31-35, 44-45). Mount Zion, the kingdom of God's elect, is sometimes portrayed as a mountain (Psalm 2:6). Lucifer, as Satan, is cast out from the presence of God, and cast to the earth after his defeat at the cross (Ezekiel 28:16; Revelation 12:7-9). This particular mountain, or kingdom, was in complete judgement *as* a kingdom (see Jeremiah 51:25b). The mountain was thrown in to the sea. The sea is first mentioned in chapter four, and in other places in the book of Revelation (see discussion above, and Daniel 7:3, 17; Isaiah 57:20). The result of this mountain being thrown into the sea brings the sea into this time of testing. The fact that the sea became blood confirms that it was found to have no life. Life, being that state of redemption and quickening of the spirit.

Ships were, and still are, a means of doing commerce and travel. The means by which the sea is able to sustain itself, for itself, is taken away. The Greek word translated "destroyed" has in its meaning, to become corrupted, immoral, and to be confirmed in deceit and decay. Separation from what God had intended and planned is being confirmed in unbelievers. The first two trumpets confirm what will happen in the future, when a final anti-God kingdom will be established. This will usher in the final rebellion that will result in the Day of the Lord (Revelation 13:1-10). This kingdom will cause all to make a decision, for or against the will and word of God. This

time of decision will cause the final separation (Revelation 13:9-10).

8:10-11   The third angel issues a messenger, or message, fallen from heaven. The key to this action is in the fact that it has come from heaven. The source is heaven, and the mission of this star is for judgement. The star is burning like a torch, or a fully lit lamp. This is the same Greek word that is used for something that gives illumination. What this message contains is best interpreted by what it does. The lamp falls on a third of the rivers and springs of water. Rivers are fed by springs, and then feed into the seas. Rivers are sometimes symbols of power, boundaries, and impassable natural elements. Springs are sources of refreshment and life. That a third of these rivers and springs are affected continues the idea of being tested for truth or error.

False teachings, and the accompanying false prophets with false messages, are often called bad sources of water (2 Peter 2:17). Living water, of which Jesus spoke (John 4:10-14; 7:38), is different than water that has no movement, and no capacity to refresh and benefit life. These springs of water and rivers in the third trumpet fall prey to the deceit of a false message. That the message has its origin in heaven must be understood. There are times that God tells His people that He will test them with false teachers (Deuteronomy 13:1-5). And there are times, and there will be a time, that God Himself will send a delusion to test and confirm a wicked generation in their sin and apostasy (2 Thessalonians 2:11-12). God sent an evil spirit to torment Saul (1 Samuel 16:14-16). Pharaoh hardened his heart, and it is narrated that God hardened Pharaoh's heart, that is, gave Pharaoh what he wanted. Many times, it is stated that "God gave them over" (Romans 1:24-28; 1 Timothy 4:2; 2 Timothy 3:8).

The star, or message, is called Wormwood. The Lord used Wormwood to inflict judgement on His Old Testament people for rejecting His commandments and following false prophets (Jeremiah 9:13-15; 23:8-15). Wormwood is a substance that may have an appealing taste when first experienced. Continuing to consume Wormwood leads to death. False prophecies and teachings that lead others away from God's truth will always lead to spiritual illness and death.

8:12-13 The fourth trumpet's sounding affects the sun, moon, and stars. It will be remembered that the sun, moon, and stars are affected during the sixth seal. If what is being described in the sixth seal is an actual, literal, physically seen event that happens in the spatial heavens, then we have a consistency problem with the text if we use a literalistic interpretation concerning the stars. Of course, we must remember that the book of Revelation describes itself as a symbolic, signified presentation (Revelation 1:1). Therefore, what is happening to the stars in the sixth seal will not preclude how they are affected in the fourth trumpet. Stars can represent, or symbolize metaphorically, messengers, princes, angels, or any means of guidance used and allowed by God towards humanity (Hebrews 1:13-14). All of these bodies of light, or light-bearers of illumination succumb to the testing and do not give the light they were intended to give. That they were darkened reminds us of the words of Jesus about the eye, or of being cast into outer darkness (Matthew 6:23; Luke 22:53). Paul speaks of the darkness of the mind and heart in reference to people who reject God and His commandments (Romans 1:21; 11:10; Ephesians 4:18). The darkness here is a metaphor for ignorance, deception, spiritual blindness, evil, and ultimately eternal death.

At this point, there is an angel flying through the midst of heaven with a message for the whole world. The Greek term for "midst of heaven" has the meaning of: at the zenith of the sky. This angel, or the message, is at a point of observation that all will be able to know. God never issues judgement that is not consistent with His perfect justice. In a way that only God can work, He will leave no doubt in the minds of people and angels Who is in sovereign control. The angel, or message, conveys the impending warnings of the last three trumpets. The threefold "woe, woe, woe," carries the fullness of a complete warning. It is similar to the threefold "holy, holy, holy" of the Seraphim in their song describing the fullness of God holiness. Woes are always directed towards the wicked and unbelieving (Matthew 23). The last three trumpets are the three woes and include the fullness of trumpet judgements on the unbelieving population (Revelation 9:12; 11:14; and the seventh trumpet). These will have effect on the inhabitants of the earth, or those whose citizenship has not been "established in the heavenly places."

9:1-2 John narrates the fifth angel sounding his trumpet, and sees an associating star fallen from heaven to the earth. Stars are often used to represent angels (as in Job 38:7). The past tense sense of the verse takes us back to the great exchange that occurs at the Ascension and Exultation of Jesus portrayed in a later narrative (Revelation 12:7-9). Jesus is exalted to the right hand of God, and Satan is cast down from the position of accuser. The accuser was also positioned at the right hand of the judge (Zechariah 3:1). The format and structure of the book of Revelation is not chronological, but recapitulative.

This star, Satan, is given a key to the bottomless pit. One of the many themes in the book of Revelation, is that agents and beings are only "given" while the sovereign Christ takes and initiates (Revelation 5:7; 6:1). Keys are symbolic of authority. The star is given authority to open the bottomless pit. The bottomless pit is the place of the worst incarcerated demons (2 Peter 2:4-8; Jude 6-7). This scene is described as a pit being opened and smoke coming out of the pit like a great furnace. Smoke is usually associated with anger. One can imagine the heat of a furnace and the accompanying smoke filling the air. The sun and the air were darkened because of the smoke of the furnace. Here again, to be darkened is to grow corrupt, create blindness and deception, and to become ignorant of divine things. The major source of revelation, how things are seen, and the spiritual realm, the air, are given over to evil beings and their activities. The Devil is the prince of the power of the air (Ephesians 2:2).

9:3-11 To be sure, the next verses are difficult for a number of reasons. The event is yet future. It is allowed by God as judgement and warning. The descriptions given in these verses certainly describes that which is evil, and that which is primarily of the spiritual realm. To describe that which is primarily in the spiritual realm does not imply that it is spiritualized. Many places in the Scriptures inform us that what happens in the corporeal realm has bearing on the spiritual, and so the reverse is also true (Matthew 16:19; 18:18; Hebrews 8:4-5). John uses earthly language to describe the characteristics of these evil, spiritual creatures. We are not left without direction, for the Bible is most helpful in giving us insights into what is represented by the language John uses.

Out of the smoke, or with anger, locusts come upon the earth. To the original readers locusts were a source of terror and destruction. Locusts were uncontrollable, could not be stopped, and consumed all in their path. They swarmed across the earth, eating, consuming, and leaving nothing but destitution in their wake. Locusts are often used in the Old Testament as a metaphor for invading armies used by God for judgement (Jeremiah 51; Joel 2:1-11). These locusts "were given" the power of scorpions. Scorpions usually strike from the unseen. The sting and agony from a scorpion are known only to those who have been inflicted by them. It was considered as a prelude to certain, and painful, death. However, these locusts were given a particular limitation to not harm the grass, or any green thing, or tree, but only those who do not have the seal of God on their forehead. The wording of this sentence, in any translation, makes an association of the grass, green things, and trees, as being part of a group of things that includes any person who is not part of the select sealed by God. This symbolism harkens back to how we interpret the grass and trees of the first trumpet.

The Greek word translated "seal" is the same word used in Revelation chapter 7. It is the word used to identify the ones who are of God's elect, and, are therefore His possession and protected people (2 Corinthians 1:22; Ephesians 1:13; 4:30; 2 Timothy 2:19). Therefore, to not have the seal is not to be elect or redeemed. The book of Revelation reveals that every person is acknowledged, either with the seal of God, or the mark of the beast and Satan. There are eight uses of the word forehead in the book of Revelation. Four are in the positive, used by God to show the redeemed (Revelation 7:3; 9:4; 14:1; 22:4), and four are in the negative, to indicate opposition to God (Revelation 13:16; 14:9; 17:5; 20:4). The forehead, to the Hebrews and the Greeks, was the seat of thought and devotion. If green things represent that which has life from God, the demons were only to have effect on those *who are not protected by God's seal of possession*.

The demons' activity was restricted. They could not kill their victims, but only torment them. The time or season of the torment was five months. The five months is also the time that the flood waters prevailed on the earth after the end of the deluge (Genesis 7:24). This is not the format for discussing demon oppression in a detailed way. Suffice it to say, that demon activity can be present at times without any ability on the part of the oppressed to free themselves from the bondage (Luke 8:26-31). This text gives the impression that people know that there are problems, but are unable to free themselves even by death. Just like the sting from a scorpion can take a person into the realm of wishing it would all just end, so the end does not come. The torment is not just physical, but spiritual as well. The demons themselves will keep the victims from ending their existence.

The locusts were like war horses prepared for battle and with great authority. Their movement was like a great army of soldiers (Jeremiah 46:4-23). The appearance of this army gives the impression of being unstoppable. Their teeth were like lions' teeth. The victim they grasped was not in any way able to escape. These demons assumed a certain authority and position of torment that was not theirs by design, and it could not be decreased by human means. Hair for a woman is her glory (1 Corinthians 11:2-10). Hair in the Old Testament was also a means of ascertaining or determining a malady, or sickness, or uncleanness (Leviticus 13). The breastplates were of iron. The breastplate protected the warriors' vital organs of life. Iron was the hardest substance known to the readers of John's day. The demons were not able to be killed. Their capacity for terror and coverage was like that of an army of chariots in motion. The end result of the onslaught was the sting of pain, and then death. The Greek word for sting, *kentron*, is also translated as goad, or prick, and is an instrument of authority that drives the oxen. It carries the idea of a power and authority to drive another. The end result, is that the ones being stung are driven to serve the demons who sting them. They want release, but are unable to effect it (see Revelation 9:6). Paul is aware of another authority that drives him to the ground while on his way to Damascus (Acts 9:5; 26:14). We are informed of the sting of death, which is sin. Sin drives death. When sin was dealt with, death loses its authority (1 Corinthians 15:55-56).

These locust demons have a king and leader over them. The king and the one who released them are one and the same. He is given his characteristic names in both Hebrew and Greek, Abaddon and Apollyon, meaning Destruction and Destroyer. Jesus said the enemy, or Satan, comes only to kill and destroy (John 10:10). The book of Proverbs says that normal locusts have no king, but still advance like an army (Proverbs 30:27). It is clear from the type of book Revelation is, that these are not ordinary, literal, locusts. They have a king, have an origin, and they are from the bottomless pit. They are demonic.

9:13-21 As we look at the sixth trumpet it will be important to be reminded of the context of these verses, and where they are in the structure of the book of Revelation. This trumpet occurs within the series of trumpets, during the last week of Daniel's seventy-week prophecy (Daniel 9:24-27). The first four trumpets are judgements sent by God in order to test and purify those on the earth. The last three are specifically directed towards the unbelievers (Revelation 8:13; 9:4). There is a progression of testing, in the form of hardship, then a deceptive kingdom, deceptive teaching leading to a false worship, and then to the arrival of a false world leader who is followed by his demonic host. The sixth trumpet is a continuation of testing that will confirm unbelievers in their unbelief.

There is much debate as to whether the elements in the sixth trumpet are demonic in origin, as in the fifth trumpet, or, are angels that come directly from the presence of God with the duty of destruction. The context gives direction to the answer. The voice giving the command is coming from the four horns of the golden altar which is before God. The golden altar was the place of incense and prayers. The golden altar is also the place where the blood of the atonement was sprinkled once a year to take away the sins of the people. In chapter 8, verses 3- 5, the angel takes fire, with the prayer of the saints, and casts it to the earth. This initiates final judgement and the end of the seals. We remember the prayers and petitions of retribution from the beheaded souls under the bronze altar of sacrifice (Revelation 6:9-11). This trumpet begins the fulfillment of these prayers. The four horns represent the power of these prayers and petitions, as related to the golden altar.

The voice associated with the altar commands the sixth angel to release the four angels that are bound at the great river Euphrates. Rivers were natural boundaries that most times restricted invading armies from conquering certain areas or nations. (At the time of the writing of Revelation, the Euphrates hindered the great nation of Parthia from invading the Roman provinces.) The symbolism of a river represents a great barrier being overcome to invade and conquer. The release of the four angels at the exact year, month, day, and hour is reference to the plan, will, and exact sovereignty of God in allowing the coming of the Day of the Lord. These four angels are also mentioned as being held back in relation to the completed sealing of the 144,000 before any earthly calamities can occur (Revelation 7:1-3). Once the angels are released, John declares that he sees and hears the number of the army that is of myriads, that is, an uncountable number. He declares that he *hears the number*, or that he *hears the sound* of their number.

Is this army demonic in nature? Is this army from the presence of the throne? This author believes the wording and context lends support that this army is the destroying army of God. The origin of the commands come from the golden altar before God. The idea of atonement is beginning to be executed. The next element to occur will be the seventh trumpet, which will be the final wrath of God. If we remember that this is a season of testing and purifying, then we have other references that will help us understand what is happening.

In the book of Isaiah, the prophet sees the Lord high and lifted up on His throne and the accompanying Seraphim who continually say "Holy, Holy, Holy" (Isaiah 6:1-7). Some relate these angelic beings, called Seraphim, as being the same as the Cherubim of Ezekiel (Ezekiel 1). The Seraphim and the Cherubim are different beings, as the texts will reveal.

In the Isaiah passage, the Seraphim are above the throne. In the Ezekiel text, the Cherubim are around the throne, as they are in Revelation chapter 4. The prepositions that are used portray the positions of the creatures in relation to the throne. They portray relationships, and not visual pictures. In the Isaiah passage, God *is between* the Seraphim and His creation. In the case of the Cherubim, they give boundaries and *are between* God and His creation. Cherubim provide separation. In Isaiah, God provides the separation. Why? Because the Seraphim are created to carry out judgement and purification. In Isaiah, accordingly, one of the Seraphim takes a coal from the altar and touches Isaiah's lips, thus cleansing him for ministry among an impure people who are not trusting in God.

The Hebrew word for Seraphim in Isaiah 6, is the same word used for "fiery serpents" in the narrative of the bronze serpent in Numbers 21. In that story, the Israelites were complaining again about the bread from heaven, thus bringing down the wrath of God upon them. It is narrated that "fiery serpents" bit the people and they were dying. Moses intercedes, and is commanded to make a bronze serpent, put it on a pole, so that anyone who looked at it would be saved. Were these "fiery serpents" actually the Seraphim sent by God to carry out destruction and purification in the midst of His people? There are other texts that use the same Hebrew word for Seraphim in the same way (Deuteronomy 8:15; Isaiah 14:29; 30:6). Are these Seraphim angelic beings created by God for the specific purpose of the destruction of His enemies? In context, this trumpet narrates the final and fatal destruction before eternal judgement is meted out in the seven bowls.

These beings are described in similar fashion to the demons in the fifth trumpet. They are described in terms of an army, horses in military use, and with riders of particular means. The fiery red, hyacinth blue, and sulfur yellow, are all associated with fire and brimstone. These are elements of judgement and destruction. While the fifth trumpet sends demons to terrorize certain people, these creatures are sent to kill those who have given themselves to the system of the beast. The word brimstone means: fire from heaven (Genesis 18:24-28; Luke 17:29). The head of a lion portrays great strength and ferocity. In the fifth trumpet, we are told that the demons are not allowed to kill, but only to harm those who do not have the seal of God on their forehead. In the sixth trumpet, the spiritual beings are sent to specifically kill during the time of testing. They are to physically kill those who are spiritually dead. The end result of the experience for the unbelieving unsealed victims of this event, is confirmed unbelief and destruction. The unbelievers who do not die during this activity do not repent, even though they see the results of the conflict is destruction. They remain

firm in their idolatry, and continue practicing that which idolatry, and their demons, promote.

Verse 20 is the first instance of the word plague in the book of Revelation (Revelation 11:6; 15:1-8; 16:9, 21; 18:4-8). Plagues are used for punishment and wounding. Plagues are reminiscent of the judgements that fell on Egypt before the Exodus. God used them to confirm the hardness in the heart of Pharaoh (Exodus 7:14; 8:15; 9:14). They are used here to confirm the hardness of the earth-dweller's resistance and rejection of God.

The trumpet judgements issue forth during the time of the Great Tribulation. The believers are sealed against any harm from any of the trumpet judgements during this time. There is opportunity for those who do not believe to repent before the seventh trumpet. It is during this time that those who follow Christ will give their greatest testimony, both in word and sacrifice (the next chapter). Be encouraged! The book of Revelation was given to prepare us for these times. May we continue to pray for insight and courage from the Lord!!

14

The Testimony of the Two Witnesses
Revelation 10:1-11:19

As we move into the next section of the book of Revelation, it will be important to continue the focus of observing the structure of the book. Remember that there are four major groups of sevens: the churches, the seals, trumpets, and the bowls. We have noted that in the progression of the seals, there is a parenthetical section, or interval, that is placed between the sixth and seventh seal. This represents the sealing and glorification of the people of God. This is portrayed in chapter seven of the Revelation. The trumpets contain the same pattern as the seals.

Just like the opening of the seventh seal did not occur immediately after the opening of the sixth seal, so the seventh trumpet does not occur immediately after the activity of the sixth trumpet. There is a parenthetical section, or interval, between the sixth and seventh trumpet. This parenthetical section is chapter 10, verse 1, through chapter 11, verse 14 (see Diagram #4, Pg. 36). Though the insertion is in a literary form, the activity is concurrent within the first six trumpets, and concludes with the seventh. Just as the activity of chapter seven is concurrent, or simultaneous with the seals, ending with the seventh seal, so, the activity of chapter 10 through chapter 11, verse 14, is concurrent, or simultaneous with the first six trumpets, ending with the seventh trumpet. It is also part of the second of three woes (Revelation 8:13; 9:12; 11:14). All three woes are directed specifically towards the unbelievers of the world (see Matthew 23).

10:1-3 John sees another strong angel who cries with a loud voice. The first strong, or mighty, angel that John had seen was also associated with a loud voice and the throne of God (Revelation 5:1-2). There will be a third mighty angel who deals with the final destruction of Babylon, although there is not a loud voice attached (Revelation 18:21). Note that John must be on earth for the angel to come from heaven. It must be remembered that in the narrative of the book of Revelation, that the association of an important dignitary or messenger, and their message, was one and the same. To mistreat, or ignore, the messenger was as if one were mistreating, or ignoring, the very dignitary who sent the messenger. So as will be noted, this angel is highly representative. He comes with a description like the one on the throne, and as the glorified Christ. Is this Jesus Himself?

The mighty angel is clothed with a cloud, as only the Son of Man and God Himself are seen (Daniel 7:14; Revelation 1:2; 14:14). He has a rainbow on his head, similar to the description of the sovereign throne (Revelation 4:3). His face is like the sun and his feet as pillars of fire (Revelation 1:14-15) To describe this angel as coming from God the Father and from Christ the Son is to make the Father and Son equal in deity.

Everything about Revelation chapter 10 picks up where Daniel chapters 10-12 leave off. The man in Daniel is clothed with linen and has the same characteristics as the angel in Revelation 10, specifically: the pillars, the feet, the oath, etc. (see Daniel 10:4-6; 12:7). It is interesting, that when the Lord talked to Moses from the burning bush, He is called the Angel of the Lord (Exodus 3:2). Joshua is told to remove his sandals when standing before the Angel of the Lord (Joshua 5:13-15). It is noteworthy that the strong angel of Revelation chapter 5 is associated with a *sealed scroll* in the hand of the One on the throne.

This mighty angel is associated with an *open scroll* which John is to consume.

Much has been written about the little book, or scroll, open in the hand of the mighty angel. It is in the structure of the book of Revelation that we can narrow the meaning of this representation. We are reading and hearing of the activity within the blowing of the trumpets. We know from the structure and the pattern, that the seven trumpets are within the seventh seal. The seven trumpets represent the seventieth week of Daniel. Therefore, the scroll in the hand of the angel represents a shorter length time and a more intense portion of the scroll taken by the Lamb in chapter five. The scroll is opened with the breaking of the seventh seal. The scroll lays open, representing that which John himself is required to make known (see Revelation 10:11). As such, the little scroll is a brief part of what the whole represents. The little scroll, opened, represents the written interior contents of the scroll mentioned in Revelation chapter 5.

The angel sets one foot on the sea and the other foot on the land. To have a foot placed on something has the idea of having authority over, or, of having something or someone in subjection. The angel's message and activity involve all the subjects represented by the land and the sea. None are outside the effects of the proclamation. The angel cried out, "as when a lion roars." This picture is also representative of the Lion of the tribe of Judah (Revelation 4:5). When the cry is made, seven thunders are voiced. The Lion and the thunders are references not only to the source of the cry, but also to the identity attached to the message.

10:4-7 Everything about the following verses contains the idea of greater intensity, scope, and finality. In obedience, John is about to write what the seven thunders uttered, but is told not to write. Instead, John is told to seal them up. This is an interesting contrast to his original command given at the beginning (Revelation 10:11; see also 1:1 and 22:10). Remembering that the number seven represents completeness, or a completed series, whatever is communicated by the thunders is a complete idea of its own. It is often discussed that something was heard by John, and then denied scribal expression by the Voice from heaven. Therefore, the thought is that there is something that we are not to be privileged to know.

Thunder is often associated with an accompanying occurrence of the voice of God being heard (Exodus 19:16; 20:18-19; Job 37:1-5; Psalm 77:18; 104:7; John 12:29). Thunder is associated with the throne of God (Revelation 4:5; 14:2; 19:6). Thunder also part of the activity of the seventh seal, the seventh trumpet, and the seventh bowl. This is the connection with the seven thunders heard by John.

These seven thunders represent the last, final, and complete command from God. Within the context of this event is included the statement that: "there should be delay no longer," or, "time no more" (Revelation 10:6b), and that "the mystery of God would be finished" (Revelation 10:7). But why is John told *not* to write them down? Because the completed, final, and fulfilled plan and destiny of redemption, and when it ends, is and always will be the prerogative and knowledge of God the Father, and His alone! We will not know the times and seasons that are known only to the Father (Matthew 24:36; Acts 1:7; see 2 Peter 3:1-7). It is enough for the original readers, and for us, to know that the end is part of His sovereign plan. The Creator of all things will indeed bring things as we know them to a conclusion, as the angel gave testimony by the One who lives forever (Revelation 10:6a). The unbelieving world does not look for, or, anticipate this.

The seventh trumpet brings another element that portrays the end. "But in the period of time of the seventh trumpet, when it is *about* to sound, the mystery of God will be complete, or finished." Notice that the mystery of God will be complete, or finished, when the seventh angel is <u>*about*</u> to sound his trumpet. What mystery of God is being mentioned? The Bible does not leave us without an answer. Although the answer challenges and brings tension to many interpretations given concerning the book of Revelation. A thorough, expositional, systematic, non-contradictory, all-inclusive treatise of the Scriptures will teach us.

What is the mystery that will be finished? And does it qualify as being a mystery declared to His prophets? The mystery being referenced here is one that brings many dynamics from different places in Scripture. Keep in mind that the mystery *will be completed* (Revelation 10:7). In Matthew and Mark, Jesus stated that there is the mystery of the kingdom of heaven (Matthew 13:11; Mark 4:11).

Paul teaches about the mystery of the "blinding in part" of the people of Israel, and the Gentiles believers being combined and included so that all Israel will be saved (Romans 11:25-27; see Hosea 1:10-11). This includes those from all nations (Romans 16:25-26). Paul then states that a mystery includes the resurrection at the *last trumpet* (1 Corinthians 15:51-52). Paul, in Ephesians, makes much of the mystery in which the constitution of the body of Christ is made known (Ephesians 1:9; 2:11-3:1-7; see 3:5-6). Then, in 1 Thessalonians, Paul brings another dynamic of the mystery being finished to bear in his discussion of a trumpet call of God (1 Thessalonians 4:15-16). His use of the voice of an archangel, and the trumpet of God, is very similar to the scene portrayed in Revelation chapter 10.

In the passage of 1 Thessalonians mentioned above, we must see the return, the resurrection, the rapture, and the reunion, in that particular order. This must fit with any interpretation we may have of Jesus' return within the book of Revelation. Any other additions to the events are dangerous and confusing (Revelation 22:18-19). Paul even includes the mystery of lawlessness as a current, ongoing, dynamic that will be concluded (2 Thessalonians 2:7-8). It is very certain in that passage that the mystery of lawlessness will also be finished, and that judgements are to follow (IE. The bowls of wrath).

What must be included, and is probably primary to the explanation, is the mystery that Daniel wanted to understand about the future fulfillment (Daniel 12:8-10, 13). Daniel wanted to know the meaning of what he was shown. The period of time, times, and half a time. What was given to Daniel has arrived. It will be referenced several times in the following narrative of the book (Revelation 11:2-3; 11:9-11; 12:6; 12:14; 13:5). It is this authors' assertion that all of the above can coalesce in the meaning of Revelation 10:7. The mystery is being shown when it will be fulfilled. The final decrees that bring the eternal kingdom of God to earth will be executed (Matthew 6:10; Revelation 22:17).

10:8-11 The voice which speaks from heaven instructs John to take the little book which is open from the hand of the angel. It is an interesting contrast that John is commanded to take the book, instead of assuming the authority that Jesus has when He *takes* the book from the One seated on the throne (Revelation 5:7).

John is told to eat the little book, and that it will taste sweet to his mouth. As a result of his ingesting the book, his stomach became bitter. We have a similar picture from the Old Testament when Ezekiel is commissioned to bring prophetic judgement to his people (Ezekiel 3:1-14). The receiving of God's word is sweet to our taste. Experiencing and appropriating it can mean times of bitterness and judgement for those who are meant to live through it (Psalm 19:10; 119:103; Jeremiah 15:16; see John 15:20).

John is told that he is to prophecy about, or to many peoples, nations, tongues, and kings. To prophecy can be both to forthtell and foretell the condition, warning, and future of a specific situation. This adds to the intensity, directness, and the greater gravity to which the structure of the book lends itself. The addition of kings strongly suggests that the context of the use of these nouns will, from now on, be for all those who are worldly and have rejected the presentations of the Gospel. Instead, they follow the false system of worship to the beast and the dragon (Revelation 18:3-9). The worldly kings are always, from an earthly perspective, described as being in opposition to the King of Kings. This is a clear judgement announcement scenario that will be given in more detail in Revelation chapter 11. This judgement is given by the two witnesses and will complete the picture of the second woe.

11:1-2 John is told that he will prophecy about many peoples, nations, tongues, and kings. This moves us right into the means by which this will occur, the service of the two witnesses. This part of the book of Revelation, and its' understanding, has at its core the use of symbolism (see explanation of Revelation 1:1). Misinterpretation of this section has led to much speculative possibilities and scenarios that are difficult to reconcile with the narrative. Being reminded, for something to be signified does not mean that it has been spiritualized. There is still a literal reality behind what the symbol represents. This part of the narrative is a continuation of the second woe (Revelation 11:14). The woes are directed towards those who dwell on the earth, that is, those who do not have an identity in heaven. They call earth their home. What the witnesses do, what is done through their ministry, and what is done to them, is both a testimony about God directed at and against the earth-dwellers.

John is given a reed like a measuring rod. He is told to rise and measure the temple of God, the altar, and those who worship there. This idea of measuring has its counterpart in the Old Testament. The prophets are told to measure things. This represents God's ownership, knowledge, protection, and of being set apart for Him (Ezekiel 40:1ff; Zechariah 2:1-5; see also Revelation 21:15). Does God need to measure anything to know its literal dimensions? Or, does God mean to convey something else by the symbolism? Anytime God sets out to do anything He always sets apart His chosen vessel(s) for His work. The 144,000 are a measurement (Revelation 7). The holy city is also measured (Revelation 21:12-17). It is easy to focus only on the literal physical dimensions. But there is something else being conveyed.

What is being measured is specific in detail. He is to measure the structure *and* the people. What is being measured is also significant by that which is left out of the measurement. What is left out is not claimed by God. That which is measured represents only those people who have entered into the temple proper for the worship of the only true God. These people represent the corporate and covenant people of God. There is a separation within mankind that is being pictured here between those who are the true worshippers, and those who are not. (To bring into the interpretation the multiple temple divisions of the Old Testament leads to confusion of this simple separation.) A literalistic temple in Jerusalem, past or rebuilt, is not being represented here.

The temple was the mediating location for meeting with God. The garden of Eden was a temple of sorts. The Tabernacle during the time of Moses, and Solomon's temple were both places where God met with His people. Jesus uses the metaphor of a temple to describe His earthly body (John 2:19-21). Jesus, in talking to the woman at the well, declares that there is a time coming and now is, when true worship will not occur at any specific geographic place, or on any mountain (John 4:21). The picture of the temple is continued in the New Testament, described as the individual and corporate people of God in authentic communion, obedience, and worship of God (Acts 7:48-49; 17:24; 1 Corinthians 3:16-17; 6:19-20; 2 Corinthians 6:16; Ephesians 2:19-20;

1 Peter 2:4-10). The physical temple buildings were needed no longer (Hebrews 8:7-13). The temple here is of an internal, spiritual reality of God's people who are His because of a heart relationship.

The part that is not measured represents those who do not worship the true God, symbolized by the term Gentiles. The term Gentile is used to describe those who are not part of Israel, the covenant people of God. The term Gentiles is also used to describe those who are not part of the covenant people of faith and not part of the church, the body of Christ (1 Corinthians 10:32; 12:2; Galatians 6:16; Ephesians 2:11-13). This group, called Gentiles, will trample and tread upon the holy city for 42 months. The Holy city is Jerusalem. But the holy city, Jerusalem, does not only mean the geographical location in the middle east.

The Hebrew and Greek words for city primarily mean: the community, the inhabitants, or the population of a distinct description or location. They may, or may not, reside in a specific geographical location. Jerusalem can be a composite multitude of cities (Zechariah 2:4). The whole city came out to see Jesus (Matthew 8:34). We can have a city coming together to hear the Apostle Paul (Acts 13:44). There is a heavenly Jerusalem, described not in terms of physical brick and mortar, but as consisting of persons and personalities as its composition (Hebrews 12:22-24). The holy city, Jerusalem, descends from heaven, described as the bride of Christ (Revelation 21:2-10). Holy has the idea of being set apart, or sanctified. The holy city being described in chapter 11, verse 2, is the corporate covenant people of God. (Being a part of Israel was *never only* about being a *physical* descendant of the Patriarchs). They, *the inhabitants of the holy city,* Jerusalem, will be tread upon and oppressed and persecuted by the unbelieving world of Gentiles during the second half of Daniels' seventieth week. Evidence that it is the second half of the week will become apparent as we look at the ministry of the two witnesses as a whole.

11:3-6 The voice of the angel continues the message that two witnesses will be given a position and a posture to prophecy for half of the seventieth week of Daniel. Their prophesying will include that of mourning and seeking penitence. The witnesses are just that, a witness of something for others to see and hear.

Their message is similar to, and related to, the interior contents of the little scroll, or the little book.

The two witnesses are described as the two olive trees *and* the two lampstands. There is a very strong Old Testament reference for our understanding of this picture from the book of Zechariah, chapters 3 and 4. In Zechariah's prophecy, the prophet sees two anointed ones who stand beside the Lord of the whole earth. These two anointed ones receive oil from a common lampstand (Zechariah 4:2-3). The lampstand is that which supports the light. The light is fueled by the Holy Spirit. The light is that which provides the leadership and guidance of God by His Spirit. The two anointed ones are also called the two olive trees (Zechariah 4:11-14). These two are named as Zerubbabel and Joshua. Zerubbabel held the place of governor and is also mentioned in the kingly line of Jesus Christ, and therefore could have ruled as king (Matthew 1:12). Joshua was the high priest at the time of the return from Babylonian captivity. Joshua is the Hebrew name Jesus. During the time before Christ, the kingly and priestly functions were separated. That is why many kings found themselves on the wrong side of God's wrath by performing the priestly functions (1 Samuel 13:1-14; 2 Chronicles 26:16-23). There are only three occasions where the kingly and priestly titles are given to a person. The first is Melchizedek (Genesis 14:18). The second is Jesus Christ as Prophet, Priest, and King. The third gives the promise that we each are co-heirs with Him, a royal priesthood of believers (Romans 8:17; 1 Peter 2:9).

The two olive trees represent the kingly and priestly functions of God's economy. The olive tree always represents the people that God chooses (Romans 11) The lampstands have already been identified as the churches that hold up the light, guidance, and testimony of God (Revelation 1:20). The light itself is the person, work, and word of the Holy Spirit. Note that only two churches held a testimony about Jesus with no condemnation.

The number two has the symbolic representation of a secure and firm witness and testimony (Deuteronomy 17:6; 19:15; Matthew 18:16). The two witnesses are the corporate witness and testimony of the church during the time of the trumpets. They represent the people of God. The number two gives the description of their function, not the cardinal count of witnesses. For those who want to name the two witnesses as individuals, much is made of who they could be. Little is made of the place and role of their prophecy. (If the 7 churches, which *are* named, are representative of the whole church, why do we want to limit the 2 witnesses, which *are not* named, to just 2 individuals?)

During the first half of the seventieth week the witnesses are given the words, the power, and the protection that are equal to the roles that prophets of the past have had. The significance of their power is equal to the most famous of prophets, Moses and Elijah (Exodus 7:14-25; 2 Kings 1:10-11). Moses and Elijah both served at critical times in the life of God's people. The two witnesses' message and testimony are also an allusion to the Prophets Isaiah and Jeremiah (Isaiah 1:9-10; Jeremiah 5:14).[1] The two witnesses are protected in such a way, that they can inflict judgement and punishment upon their adversaries equal to the harm that is attempted towards them. It is interesting that both witnesses are described as having both sets of miraculous judgements. This adds to the corporate nature of their ministry.

It should be noted that at the beginning the witnesses have freedom, per se, to witness and testify about what is coming (verse 3). This is during the first half of the seventieth week. Then, they will be persecuted and oppressed during the second half of the seventieth week (verse 2). This is in accord with Daniel 9:27, where, the prince who will come will make a covenant with the many, and then in the middle of the week will break the covenant and bring an end to sacrifice and offering, thus bringing his desolation. Paul speaks of this time when he states that at some point the man of lawlessness will be revealed (2 Thessalonians 2:1-4).

11:7-10 The witnesses' testimony lasts for a determined length of time, 1260 days. This is the first half of Daniel's seventieth week. The beast that ascends from the bottomless pit makes war against them, overcomes and kills them (Revelation 13:7). The origin and activity of this beast is mentioned many times (Revelation 9:1-3; 12:17; 13:7, 15; 20:7, see Daniel 7:21, 25). Their dead bodies are part of the scenery of the great city for three and half days. The great city is spiritually, or prophetically,[2] called Sodom, for its perversity, and called Egypt, for its oppression of the people

of God. The same title is given to the false system of worship called Babylon (Revelation 14:8; 16:19; 17:18; 18:10; 18:16-21). In the book of Revelation, there is the great city, contrasted with the beloved city. Both cities are symbolic of their respective inhabitants. One follows the true God, and the other follows the beast. Babylon represents all false systems of worship, and, has in its origin the tower of Babel.

The three and a half days has not been understood clearly by most expositors and teachers. The original prophecy given to Daniel was given in seventy sevens, or weeks of years. Three and half days is still half of a week. Therefore, the witnesses being a corporate body, are killed for the whole second half of the final week of Daniel. If believers exist all over the globe, then it is not impossible that this represents a world-wide persecution of believers during the second half of Daniel's seventieth week. The witnesses, being a corporate body, are being killed, and are seen dead and dying for this period of time. This is equal to the statement made in chapter 11, verse 2. (See also Daniel 7:25 and 12:7.) The fact that the witnesses are not allowed burial communicates the most heinous of repute, scorn, derision, and disrespect towards the witnesses (Psalm 79:1-6). Note, the body of Jesus had to be taken down because of regulations given early in the Old Testament, and for contemporary respect (Deuteronomy 21:22-23).

The joy and celebration of the people of the earth over the demise of the witnesses is apparent from their actions. This coincides with the persecutions and ultimate killings of the witnesses. The people of the earth celebrate by sending gifts. This is a parody of the Old Testament celebration of Purim. In the book of Esther, the Jews celebrate and send gifts as part of their joy in preserving their lives from the edicts of death (Esther 9:16-19). They thanked each other for what they collectively had done. Similarly, the earth dwellers sense that they have spared their own lives by killing the two witnesses, thus saving themselves from the edicts of their judgement. The problem is, those on the earth have failed to consider what is certainly next on the eschatological schedule.

11:11-14 After the three and a half days, the breath of God enters the witnesses. The witnesses stand on their feet, and great fear fell on those who saw them. Here again, the three and a half days represents a half week, the second half of the seventieth week of Daniel. The witnesses' prophecy during the first half, are persecuted and killed during the second half, and are resurrected at the end of the second half just before the seventh trumpet. The seventh trumpet contains the judgement and outpouring of God's wrath represented by the bowls. The two witnesses are removed before the wrath (1 Thessalonians 5:9). Any Biblical principle must be true for all saints, at all times, for all seasons, and for all circumstances. This is certainly a resurrection of the highest order. This is a strong inference to the final catching away of the saints without using the term rapture. There is a loud voice from heaven (1 Thessalonians 4:16-17). It is the martyred, and all those living witnesses at the time of the end, the corporate body of believers. It is just before the seventh trumpet (Matthew 24:21; 1 Corinthians 15:52; Revelation 10:7). The witnesses ascend with the visual power of the glory of God. At the same period of time there was a great earthquake, a changing of the environment, and the (great) city of the earth dwellers fell. Complete death occurred, and the remnant gave reverence and glory to the God of heaven. The second woe is completed.

11:15-19 Immediately following the two witnesses ascending to heaven the seventh trumpet is sounded. The seventh trumpet will be the completion of the trumpet sequence. The contents of the seventh trumpet are similar to the seventh seal and the seventh bowl (Revelation 8:1-5; 16:17-21). The seventh trumpet increases in intensity that which is portrayed by the seventh seal, but not as intense as the seventh bowl. All three provide the sense that something has come to an end.

The seventh trumpet issues praise and worship. It is the end, the coming of the Kingdom of God, the rewards of the servants of God, and the punishment of the opposition to God. "Who is to come" is left out. He has come (Cf. Revelation 16:5)! It is written as if it has already occurred. It is of great importance that we understand that the prophecies that God decrees are as good as done in the mind of the Creator. His timing is not our timing. The kingdoms of the world *have become* the kingdoms of our Lord and of His Christ. The twenty-four elders, who have close proximity to the throne, also worship

(Revelation 4:10; 5:8-14; 19:4). What the twenty-four elders proclaim gives us information to consider about who they represent (see Revelation 4:9-10). They proclaim the deity of the One on the throne, and to His Christ, by the titles given in their praise. The nations being angry, but to no avail, takes us back to the words of Psalm 2. In the seventh seal, the activity is at the altar. At the seventh trumpet, the scene is inside the temple where the ark of His covenant is seen. When we get to the seven bowls, the seven angels who have the bowls come from the opened ark, or the temple of the testimony in heaven. And there were noises, lightnings, thunderings, an earthquake, and hail (also Revelation 8:5;16:18-21). Be encouraged! God always has a plan for His people!!

15

The Wondrous Signs
Introduction

It would seem strange to offer an introduction to the next four chapters, if it were not so important in understanding the structure of the book of Revelation. How *do* we read the book from chapter 12 going forward? Does the book continue in a linear timeline, or does the narrative recapitulate to events already covered? Many books of the Bible cannot be read from one chapter to the next without understanding how the book is structured. One case in point would be the book of Daniel. The first six chapters of Daniel are a historical narrative of Daniel's life and experiences. The last six chapters consist of prophecies that dovetail into the first six at various points. The structure of the book of Revelation is primarily seven church letters, seven seals, seven trumpets, and seven bowls. As has been shown, the seventh seal contains the seven trumpets, and the seventh trumpet contains the seven bowls. The seventh of each representing the completed set.

The seven bowls will be the climax of God's dealings with the world and with time as we currently know it. Why so much narrative from the seventh trumpet to the activity of the seventh bowl? There may be many reasons, primary among them is the reason and purpose of the book itself. All that is final and eternally significant associated with the Second Coming of Jesus reverses the curse. His desire is to inform His followers to persevere, endure, and overcome. With the terrible calamities of judgement to befall the world, the grace of God encourages His people. With chapters 12-14, God gives us the origins and details of the subjects that will be operative until the end. The seven bowls of judgement are not executed without an appropriate historical background, and the unfolding of the details of all who will be part of the final act. It is the pattern of God to give warning and announcement to His people regarding His dealings of judgement on the world. In the time of Noah, He gave a "heads-up" to Noah many years before the event of the great Flood (Genesis 6:13). When God was about to destroy Sodom and Gomorrah, He informed Abraham of the event (Genesis 18:17-21). Amos declares that the Lord does nothing without revealing it to His servants

(Amos 3:7). Jesus informs His followers about the signs of the times (Matthew 24:25). Paul, in his encouragement to the persecuted believers, gives an order of events that will be before the return of Christ stating that the day will not come upon them as a thief in the night (1 Thessalonians 3:2, 1 Thessalonian 5:4; 2 Thessalonians 2).

The seven bowls are framed with three "great, or wondrous, signs." The first two will be early in chapter 12, in verses 1 and 3. The third one will be early in chapter 15, verse 1. It will be the angels who have the bowls who will then give narrative to the rest of the book, showing the eternal separation that will occur, including both the judgements and the rewards (Revelation 17:1; 21:9).

It is of serious concern that many interpreters will address a particular subject of these last chapters, take them out of the context, and build an elaborate eschatological scenario and theological understanding with them. Then they try to re-insert them back into the larger context where they can no longer fit. The results promote incongruence and confusion with the rest of the passage while omitting other Scriptures. Another concern is the attempt to understand all the events of chapter 12, specifically, as something yet to happen in the future. Therefore, it is the view of this author that the two signs that start chapter 12 are past tense. They give foundational understanding for the conflict, the perseverance, and ultimate separation of the two people groups. The judgement and reward events will then be narrated in the last chapters of the book of Revelation.

The first group of people are the followers of the true God and His Christ. The second, and opposing group of people, are the followers of the world system led by the dragon. These two groups, and only two, are seen as being separated in their respective worship and devotion. They are separated in devotion and whom they follow. One will take the seal of the Lamb and will incur the limited wrath of the beast. The other will take the mark of the beast and will incur the eternal wrath of God and the Lamb.[1] They are separated eternally by the end of the book of Revelation (Revelation 17:1ff; 21:9ff). (See below: TIME OF SEPARATION, Diagram #5, Page 120.)

Diagram #5

TIME OF SEPARATION

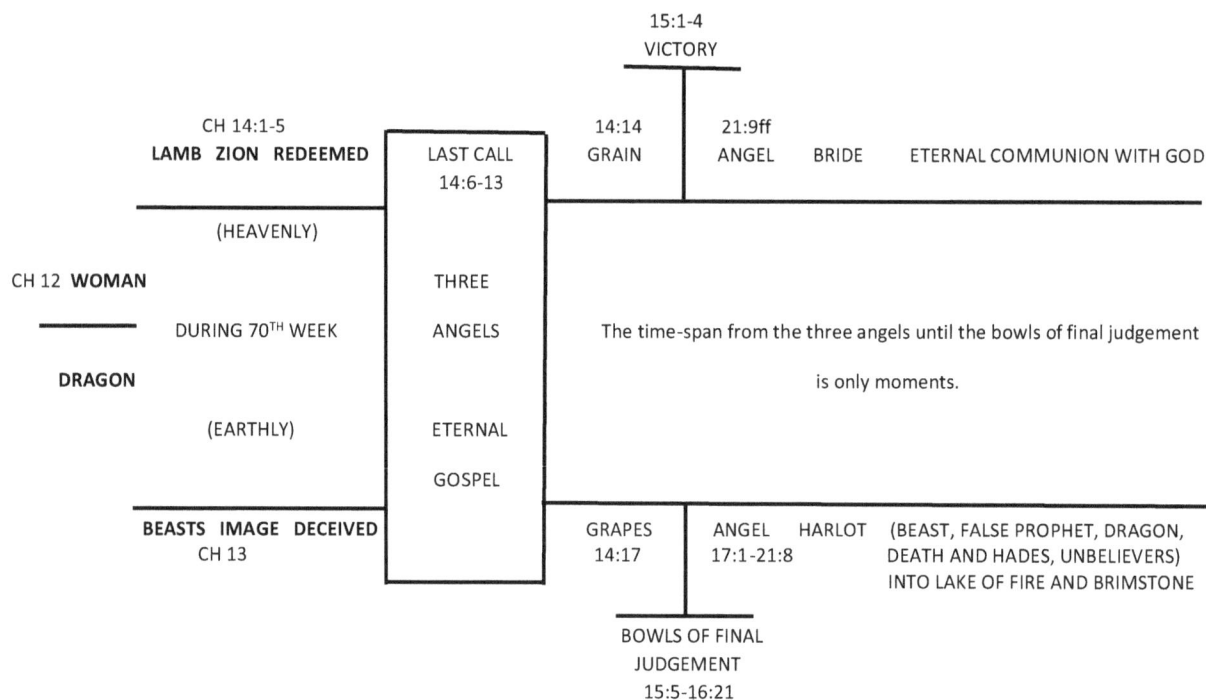

```
                                          15:1-4
                                          VICTORY

      CH 14:1-5                  14:14        21:9ff
  LAMB  ZION  REDEEMED  LAST CALL GRAIN       ANGEL    BRIDE   ETERNAL COMMUNION WITH GOD
                        14:6-13

         (HEAVENLY)

CH 12  WOMAN            THREE

         DURING 70TH WEEK  ANGELS   The time-span from the three angels until the bowls of final judgement

  DRAGON                                              is only moments.

         (EARTHLY)         ETERNAL

                           GOSPEL

  BEASTS  IMAGE  DECEIVED   GRAPES    ANGEL   HARLOT   (BEAST, FALSE PROPHET, DRAGON,
         CH 13              14:17     17:1-21:8         DEATH AND HADES, UNBELIEVERS)
                                                       INTO LAKE OF FIRE AND BRIMSTONE

                           BOWLS OF FINAL
                           JUDGEMENT
                           15:5-16:21
```

The above diagram illustrates the structure of the book of Revelation from Chapter 12 to the end of the book. There is a brief narration that explains the initial conflict between the covenant people of God and the Dragon. The first coming of Jesus and His ascension and exaltation are narrated briefly. The Dragon is casting to earth, and the celebration of Heaven is shown. The narrative moves quickly through the Dragon's subjugation of the earth, and the persecution of the saints. Chapter 13 narrates the rise of the final world kingdom that will be present during the 70th week of Daniel's prophecy. This is a time of significant testing and separation. The box represents the last call initiated by the message of the three angels announcing the Day of the Lord. The separation is solidified by the two separate harvests, followed by the victory of the Saints and the final bowls of judgement. Two separate eternities are then explained by the angel(s) of the seven bowls. From the time of the three angels until the final judgements *is only moments*, if not instantaneous (1 Thessalonians 5:1-11).

The Three Great Signs
Revelation 12

12:1-6   John sees a great sign appearing in heaven. The sign appears as a woman clothed with the sun, the moon under her feet, and with a crown of twelve stars on her head. The covenant people of God are always portrayed as a female figure whether it be the wife of God, the virgin daughter of Yahweh, or the bride, the wife of the Lamb. Her attire and position here uses the symbolism of the light-bearing heavenly bodies. This is not the first time in the book of Revelation that the sun, moon, and stars are mentioned together (Revelation 6:12-13; 9:12). Revelation is not the only book of the Bible where they are mentioned together. In Genesis, Joseph's dream of the sun, moon, and stars is interpreted by Jacob as being Joseph's father, mother, and brothers (Genesis 37:9-11). The sun, moon, and stars play a prominent role in the prophecy of Joel (see Joel 2:10; 3:15). In the Olivet Discourse given by Jesus, the sun, moon, and stars, are grouped together in His prophecy of the days to come (Matthew 24; Mark 13; Luke 21).

The sun, moon, and stars are light bearers, or agents of light. They are given to us by God. The light they give is what we need to see, to apprehend, to understand and negotiate that which is around us. God is light, the source of revelation. Jesus is the light that has come into the world, that is, He is the revelation of God in the world. The light bearers were given to rule, to lead, to guide, and as a means of general, visual revelation.

The woman, as the covenant people of God, is clothed as an agent of revelation. The moon, under her subjection and agency, is only a reflection of the primary source of light. The moon was the clock by which the heavenly pattern was practiced in the temple system and its ceremony. It was by the cycles of the moon that the temple system was ordered. The temple was an earthly shadow of the heavenly (Hebrews 8:4-5). The stars, being 12, represent the divine administration of God, given through the people who give leadership and guidance to His spiritual community. There are 12 tribes in the Old Testament, and 12 Apostles in the New Testament. Paul, when describing his brethren in the flesh, says: to them was given adoption, the covenants, the Law, the service, the promises, the fathers, and the Christ (Romans 9:1-5). The covenant people of God are to be the light bearers, agents of light, and emissaries of light in the world. They were to be a kingdom of priests before the rest of the nations, and to be a testimony to the nations about God (Exodus 19:5-6; 1 Peter 2:9). Light, as revelation, can be good or bad, helpful or dangerous, guiding or deceitful (Matthew 6:22-23). Christians are to be children of God's revelation (Philippians 2:15; 1 Thessalonians 5:4-7).

The woman is in pain and cries out as one who is in labor to deliver a child. Israel, as a people, were often described as one to bring forth a child described as the Messiah (Isaiah 26:17-18; 54:1; 66:7-12; Micah 5:2-3). The pain of the woman describes her experiences throughout her history. Many obstacles, both internal and external, would be experienced through her history before the Messiah would ultimately come (Hebrews 1:1). The Messiah will fulfill the initial prophecy of the destruction of the serpent (Genesis 3:15-16).

John sees another great wonder that appears in heaven. A great, fiery red dragon having seven heads, ten horns, and seven diadems on his heads. The dragon is a symbolic image of Satan. The heads, horns, and diadems associate this dragon with other elements that are images that are also in opposition to the will, purpose, and plan of God (see Revelation 13:1). The dragon is described as having a tail that casts the stars of heaven to the earth. This is a reference to his leading groups of angels in a series of rebellions. These rebellious angels are known as the false gods of the Old Testament. Also, they are responsible for the appearance of demons.

The dragon takes a position and a posture to destroy the Child when it is delivered. The dragon wants to consume the Messiah. From the beginning, the work of Satan has been to destroy, kill, corrupt, and hinder the work of God to bring forth the Messiah into the world. This enemy of the woman, and the Child that she delivers, has manifested himself in the work of the many kingdoms that have oppressed the people of God throughout their history. There are many times in the Gospels that Satan is overtly, or covertly, trying to kill, tempt, or destroy the work of Jesus. The primary means were through Herod, the temptations in the wilderness, and the cross.

The woman delivers the Child. The descriptions of the Child are filled with prophecy. The male Child, who would rule with a rod of iron, is a Messianic picture from the Old Testament and is used many times in the book of Revelation (Psalm 2:6-9; Revelation 2:27; 19:15). The Child is caught up to God and to His throne. These first verses of Chapter 12 are a synopsis of the purpose and journey of the nation of Israel, of whom Jesus is physically born. His coming, life, death, resurrection, and His ascension are portrayed in a few brief verses. This gives the foundation of the covenant people of God as they are narrated through the next chapters. The woman then moves into a time of testing, to be cared for during a time of tribulation.

The Two Signs in Conflict

12:7-12 The next part of the drama, the war in heaven, is as a *result* of the exaltation of the male Child (see chapter 12:5). John narrates the event of this war that occurs in heaven. It is being fought between Michael and his angels, and the dragon and his angels. The dragon and his angels were not strong enough to win the war and were cast out of heaven. Significant also in the narrative is the fact that: nor was a place found for them in

heaven any longer (Revelation 12:8). Whatever status, position, and place of operation the dragon had occupied, he no longer held. We are given a description and a definition of the symbol of the dragon. He is that serpent of old, the Devil and Satan (Genesis 3). The dragon's history is that of being the deceiver of the nations of the whole world (John 8:44). He is cast to the earth along with the angels who had followed him.

Michael is one of the two Archangels mentioned in Scripture, along with the Archangel Gabriel. It is Michael who is called the protector of God's people (Daniel 10:13,21; 12:1; Jude 9). From reading Scripture, there appears to be angels assigned to have effective authority over nations, and people groups, as well as individuals (see Daniel 10; Matthew 18:10). The timing of this war in heaven and its results, along with the ultimate judgement of Satan given at the end of Revelation provides additional information as to his personal history.

Satan is a created being (Genesis 1:31-2:1; Ezekiel 28:15a; Colossians 1:16). Whether Satan was created during the creation week of Genesis (Genesis 2:1), present for it (Job 38:4-7), or created prior to it, we understand from Scripture that he was in, or had access to Eden before he fell (Ezekiel 28:13-15). Did Satan fall before Adam and Eve were created, or, was the fall of Satan *because* he tempted Adam and Eve? If we understand that the Fall of Satan was *because* he tempted Adam and Eve, it explains the struggle and conflict between the sons of Adam and the Devil all throughout the Bible (Genesis 3:14-15). It also informs us about the struggle between Satan and the last Adam, Jesus Christ (Matthew 4:1-11).

Satan tempted Adam and Eve because they were created, for a little while, lower than the angels. They were created to have dominion and would eventually rule over them, including Satan (Psalm 8:4-6; 1 Corinthians 6:3). Mankind was created in the image and likeness of God, and, given dominion as God's stewards (Genesis 1:26-38). Angels are created as ministering spirits, and as such, any authority is derived or given (Hebrews 1:14). Satan, not his name before the Fall, would not take this dominion mandate without a fight. He tempted Adam and Eve, leading them to disobey God, and thus has taken the dominion that was given to them as his own (Matthew 4:9; 1 John 5:19). It was at the Fall that Satan lost his position in heaven as the anointed cherub who *covers* and guards, beautiful and perfect in all his ways (Ezekiel 28:14-15). He wanted to be *like* God, being exalted and being worshiped by mankind, not ruled by them (Isaiah 14:12-15).

After the Fall, and prior to this war in heaven (Revelation 12:7-12), Satan had access to heaven as the accuser of the brethren (Job 1:6-12; Zechariah 3:1-2; Luke 4:3; Jude 9). All of these are before the birth, life, work, cross, and ascension of Jesus (Revelation 12:5). It is at the point of the ascension of the Child that Satan is cast out of heaven, as accuser of the brethren (see Zechariah 3:1-2; Revelation 12:10). It was precisely because of the cross, and the ascension of the man Christ Jesus, that everything in heaven changed. It is interesting that Michael did not have the power to handle Satan with regards to the body of Moses before the cross, but could then overpower Satan after the cross (see Jude 9).

Jesus, the last Adam, now has dominion. Jesus speaks of Satan's fall in the past, and, predicted Satan's defeat and casting out of his position in heaven at the cross (John 12:31; 16:11). Now, instead of having an accuser at the right hand, we now have Jesus as our personal advocate at the right hand of the Father (Acts 7:55-56; Romans 8:34; Ephesians 1:20-21; Colossian 3:1; Hebrews 1:3, 13; 8:1; 10:12).

John hears a loud voice in heaven declaring the joy that heaven has over the casting out of Satan from his position in heaven. Now, salvation, strength, and the kingdom of our God, and the power of His Christ have come. The only way to overcome the accuser of the brethren, past or present, is by the blood of the Lamb and the testimony of Jesus. Even if it costs physical life. There is a warning of woe to the earth and to the sea. The devil is cast down to them. He has great wrath, for his time is short. In the context of the whole book of Revelation, this short time that Satan has is yet to be played out. This short time is equal to the period he is released to deceive the nations for one last time (Daniel 9:27; Revelation 17:10; 20:3, 7; also see commentary on Revelation 8:1). Satan will afterwards be cast into the eternal punishment called the lake of fire and brimstone (Matthew 25:41; Revelation 20:10).

The Results of the Conflict

12:13-17 John now briefly narrates the history of the woman and her seed from the time of the war until the present, and then on to the time of the final world empire (Revelation 13). The dragon specifically targets the woman who gave birth to the male Child. There have been hundreds of years of history to corroborate the targeting of the ethnic, particular nation of Israel. Some of these events include the destruction of Jerusalem in A.D. 70, the historical pogroms of various times, anti-Semitism, and the events of World War 2, just to name a few. In all these, God has provided protection of all sorts and provision of all kinds, similar to the times of the Exodus and their journeys through the wilderness under the leadership of Moses (Exodus 19:4). The purpose of the wilderness is to purify and test. This testing time will continue until the time of the end (Daniel 7:25; 12:7). This testing which God uses is initiated by the dragon to overtake the woman. Many times, a flood is used as a symbol to represent oppression and persecution (Psalm 18:4). The earth and the leadership of the nations is used by God to aid the woman from the wrath of the dragon. The dragon then continues his wrath by making war with the offspring of the woman, called her seed. This seed is specific, and is described as the ones who keep the commandments of God, *and* hold the testimony of Jesus. This is the church that Jesus said He would build (John 10:16; Romans 4:16; Galatians 3:28).

The statement that they keep the commandments of God, *and* the testimony of Jesus, is significant. One without the other is powerless. It should be the natural and obedient process for those who have waited for the Messiah, to follow the Christ that was sent for them. There were many judicial statements that Jesus declared because of the rejection of His person and ministry (Matthew 8:11-12; 21:43; 23:37-38; Luke 19:42-43). He held them responsible for the event of His first coming. We will be held responsible for the event of His second coming.

13:1a The first part of chapter 13, verse 1, states that he, the dragon, stood on the sand of the sea. This statement has three dynamics that should be noted carefully. First, it is a continuation of the dragon pursuing the woman and making war with the seed of the woman. (The chapter and verse divisions do not help in some cases.) Secondly, to *stand* can mean to take an opposing position or place of authority over something or someone else. The dragon takes a position of authority, as in a ruler or oppressor, over the sand of the sea. Thirdly, the sand of the sea is used often to describe large numbers of people (Genesis 32:12; Isaiah 10:22; Hebrews 11:12; Revelation 20:7-8). Going back to the symbolism of the sea in chapter 4 and 5, the sea represents the world system, and its members, in opposition to the will and purposes of God. Therefore, part of the dragons' current activity is waiting for his short time to be loosed. He is all the while working his given authority in the world, albeit in a restricted sense (1 John 5:19).

As noted, chapter 12 is a jet tour from the time of Jesus' first coming until the coming of the last world empire. The last world empire is symbolized in chapter 13. Therefore, this verse is pregnant with the time span and activity of the work of the dragon during our current experience. The dragon is waiting for his time to gather the nations again. Be encouraged! God is sovereign over His timetable!!

16

The Beasts
Revelation 13:1-18

It will be important to remember that chapters 12-16 are a unit. They are framed by the three signs. Chapter 13 of the book of Revelation picks up where the woman, and then the seed of the woman, are under the pursuing wrath of the dragon. At the end of chapter 12, or the first part of chapter 13 (verse 1a), we find the dragon standing on the sand of the sea. This phrase is not passive, but filled with the activity of the dragon known as Satan, during our present dispensation (Ephesians 3:1-7; Colossians 1:19-29; 1 John 2:18). His activity is in accord with his waiting for the short time he will be given to gather all those that oppose the Lamb (Revelation 12:12b; 17:10). Chapter 13 as a whole describes the means by which Satan gathers the world to stand against the word, will, and final decrees of God. This will be the ultimate time of division between those who follow the beast and those who follow the Lamb. It will be during this chapter that we will find out how the separation is initiated and then carried out. The final scene will be the eternal separation and the eternal judgement of the unbelieving world as executed during the seven bowls (Revelation 15-16). Each person will either stand for the Lamb or stand for the beast. What each receives, the Lamb or the beast, is what their followers will also receive.

Chapter 13 continues and intensifies the struggle and conflict between the followers of Christ and the followers of the beast. The beast is energized by Satan. And there are saints present in chapter 13. During the discussion of the seven churches, there are believers and unbelievers comprising the church in general. During the seven seals, we have believers who are sealed (Revelation 7). In the same way, there are believers and saints who are protected during the trumpets from the effects of the demonic host that is released in the fifth trumpet (Revelation 9:4). Then, during the reign of the beasts, saints are killed and martyred for not following the beast (Revelation 13:7, 15).

Coming to this section of narrative, it is important to think through our theology and our understanding of the mind of God. Can we know the mind of God? Yes, in what He reveals to us (Deuteronomy 29:29; Amos 3:7). There are many who teach that *the church* will not be here, but will be taken out and not experience any of this intense future. We must consider if this promotes subsets of believers that are nowhere else mentioned in Scripture. If we say that the church will be taken out, what part will be taken out? As in the seven churches, there are those who will be left to the hour of testing (Revelation 3:3). Others are told to hold on, and that death will be a part of their experience (Revelation 2:10). No, it is about not being deceived more than it is about preserving our lives. There is an argument that if we are not in a time of need, or do not anticipate a time of testing, that we will not be motivated to prepare ourselves. It is then that we will fall to the deception.[1] Note: The great tribulation is about what the dragon will do to the elect of that time. The wrath of God is what unbelievers will experience because they have rejected Him and, persecuted His elect. We can be prepared, strengthened, and encouraged, by knowing what will happen ahead of time. That is the whole purpose of the book of Revelation.

The order of events that are described in chapter 13 may well be contained in the final week of Daniel (Daniel 9:27).

Or, as could be the case with the narrative of chapter 12, the events occur in brief. The events of chapter 13 begin to occur slowly, then at an ever-increasing rate. As within our own recent history, there are more people being led to Christ in the last century than in the combined eighteen centuries before. There are also more people being killed for their faith in the last century than in the previous eighteen combined. Jesus said that the wheat and the tares will grow together until the end, then they will be separated (Matthew 13:14-30). It would be hard for us to imagine a beast kingdom that would envelope the whole world in its grasp. Let us remember the recent past. In World War II, the whole world was engaged in a conflict that only took a few years to develop. That war came about without many of the advanced communications and inventions of movement we have today. We must not be deceived and distracted, and caught without oil.

The Rise of the Beast from the Sea

13:1-4 John sees the dragon standing on the sand of the sea (see discussion in chapter 12). John then beholds a beast that rises up out of the sea. It is important, and vital, to understand the allusions to the Old Testament that are given throughout the book of Revelation. The sea represents the world system opposed to God, and all of its component parts and philosophies. The people of John's day generally saw the seas as a source of chaos and evil. The beast is a kingdom that is derived from the sea. We must go to the Prophet Daniel to get our foundational background for this symbolism.

The prophet Daniel is given a vision of the four world empires that would exist until the coming of the Messiah. In the vision, the four world empires are described as four beasts that rise up out of the sea (Daniel 7:2-8). Each of the four beasts are representative of a single empire that will have a significant impact on the world and the plans of God. The end of the vision includes the little horn who is destroyed, and the kingdom of God being set up on the earth (Daniel 7:9-14). The interpretation given is that the four beasts represent four kings who will rise up out of the earth. These kings will rule, but the saints of the Most High will ultimately prevail (Daniel 7:17-18). It is revealing that the four beasts are also represented by the image in Nebuchadnezzar's dreams (Daniel 2). The four kingdoms are Babylon, Persia, Greece, and Rome. These kingdoms ruled the known world, oppressed the people of God, intended to thwart the purposes of God, and exalted their leaders as gods. The Bible presents these beasts as concrete, historical, opposition to the covenant people of God. They are agents of Satan sent to kill, to corrupt, or distort the plans of God in redemption. The same scenario will occur before the second coming of Christ. Out of the world system and the sea of humanity there will be a world kingdom that will dominate all nations, oppress the people of God, and blaspheme in the sight of God. The leader will exalt himself as God (2 Thessalonians 2:2-4). Satan has always had his various people in place since he was cast from heaven. Many of his pawns are well known throughout the last 2,000 years. It will not be until God allows this, that this final world kingdom and its ruler be allowed to fulfill this prophecy.

The beast rising out of the sea has seven heads and ten horns. On the horns were crowns, and his heads had blasphemous names. These blasphemous names were titles of deity only attributed to God and God alone (Lord, Savior, Son of God, Our Lord and God, etc.). The heads of the beast assume these names in an attempt to deceive the nations, thus claiming deity. It is interesting that all the historical empires mentioned in the Bible had rulers who eventually claimed deity (as did all of the Pharaohs, Nebuchadnezzar, and the Caesars).

We must notice that the description is similar to the dragon but with significant differences (Revelation 12:3, see also 17:3). The dragon had crowns on his seven heads, while the beast has the crowns on his ten horns. The seven heads represent the complete number of world kingdoms that God will allow to exist (see Revelation 17:3). The ten horns are the makeup of these world kingdoms, namely, through the agency of all of mankind. Any form of man as the ultimate source good is idolatry. The crown is a symbol of ruling authority. What is being portrayed here is the way in which the dragon, or Satan, will manifest his power and authority. In the scene of chapter 12, the crowns are on the heads. In particular, the head which exists at the time of the birth of Jesus is the empire of Rome. In chapter 13, the crowns are on the horns, which is the world kingdom manifested through the authority and rule of mankind united under one leader.

John sees the beast as having the appearance of a leopard, the feet of a bear, and the mouth like a lion. This is in reverse of the vision in Daniel (Daniel 7:2-6). What John sees is a composite of these beasts, in reversed order, reconstituting a beast that can only be described in the terrifying terms that are given in chapter 13. The beast of chapter 13, as a world empire, will be everything these former kingdoms were combined. The dragon will give his power, his throne, and his authority to the beast. Satan will throw everything of his, and everything he has done, into and behind this world kingdom.

John sees one of the heads as if it was mortally wounded. It appeared as if it had received a mortal wound, and yet, was alive. The wound was healed, and the world was amazed and followed the beast. It is important to understand that one of the heads was wounded, but, the marvel of the world was for the beast and not the wounded head. It was because the beast, in its manifested time as a particular kingdom (Rome), was wounded as though dead. It is the final head representing the sea beast that causes amazement. The last time a kingdom ruled the known world was during the Roman Empire (Revelation

17:10). This coming head of the beast will be that, and much more. What is happening?

The world will come together to give allegiance to a world kingdom, an empire, that involves all the nations of the world. All nations will be deceived into believing the dragon will give them what they need and desire. So, as the world gives allegiance to the beast, they are in turn giving worship to the dragon who empowers the beast. The mentality of the world will be that there is nothing else that can be compared to the beast. This is very close to the declaration of Scripture, as given to the one, true God (Psalm 71:19; 81:8; Isaiah 40:25).

13:5-10 The beast was given a mouth. This is a way of saying the beast has a message, and, has the means of communicating great things and blasphemies. Careful discernment will give evidence of the source and heart of a personality (Matthew 15:18-19). Blasphemy can either be saying things of God that are not true, or, saying things of yourself that are only true of God (Daniel 4:30). The beast communicates that it can, and does, meet the needs and desires that in reality can only be met by God. This blasphemy correlates with the time of the treading of the holy city (Revelation 11:2). The beast then opens his mouth to blaspheme against God himself, His name, His dwelling place, and those who are heaven (see Daniel 7:25). The beast will make war against the saints, and, overcome them (Revelation 11:7). It is not usually in our mindset to realize that the devil must be endured, but God is still sovereign. It must also be remembered that whatever the dragon or the beast can do is always in a limited time span. The beast will have authority over all kinds of people, and in all kinds of places. All those who are called earth-dwellers, those who refuse God and His future, will worship the beast. The earth-dwellers will trust in, and make an idol of any government that meets their need. They do so because their names are not written in the Lamb's book of life. They have chosen the beast instead of the Lamb, and have chosen temporary security instead of God's plan. The redemption through the Lamb from the foundation of the world.

Then comes a statement similar to the encouragements given to each of the seven churches. This is a crucial time of division. From this point in God's unfolding of history, there will be a separation that has eternal implications. The time for waiting is dangerously short. The separation is between those who choose to follow the beast and be captivated by his deceit, and those who follow the Lamb. The patience and faith of the saints is to endure this time of deceit, struggle, and division. It must be remembered, and the original hearers of this prophecy would have been encouraged to know, that God has sanctioned this time in world history. Victory is won by being faithful, even if it means death. Earthly institutions and conditions, good or bad, must never take precedence over, replace, or marginalize the plan and Gospel of God (1 Corinthians 7:29-31). These verses, and many like them, are proof that the book of Revelation was given to those who are encouraged to endure, persevere, and overcome. The time of decision is about over. The final judgements for those who choose the beast are at hand. God has set a day that He will not relent (see Jeremiah 15:2). Judgement will be non-deferred.

The Rise of the Beast from the Earth

13:11-18 John then sees another beast rising out of the earth. This is similar to what was seen by Daniel in his vision (Daniel 7). Daniel first sees beasts rising up out of the sea, and then sees beasts who rise up out of the earth. The two beasts that John sees are connected, as are the beasts that Daniel saw. Both beasts are agents of Satan. While the beast that rises from the sea represents a world empire or kingdom, the beast rising from the earth represents the notable leader of that empire. The beast from the earth provides organization to the chaos of the sea. This earth beast has two horns like a lamb, but speaks like a dragon. The imagery symbolizes that there will be a counterfeit of Christ, a counterfeit of the Lamb of God. Jesus was the Prophet spoken of by Moses. This earth beast is called the false prophet later in the book of Revelation (contrast Deuteronomy 18:15 with Revelation 16:13; 19:20; 20:10). The power in his testimony is that of a beast coming as a lamb. But this beast speaks as from the dragon, who is Satan. Many interpreters label the beast from the sea as the Antichrist. It is, in reality, the beast from the earth, the designated ruler, who is the Antichrist. The Antichrist is one who comes instead of, or, in place of Christ. This whole picture of the two beasts is a parody of the relationship of the Father and the Son.

The beast from the earth is directly associated with the beast from the sea in all that he does. He works on behalf of the first beast. His specific task is to draw all worship and allegiance of the earth-dwellers to the first beast and away from God. He is given the ability to perform great signs, as Jesus did, to persuade the world of his message. The signs that Jesus performed pointed to point to Who He was, and Who had sent Him. The signs that the beast from the earth performs are a counterfeit to mask his origins, his intentions, and who empowers him (John 3:19; 2 Corinthians 11:14). The results of these great signs will deceive those who dwell on the earth. They give to the sea beast status and position as the be all, provide all, and protect all. This designation is in direct opposition to what God demands and is due as the Creator. The doctrine of Creation demands our accountability to the Creator. Those who dwell on the earth replace God with their world kingdom, making it their God.

We are commanded not to make an image of God, or of anything that we can call a god (Exodus 20:4-6). The earth dwellers make an image, or a representation of their god. The image, or likeness, of their god is of their own making. The earth beast, using deception, causes the followers of the beast from the sea to make a

god of their self-governing world institution. The image represents themselves as the final arbiter of their safety and security. The image has the purpose of forcing conformity to the world system (Daniel 2). This is similar to the mentality that was behind the tower of Babel (Genesis 11:1-6). Mankind governing himself without God.

The earth beast, or false prophet, was granted to give spirit to the corporate activity of the sea beast. This corporate activity did not allow any dissidents or opposition to the allegiance of the sea beast. Somehow, corporate compliance will be promoted. Any violation to this god-like status of the beast would be fatal. The opposition is identified as anyone who will worship the true God and speak against the beast.

Those who align themselves with the beast receive a mark on their right hand or on their forehead. The mark is the parody of the seal on the forehead. It is important to realize that those who worship the beast are *caused* to receive the mark. The seal protects, the mark does not. The mark is not forced. The purpose of the signs is to produce a "buying into" the counterfeit scheme of the dragon. It is caused by deception, but its acceptance is voluntary. Of note is the result: to take the mark of the beast is to incur the wrath of the Lamb, and, to receive the seal of the Lamb is to incur the wrath of the beast.[2]

There are eight places in the book of Revelation where the forehead is mentioned (Revelation 7:3; 9:4; 13:16; 14:1, 9; 17:5; 20:4; 22:4). Four of them are in a good context, and four of them are in an evil context. Is it the literal forehead in all instances? The forehead was the front part of the head and seen as the seat of perception, the place of thought, logic, and judgement. This is the part of the mind that gives adherence and loyalty to what each person maintains in devotion (Ezekiel 3:7-9). The mark and the seal, are not seen, but are each a spiritual stamp of ownership. In the Old Testament, the Hebrews were to attach phylacteries to their foreheads and to their hands. This was not a means of show for others, or as a sort of talisman. They were for a remembrance of what they were to follow and by what devotion they lived their lives. They were used as a symbol, or sign, for something they maintained *internally* (Deuteronomy 6:8; 11:18).

When those who dwell on the earth give worship and adherence to the beast, this *causes* them to receive the mark. They have given themselves over to the beast. This is in contrast to the believers who follow the true God, and who receive the seal of the Holy Spirit after receiving Christ as Savior (Ephesians 1:13; 4:30). The same word for seal is used for the sealing of the 144,000 (Revelation 7). Ezekiel sees the same type of marking, albeit for safety, when the people who sigh and grieve over the sin of Jerusalem are spared from destruction (Ezekiel 9:4).

The hand is often used as a symbol of the function of a person's will, control, or care. For example, we are saved by God's right hand (Psalm 18:36; 60:5). The right hand was the place of honor and privilege. Those who dwell on the earth are not only giving their allegiance and adherence to the beast with their mind, they are giving the beast honor by what they do. It is of great contrast that those who are sealed by God on the forehead are not also sealed on their right hand. That is because our salvation and sealing by God is entirely by what He does for us, not in anything that we can do (Ephesians 2:8-9).

The mark on the forehead or the hand allows one to participate in the business of the beast. Those who do not receive the mark, and have the seal, will not be allowed, or will choose not to participate in the business of the beast. The business of the beast is to promote the agenda of the dragon in all his evil ways.

John is then given some wisdom in knowing the identity of the beast from the earth. This identity is not related to a specific name or person. The wisdom is being able to decide or discern who the beast is, and who he is not. This is discerned by knowledge of the Truth. The book of Proverbs declares that the fear of the Lord is the beginning of knowledge (Proverbs 1:7). And, the fear of the Lord is the beginning of wisdom. And again, the knowledge of the Holy One is understanding (Proverbs 9:10). During this critical time of the end, two things will be important: knowledge and wisdom. Both of these are only acquired by knowing the Word of God. When we know the Truth, The Holy One, the counterfeit will be readily seen.

John is also told that there is calculation to be done. The Greek word for calculation, *psephizo*, means to decide, vote, choose, and pronounce. The work of calculating, as we would do in a computation, and the discernment of the facts has already been done ahead of time. The counting, or calculating of the number of the beast is not a calculation of the facts at the moment. It is a *knowing* of the facts and their significance ahead of time, and having the wisdom to *choose* correctly at the time it is needed (Matthew 24:15ff). (It would be similar to studying legal currency in order identify any counterfeit currency when it appears.) The gematria number of man is six. The number 666, given in triplicate for emphasis, reveals to us that the earth beast is the entirely a man. Jesus came declaring that He was God, the divine Son of God. This beast will be a man indwelt by the dragon to deceive. He will be the ultimate counterfeit of Christ, and a beast from the earth (Matthew 24:24-25). We, who know in Whom we have trusted, will not be deceived (Matthew 24:24; 2 Timothy 1:12).

Chapter 13 of the book of Revelation is the narrative of the final world empire of the Antichrist. This world empire is yet in the future. We have God's word to inform us and prepare us for that time. Let us be faithful and wise in passing on the testimony of Jesus to those who follow us. Be encouraged! We are in His hands!!

17

Separation
Revelation 14:1-20

Chapter 14 is part of the section that began with the two signs at the beginning of chapter 12. The section ends with the bowls of God's wrath being completed in chapter 16. Chapter 12 opens with the narration of history from the time of Jesus' first coming. Chapter 12 introduces the current struggle and conflict between the dragon, who is Satan, and the woman and her seed, who represent the covenant people of God. Chapter 13 opens with the dragon having a position of authority and subjugation over the sands of the sea. This is a statement concerning our current dispensation of time (1 John 5:19). Chapter 13 then narrates the developing final world kingdom that will become ruled by the false prophet, or antichrist, the man of sin and lawlessness. Chapter 13 ends with the characteristics of the two kinds of people who are present on the earth. There are those who *receive* the seal of the Lamb and are subject to the temporary wrath of the beast, or, those who *take* the mark of the beast and will suffer the eternal wrath of the Lamb. Chapter 13 ends with a call to wisdom in knowing and discerning who the false prophet is, and the false worship that he has set up.

Chapter 14 begins with the separation that that wisdom will create among people still on earth, between those who follow the beast and those who follow the Lamb. It then moves to the worldwide proclamation of an eternal separation by three angels, the events of the final harvest and gathering, the victory of those who follow the Lamb, and then the wrath of God upon those who have followed the beast. (See below: Diagram #5, Page 143.)

It will be important to notice that the events narrated in these chapters move from transpiring on earth, then to heaven, back to the earth, and then to heaven again. All the while, there are spiritual implications of what is occurring on earth, and earthly implications of what is happening in the heavens (see Daniel 8:8-12). While it takes only minutes to read the words from chapter 14, verse 6, through chapter 16, the reality is, the timespan for the harvest, judgements, and rewards, will only be moments (Revelation 16:15; 22:12). In one hour (Revelation 14:7)!

The Redeemed

14:1-5 Behold!! John then looks, and he sees the Lamb standing on Mount Zion. This is in contrast to the dragon standing on the sand of the sea (Revelation 13:1). The sand of the sea represents the population of the earth of which the dragon has dominion. The definition of the term Zion contains the idea of a citadel, fortress, stronghold, community, or group of people who stand in special relationship with God. Sometimes Zion refers to a land, sometimes a kingdom, sometimes a tribe. Zion can refer to a mountain, or a group of people (in the land, in heaven, or as exiles), or a particular city (Psalm 48; 78:68; 87:5-6; 125:1; Isaiah 51:16; Zechariah 2:7; Hebrews 12:22; 1 Peter 2:6). Zion is the assembly and community of the praising and worshipping people of God regardless of place, area, or location. Zion is called the dwelling of God, be it the chief among the mountains, the city of God, or the chief among the nations. Zion is called eternal and heavenly. What is being pictured here is the contrast between the followers of the beast and the followers of the Lamb. Zion is representative of those from the earth who belong to the Lamb, the 144,000.

It is important to notice that the number 144,000, is the same number used of the ones being sealed in chapter 7 (Revelation 7:1-8). The number represents those who are sealed prior to the four winds being released. None are lost! This number also represents the completed, full complement of redeemed on the earth up to the time of the end. These redeemed have the name of the Lamb's Father written on their foreheads (Revelation 3:12). John hears a voice from heaven. John is not in heaven. The voice is from God in all its facets. The sound of harpists represents the peace that is associated with the status of being under the agency of the Lamb.

The 144,000 sing a new song (see Revelation 5:9-10). The new song is in relation to the finished work of Christ on the cross. This is the particular song of the redeemed out of the earth and out of the deceitfulness of the times. They are not defiled by spiritual idolatry. They have kept themselves for communion with the Lamb, and, have not committed spiritual adultery against the One to whom they have been betrothed (as the church in 2 Corinthians 11:1-2). The 144,000 follow the Lamb in all His commandments and keep His testimony. To follow means to be invested in discipleship. *The Lamb is the Shepherd* (see Revelation 7:17). They are called first fruits, which is an offering of the first and the best crops given to God. Firstfruits were an act of faith and trust that God would fulfill His promise of a complete harvest. Those who are "firstfruits" in Christ are evidence of the renewal and new creation that is to come (Romans 8:18-25; 2 Peter 3:10-13). In their mouth was found no deceit, guile, falsehood, or wavering of their faith (John 1:47). They are without fault before God. God sees them in the righteousness of Christ, the Lamb. They are in direct contrast to the ones who worship and follow the beast.

Without a doubt, whoever the 144,000 symbolize here in this section, they are the same 144,000 in chapter 7, and visa-versa. Some interpreters want to make the 144,000 in chapter 7 a group of specific *Jewish* converts. Chapter 7 does not contain the term Jew in its context. That they are called Israel does not mean that they are also Jewish, just as being Jewish does not mean that they are part of Israel (Romans 2:28-29; 9:6-8). The terms are not always interchangeable. The term Jew was used long after the nation of Israel was given its identity in Joseph. The term Israel means to strive, struggle, or rule with God. There are many who were not originally of the lineage of Abraham included into the twelve tribes of Israel (IE. Ruth, Caleb, Bathsheba, Rahab, etc.). In chapter 7, the two tribes who are left out of the list of 12 tribes are left out because of idolatry (see previous chapters). In the same way, the 144,000 are described as not being involved in idolatry (Chapter 14, verse 4). The results of both criteria describe the identity of the people of God as those who do not practice idolatry. The Old Testament lessons used by the risen Christ to warn the seven churches have nothing but Old Testament allusions. If the language of chapter 7 describes the exact identity of particular, national Israel, then the seven churches must be also. This is clearly not the case. The 144,000 in both cases, chapters 7 and 14, are the redeemed who are on the earth, in Christ, and His possession.

The Proclamations of Three Angels

14:6-13 John sees another angel, or messenger, flying at the zenith (highest point) of heaven. This is a message that will be somehow received by all and cannot be mistaken or missed by anyone who dwells on the earth. The message is informing those who dwell on the earth of its eternal gravity. The events after this message will never be reversed, as it is final and forever. This is a "last call." This last call gives God the glory and credit as Creator. The angel declares an "eternal gospel," the news and arrival of the eternal kingdom of God. The Gospel is about being born again, but also includes living as overcomers in a sanctified life. The Gospel message always includes that which we are saved to inherit.

Another angel follows declaring the fall of Babylon. This statement is given as if it has already happened. It is declared twice to give certainty. This same declaration was given in the Old Testament when the specific city and kingdom of Babylon was defeated (Isaiah 21:9, Jeremiah 51:8). The context here is of a cosmic magnitude in its scope. The great city symbolism used here represents all the false worship and evil that has existed since the Tower of Babel. The tower of Babel is the root and source of all human self-reliance. This self-reliance has been the sin of all the nations in opposition to the will and plan of God.

Wine promotes intoxication and passion against the will of God.

Fornication is equal to unfaithfulness to God. This city is also in contrast to the city of God, the New Jerusalem. Babylon, whose origin is Babel, represents man's rebellion and attempt to be set free from the mandates of God.

The third of the three angels gives a final warning to those who dwell on the earth and follow the beast. They have worshipped the beast and have made it their god. They have given mental ascent and performed actions in honor of the beast. Those who have done so will share, with Babylon, the wrath of God poured out full strength upon the unrepentant. To hold a cup portrays the experience of what the cup contained. It will be given uncut, unmixed, and not diluted.

The fire and brimstone are a picture of final torment and judgement (Matthew 25:41; Revelation 19:20; 20:10; 20:15; 21:8). This judgement is before, and in the sight of, the holy angels and the Lamb (Mark 8:38; Luke 9:26; John 5:22). Smoke is associated with, and symbolic of, the destruction of both of the city and the people. There is never, ever, a hint of annihilation in the Scriptures. Hell, as the eternal punishment of the wicked will be real. We tend to be more afraid of the physical means of death by sword, disease, and genocide, than we are of hell and the eternal separation from God (Matthew 10:28).

The next statements are a strong reminder of the purpose of the book of Revelation (Revelation 1:1-8). The encouragements and exhortations are to the believers to persevere, endure, and to overcome. This gives evidence that there *will be* believers present during these events. This is needed during the darkest last days of the beast that come just before the return of Christ. These specific lines are for the ones who keep the commandments of God and the faith of Jesus (see Revelation 12:17). The faith of Jesus is what allowed Him to trust Himself to the Father (Luke 23:46). We are to have this same faith when we cannot see the next stage of our lives, especially during the very last days. We are to submit and trust the sovereign will of God the Father. The voice in heaven agrees with the statement, as this is the last minute of the last hour. The Spirit gives witness that all those who die in the Lord will be blessed and that their works for the Lord will follow them into eternity. What we do for the Lord during our earthly existence has eternal significance.

The Grain Reaping

14:14-16 Behold!! John looks again, and he sees a white cloud, and One who is seated on the cloud. The One on the cloud has the appearance of the Son of Man. Jesus' use of this title was to describe Himself in His incarnation. Jesus is the *representative man*. The use here of *with the clouds*, also includes the Messianic term used by the Old Testament (Daniel 7:13-14). When Jesus is seen with clouds He is always in an ascended, exalted context (Matthew 24:30; 26:64; Acts 1:9-11; Revelation 1:7). Clouds always accompany deity. On His head is a crown of greatness, and of worth, and of glory. Everything about Him and His person represents His surrounding value of the highest measure. In His hand is a sharp sickle that cuts, divides, and separates cleanly and completely.

There now appears an angel coming from the very dwelling place of God. The angel cries with a loud voice to the One on the cloud: "Thrust in your sickle and reap." The command comes with the description of a harvest that is ripe and ready for harvest. There is ample evidence in Scripture that the harvest of souls is usually associated with grain (Mark 4:26-29; John 4:34-

38). There is also evidence that the grain is usually associated with the converted. The fact that the Son of Man is doing the harvesting harkens back to many passages in which Jesus spoke of Himself at His return. The harvest and separation happen at the end of the age (Matthew 13:24-30; 16:27; 24:30-31; 25:31-46; 28:20).

Why an angel giving the command? Jesus, as the Son of Man, did not know the hour or the day the Father alone had set (Mark 13:32). The angel commands with a loud voice. Is there a secret, quiet coming of Jesus? The Scriptures do not portray a secret, quiet coming of Jesus (Acts 1:9-11; 1 Corinthians 15:51-52; 1 Thessalonians 4:15-17; Revelation 1:7; 10:5-7; 22:12). Are there multiple comings to accommodate different groups of believers or subsets of the elect? There are only two kinds of believers mentioned at the coming of Jesus. Those who are sleeping and those who are alive. His coming is associated with the voice of an archangel and a trumpet (1 Thessalonians 4:15-17). An angel is present here, and it is at the seventh trumpet. If any second coming scenario does not validate a visible return of Jesus, a resurrection of the dead, a rapture of the saints, a reunion of all, and a permanent

presence with the Lord, *in that order*, it must be thoroughly questioned. (Many interpreters do seem to be trying to solve a problem without letting the Scriptures speak for themselves.) So, He, Jesus, harvested.

The Gathering of Grapes

14:17-20 Then another angel comes from the dwelling of God, also having a sharp sickle. Another angel comes from the altar with fire from the altar. It must be remembered that the golden altar was used on the day of Atonement. This was a once a year occurrence where the sin of the people was removed. The picture here is sin being removed and dealt with once and for all. The angel is commanded to thrust his sickle and gather the clusters of the vine of the earth, for the grapes are also fully ripe. Gathering of grapes was often used in the Old Testament as a picture of judgement (Isaiah 24:13; Jeremiah 6:9; 49:8-10). The grape gathering is the picture of a complete, thorough, picking of every single grape. Often every single grape was particularly gathered, even the gleanings. The grapes are then thrown into the winepress of the wrath of God. The winepress is a picture of judgement in the greatest sense.

There are two Greek words for wrath in the New Testament. One Greek word, *orge*, represents the settled disposition of God against an unredeemed person (Romans 1:18; Ephesians 2:3). The other Greek word, *thumos*, used here, represents the extreme, passionate, eruptive judgement of God's anger (also verse 10). The bowls are said to be filled with this kind of extreme passion and judgement of wrath (Revelation 16:1). Jesus is also involved in this final judgement in a recapitulation of this scene (Revelation 19:15). The winepress was trod outside the city. In the same way, the scapegoat of Old Testament times was taken outside the camp (Leviticus 16:27), Jesus was also taken outside the city to die when He made atonement for sin (John 19:17; Hebrews 13:12).

The blood comes out of the winepress up to the horses' bridles for the length of 1600 stadia. Horses were the great, powerful instruments of warfare during the time of the writing of Revelation. The strength of an army was in its number of heavy horses. The bridle was the means of controlling the horse. The death and judgement left no means of resistance, control, turning back, or escape. Sixteen hundred is a product of 40 x 40. Forty was the number used to describe the time of testing, trial, spiritual preparation, and purifying (i.e., The Flood, Moses, Jesus). To use a product of that number gives a symbolic picture of completed fullness, or the complete ending of the time of testing. Then, to multiply that number by 1,000 gives the event to include all human existence until the end of time. (The same representative pattern for symbolism in numbers is used to describe the 144,000, that is, 12 X 12 X 1,000. The product of 10 X 10 is also used to convey all of man's existence, as in the 1,000 years of Revelation 20:3ff.) The separation is final. The scope is cosmic. The judgement is at hand.

Be encouraged! Jesus saves us from the wrath to come!!

Diagram #5

TIME OF SEPARATION

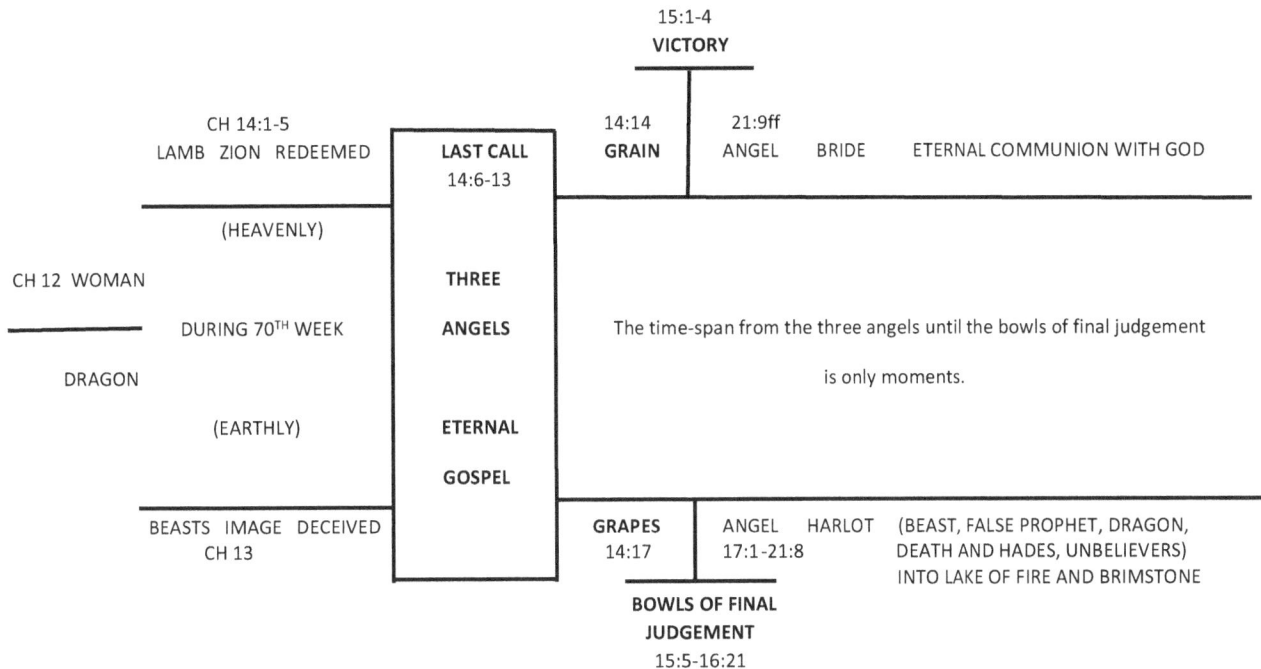

```
                                              15:1-4
                                              VICTORY

      CH 14:1-5                     14:14      21:9ff
   LAMB  ZION  REDEEMED   LAST CALL  GRAIN     ANGEL    BRIDE    ETERNAL COMMUNION WITH GOD
                          14:6-13

      (HEAVENLY)

CH 12 WOMAN               THREE

                ANGELS            The time-span from the three angels until the bowls of final judgement
DURING 70TH WEEK
DRAGON                                                    is only moments.

      (EARTHLY)           ETERNAL

                GOSPEL

   BEASTS  IMAGE  DECEIVED         GRAPES      ANGEL    HARLOT   (BEAST, FALSE PROPHET, DRAGON,
         CH 13                     14:17       17:1-21:8          DEATH AND HADES, UNBELIEVERS)
                                                                 INTO LAKE OF FIRE AND BRIMSTONE

                                   BOWLS OF FINAL
                                   JUDGEMENT
                                   15:5-16:21
```

Diagram # 5 shows the progression from chapter 12 to the end of the book of Revelation. Chapter 12 shows us the source and activities of the dragon and the conflict he initiates. Chapter 13 will be a time of global deception for the earth dwellers, and a time of perseverance for the believers. Chapter 14 begins by showing the readers the inclusive number of the redeemed and their position of righteousness in the Lamb. Chapter 14 continues with the message of the three angels giving a series of "last call" warnings to the earth concerning God, the fall of the world systems, and worship of the beast. After the messages of the three angels, the harvests of grain and grapes are concluded. Chapter 15 opens with the bowls of wrath given to the seven angels. The redeemed overcomers are shown separated from the sea, which is the symbol of cosmic rebellion. There is then victory praise and worship given to God. Chapter 16 narrates the wrath of the seven bowls being poured out on the earth. From chapter 17 to the end of the book of Revelation we have the final jugdements and rewards, the judgements of the harlot and the rewards and status of the bride of Christ.

18

The Final Wrath of God
Revelation 15:1-16:21

Chapters 12-16 are a major section that must be read and understood together. Within that narrative context, chapters 15 and 16 need to be considered together. As we proceed into the next two chapters, we observe and consider their structure and their context within the whole of the book of Revelation. Chapter 12 opens with John seeing two signs in heaven. These chapters prepare and lead us to the final set of seven, the seven bowls.

Chapter 15 opens with John seeing another sign in heaven. This is the third sign, of which the first two were seen at the beginning of chapter 12. Three is an apocalyptic number of fullness. With these three signs, we have a complete picture of the time between Jesus' first coming, and the climax of this current age. Chapter 16 consists of the seven bowls of God's final wrath. Another issue that will be noticed is the finality and completeness with which the bowls are described and implemented. It must then be noted that the same angels who held the bowls will be the ones to describe the results and outcome after the final wrath of God (Revelation 17:1; 21:9). The angels will take John to the wilderness for the judgement of the harlot and her component members. John will then be taken to a high mountain for the description and status of the bride. It is of note, that all of these passages are written as if they have already occurred.

Prelude to the Bowls

15:1-4 John sees another great sign in heaven. Seven angels having the seven last plagues. This is a complete group of plagues. Seven is the number of a completed sequence. The bowls are called the last, and completed wrath of God at the end of verse 1 (See Revelation 16:17 and 16:19). The Greek word for wrath used here is one of outburst, boiling, and retributive judgement (used also in Revelation 16:19, often translated fierceness). These bowls are future, final, and universal. The Greek word for filled-up, *teleo,* concerns the wrath of God. It is the same Greek word Jesus used when saying "it is finished," speaking of his finished work on the cross (John 19:30). It is not possible that there will be another time of God's *final* wrath, either by what is narrated here or by the structure of the book of

Revelation. The book of Revelation makes repeated use of recapitulation. Recapitulation is portraying something again from another perspective.

John then sees the sea of glass, first mentioned in chapter 4, verse 6. This time the sea of glass in not clear as crystal, but is mingled with fire. The sea being mingled with fire gives a condition of being in judgement. Those who have won the victory over the beast, his image, his number, and his mark, are standing on (above) the sea of glass. Those who have not been deceived and have not followed the beast, those who have followed the Lamb, are seen as being separated from the judgement that the sea now experiences. They who have followed the Lamb have overcome and are shown separated from the sea. The harps of God represent being at peace.

They sing the song of Moses and of the Lamb. This is a song of rescue, exodus, and deliverance. What Moses did for the particular covenant people of God, Jesus will do at the end of days for the corporate, universal, covenant people of God at the end of the age. The song is a witness and worship of God, who has the right and authority because He is powerful, just, and true.

He has the authority to manifest His judgements upon the nations. He will receive the honor due Him even from those who will be forced to recognize His sovereignty (as Philippians 2:10-11).

15:5-8 John then sees the temple of the tabernacle of the testimony in heaven *opened*. The progression from the seals to the trumpets, and then to the bowls, is apparent in the language of the texts. In the seventh seal, the scene is before the golden altar (Revelation 8:1-5). At the seventh trumpet, the scene is inside the holy place and the ark of the covenant was seen (Revelation 11:19). During the seven bowls we see that the ark is opened. Out of the heavenly temple, the dwelling place of God, come the seven angels. They are garbed as is fitting of those who minister on behalf of God.

Then one of the four living creatures gave, or allowed, to the seven angels seven bowls full of the wrath of God the Eternal One. The glory and power of God fills the temple with smoke. No one was able to enter the temple until the bowls were complete. God's anger, glory, and holiness are being executed against those who rejected Him. What is fear and dread to unbelievers, is always awe and reverence to those who are His.

The Bowls

16:1-2 John hears a voice from the temple, even from God Himself, giving command to the seven angels to go and pour their bowls of God's wrath upon the earth. The first angel pours the first bowl out, and sores came upon each person who had given themselves over to the allegiance and worship of the beast. These sores were visible, painful, and deep. This first bowl represents judgement that cannot be reversed. It affects those who have chosen permanent separation from God and cannot be redeemed. These sores cannot be healed (Deuteronomy 28:27, 35).

16:3 The second angel pours his bowl on the sea, the source of chaos and rebellion, and it became dead and without any life. The sea had no life and could not support life.

16:4-7 The third angel pours the third bowl on the rivers and springs of water. The sources of life died, along with that which carried and provided life. The angel of the waters gives us the interpretation of what the rivers and springs of water represent. The rivers and springs of water are described as *those* who "shed the blood of saints and prophets." These are people who have had the power and influence to lead, persuade and mandate behavior. These rivers and springs are those people who have had the responsibility of providing people the words that should have brought them their life. Both springs and rivers feed into the sea. The song and worship remind us of the plea of the saints under the altar (Revelation 6:9-11; 18:20). In some translations the phrase "who is to come" is left out, as with Revelation 11:17. Because He *has* come!

16:8-9 The fourth angel pours his bowl out on the sun. The sun is given power to scorch and burn with fire. The heat and scorching produced nothing but blasphemy and non-repentance. The sun is God's primary source of light and revelation. The sun, to the people of God's day, stood for God's justice and revelation. The woman is clothed with the sun (Revelation 12:1). We are protected from God's full revelation of justice. It is being held back by His grace during this dispensation (Isaiah 49:10; Revelation 7:16). There is nothing new in God's creation, under the sun (Ecclesiastes 1:9). To those who fear the name of God, the full revelation of God's righteousness in Jesus Christ will rise in our hearts (Malachi 4:2; 2 Peter 1:19). To believers, the full revelation of God will be our rescue and glorification, but to the unbelieving world, it will be His full word of justice and judgement. The promises of God are given to the believer as His grace. The promises given for unbelief will be jugdement and pain. In eternity, we will be glorified and have perfect communion with God. His full revelation will not harm us (Revelation 21:22-23).

16:10-11 The fifth angel poured his bowl on the throne of the beast. Thrones are representative seats of authority and power. The throne of the beast is Satan himself. It is from the dragon, Satan, that the beast receives his authority and his mandates. His kingdom became full of darkness. Darkness, because of the rejection of God's ways. Darkness is a metaphor of being kept ignorant and outside of the will, purposes, and plans of God. Darkness is the absence of God's presence, providential control, and His personal care and provision (Colossians 1:17; Hebrews 1:3). The beast and his sponsor will be separated from even knowing what God has in store for them until it is too late. The leaders of Jesus' day were judged in this way (Matthew 8:8-13; 22:13; 25:30).

16:12-16 The sixth angel poured out his bowl on the great river Euphrates. Rivers, and associating waters, were often used as a metaphor for the power, control, and influence of a kingdom. Many times, God says that He will dry up a nations waters as a metaphor for taking away their power and influence (Isaiah 44:27; Jeremiah 51:36; Ezekiel 30:12; Hosea 13:15; Nahum 1:4; Zechariah 10:11). God dries up the rivers and the Red Sea when He delivers His people. According to the historian Herodotus, the river Euphrates was diverted and the river bed "dried up," to allow the ancient city of Babylon to be overtaken (Daniel 5). The river Euphrates diverted, the next day there was a new kingdom in power over Babylon. In the same way, the universal kingdom of false worship called Babylon and the harlot will one day fall into judgement. God's eternal kingdom will be on earth as it is in heaven.

This calamity to Babylon will make way for the kings of the east. The kings *of the East* are not the same as those who are gathered from *the four corners of the earth* (Revelation 16:14; 19:19; 20:8). Who are these kings of the east? The Greek term used for *of the east,* is the same term used for the origin of the angel who comes to do the sealing of the 144,000 (see discussion on Revelation 7:2). These are the only two places in Revelation where this specific term is used. There is single Greek word that is used to connotate the direction on the compass called East. The Greek word used in chapter 7, verse 2, and in chapter 16, verse 12, is unique to those verses. The same Greek term, *anatole*, is used in the LXX, and is translated from the Hebrew word for *The Branch*. This is found in the Old Testament book of Zechariah (Zechariah 6:12). The term, The Branch, is used as a Messianic title of the Messiah. Is the angel with the seal of the living God sent from The Branch? Are these the kings of the Messiah, The Branch? After Babylon falls, is this the time when the believers will rule with Christ? Many times, believers are declared to be kings, a royal priesthood who will ultimately have eternal rule with Jesus (Daniel 7:27; 1 Peter 2:9; 1 John 3:2; Revelation 1:6; 3:21; 5:10). These believers are the co-reigning kings of the Messiah.

John then sees three evil spirits, like frogs, coming from the unholy trinity of the dragon, the beast, and the false prophet. Frogs are unclean and have a sound that is loud and obnoxious. The intent of this sound will to deceive those who dwell on the earth into a battle with God Almighty. It is at this point in the future that the world will be totally unprepared for the path that they have taken, insofar as to the eternal results. It will be at this point in the future that Christ comes and catches the world and its inhabitants as a "thief in the night" (Matthew 24:43; Luke 12:39; 1 Thessalonians 5:2-4; 2 Peter 3:10; Revelation 3:3). The thief in the night is connected with the "suddenly" occurrences of Revelation 17-18.

The three evil spirits, coming from the dragon, beast, and false prophet, gather the earth to the place called "in Hebrew", Har-Megiddon. (This is a cosmic event involving spiritual and physical forces united together.) This term should be understood in the Hebrew language (See Revelation 9:11). Har is the Hebrew word for mount or mountain. John uses the spelling of Megiddon and the event described in Zechariah to associate this time with great mourning and defeat (Zechariah 12:11). Megiddon can mean to "gather for destruction." The people of the earth, led by the thee evil spirits, come as one cosmic *mountain* or one *kingdom*. This is a battle and attempted takeover of God's kingdom. The Har Megiddon of this verse is a word play of Satan's past attempt on the mount of assembly, the Har Mo'ed of Isaiah 14:13. He tries it one last time. The Mountain of Megiddon is in contrast and opposition to Mount Zion (See Revelation 14:1 notes).

16:17-21 Immediately following the gathering at Megiddon, the seventh angel pours out his bowl. It is sudden, it is concise, and it is final. There is no actual war with God (See 2 Thessalonians 2:8). There is only eternal punishment and judgement. It is without escape. A voice from the temple and from the throne declares that "It is done." It is final! There were noises, lightnings, thunderings, and a great earthquake, (a massive changing of the cosmic environment). The great city of Babylon was fully and completely taken apart. All the nations fell. Babylon was remembered before God for all the iniquity and blasphemy for which she was responsible. Babylon experiences the full wrath of God. Every opportunity for escape and refuge, and every kingdom of which Babylon had been the roots, was taken from her and her inhabitants. Great hail, a symbol of final judgement, fell on each person as full judgement. Unbelievers, knowing who was judging them, cursed at God because of His justice. The end has come. Jesus has returned. The redeemed have been delivered. The final judgements have arrived. What remains is the description of the two separate eternities.

Be encouraged! Jesus will defeat the powers of darkness!!

Excursus

There are interpretations of the book of Revelation that have created many scenarios of the end that are not found in any part of Scripture. One of the key understandings that we must have, is that we are not appointed unto wrath (1 Thessalonians 5:8). Just before that statement, Paul informs the believers that the Day of the Lord will not surprise them as a thief in the night (1 Thessalonians 5:4). Only the bowls are called the wrath of God (Revelation 15-16). Tribulation and wrath are different experiences. Believers are removed just before the bowls, at the last trumpet (Revelation 10:7). We return with Jesus (Revelation 19:14).

19

The Sentencing Begins
Revelation 17:1-18

As the journey continues into the book of Revelation, three words will continue to challenge us towards the right interpretations and conclusions. Structure, structure, and structure. Structure leads to context. Context leads to meaning. The text gives us the information to interpret and explain the message that we are to understand. The following sections of narrative have been the source for some of the most divisive and contentious discussions within the church. Our Biblical understanding concerning judgement, as a corporate body of believers, is lacking because of confusion or the outright rejection of the truths that are contained in these chapters. There are times that a particular theology is developed without the congruence of narrative history. And there are times when the historical context of the issues has been at odds with a correct theology. There are extravagant, incoherent, end-time scenarios developed and expounded that do not have evidence from Scripture. God does not work outside of the historical context in which He finds His chosen people, be they a corporate group or as individuals. The same will be true for whatever is still future.

One of the hardest perspectives that one can hold is being objective. No one is completely objective. And only God is omniscient. There are times when we must dismantle or set aside the conclusions that we have already established. We can come back to them if we find ourselves chasing a rabbit down a hole. Or, we just might have to adjust our conclusions based on the revelation of the truth in God's Word. If we believe that the Bible is indeed the Word of God, then we must submit all other sources and lines of thought to that Word. If we believe that God superintended the design and truth He wanted us to have, by the Holy Spirit, and through the personalities He chose to use, then we must ask for wisdom and insight from the Holy Spirit in order to understand what He intended us to know and understand. To those who have much, more will be given, and to those who do not have, even what they have will be taken away (Matthew 13:11-12). So, there is a dynamic of receiving, by the grace of God, and in some measure by our searching, that brings forth understanding. It is our humility before God that is the basis for receiving more of what He wants us to have (Matthew 6:33).

As we have just looked at chapters 12-16 as a section, chapters 15-16 dealt with the seven bowls of God's wrath. The bowls were described as future, universal, and complete. Words like complete, completed, and finished were used to describe the holy retribution of God upon an unbelieving, rejecting, and unrepentant world system. It will be the next few chapters that will be used to describe the eternal judgements that have arrived. The angels who were given the bowls of God's wrath will be the guides, both for John and his readers. They will show the two, separate, contrasted, eternal futures. One is an eternal future for the harlot, and a different eternal future for the bride of the Lamb (Revelation 17:1; and 21:9). The theology of the judgements will be part of the discussion. The historical origins of the past, the reality of the present, and the prophetic future, will be interspersed.

Chapter 17 through chapter 21, verse 8, constitute a section that must be read as a complete section. Chapter 21, verse 9, begins another section, led by another angel who had the bowls of wrath. This second section will concern the Bride, the wife of the Lamb. This first section contains the origins and history of the harlot. It narrates the build-up to the coming of Jesus Christ in judgement, and then specifically narrates the casting of the component members of the harlot into the lake of fire. (See below: Diagram #5, Page 157.)

The Harlot

17:1-6 One of the angels who had the seven bowls comes to talk with John. It is one of the angels of the bowls of wrath who will be the guide and will narrate the results of the bowls that have been poured out. The angel invites John to be shown the judgement of a great harlot sitting on many waters. This harlot is the one with whom the kings of the earth have committed fornication and have become drunk with the wine of her fornication. The term harlot is used often in the Old Testament to describe a people, nation, or country that has rejected worshipping God, and has instead developed, or been led into, a system of worship to a false god or idol. The harlot uses seduction and alluring measures to capture her prizes and rewards. The harlot sits on, or is carried by, many waters. The many waters are described as peoples, nations, multitudes, and tongues (Revelation 17:15). These are her suitors. The book of Revelation, many times, demands and requires that we look at other parts of the book to find interpretations for the symbols (see also Revelation 1:15; 17:6). The rulers of the earth, those who were responsible for the leadership of others, led many into the false worship of anything and everything but the true God. The many waters were intoxicated with the worship of false gods and systems that rejected God as Creator and any accountability to Him. Wine can be, if used consistently and without accountability, a habitual influence towards a lack of control and a danger.

John is carried away into the wilderness, where he sees a woman sitting on a scarlet beast. The scarlet beast is full of names of blasphemy, having the seven heads and ten horns of the dragon and the beast (Revelation 12:3; 13:1). The wilderness scene here is in contrast to the bride of the Lamb who is seen from the vantage point of a high mountain, thus bringing into focus the contrast between the two (Revelation 21:9-10). The woman is sitting on, and is transported by, the beast. The beast with its' seven heads, is how the harlot is transported through history. The woman has been part of every ungodly kingdom throughout history. The woman and the beast have a close relationship, but are not the same. The dragon is seen as red, the color of judgement and death, whereas the beast is scarlet, the color of sin, of wrongful attraction and decadence. The beast being full of blasphemous names represents an entity that is entirely in opposition to the status that God holds. That she sits on the beast, and on the many waters, conveys the identity of the beast and the many waters as one and the same. The seven heads and ten horns show the relationship of the beast with the dragon, which is Satan.

The harlot's garb and attire are garish, attractive, seductive, and beautiful from an external perspective. In many ways, the appearance of the harlot portrays value and worth. Purple is the color of status, royalty, and wealth. It is a worldly counterfeit of the bride. In her possession are all the experiences and intoxicating trappings of that which God proclaims are not in His plan or purposes for His created beings. On her forehead, in her mind and her thought process, is the name that describes the identity to which she adheres. It is the name and her source of existence: Babylon the great, mother of harlots, and the abominations of the earth. The mystery is that up until now, her identity has not been exposed, but now is made known. The harlot has been in, and part of, the world system since the tower of Babel. Babel was the location of the first corporate rebellion and disobedience against the rule and authority of God as Creator. From that event has sprung up every religious and man-made system that rejects, displaces, marginalizes, or even relativizes the worship of the true and living God. Anything but the worship of God in spirit and in truth is a form of idolatry. Babylon is the name for all the false and syncretistic religions and world systems opposed to God.

The woman is intoxicated and influenced to kill the saints and the followers of the Lamb. Because this harlot is closely associated with the beast and the dragon, she has been given this purpose to her by Satan. She is in opposition to the bride of the Lamb and is the primary agent of the dragon, who uses her to persecute the woman and her seed (Revelation 12). Her one objective is the destruction of those who are part of the bride.

Christians will not submit their thoughts and actions to the beast's sovereignty, symbolized by the mark on the forehead or the hand, therefore, the harlot delights in their martyrdom.[1] John is in stunned awe and shocked at her vision.

The Supporter of the Harlot

17:7-18 The angel responds to John's amazement with a declaration that will explain the mystery of the woman and the beast that carries her, the beast with the seven heads and ten horns. The Greek word for carry, means to support or carry a burden. Thus, the woman is in need of the beast to support her mission and her purpose. It should be noted that in this instance, as in verse 3, the beast is not mentioned with crowns either on the heads or on the horns (compare with Revelation 12:3 and 13:1). The crowns are not mentioned here because the harlot has been manifested through the existence of the beast, regardless of how the beast manifests its authority and influence. Every manifestation of the beast has had the harlot with them. The angel explains that the beast John saw was, and is not, and will ascend out of the bottomless pit. The description is a parody of God, the One who was, and is, and is to come (Revelation 1:4; 1:8;

4:8; 11:17). The beast, who is the agent of Satan, is that which the inhabitants of the earth have made an image, proclaiming it to be their god, instead of God the Creator. That the beast will ascend out of the bottomless pit tells the readers of the beasts' origin, and of his evil sponsor and satanic origins (Revelation 9:11; 11:7; 20:1-3). The future judgement and destruction of the beast is also part of his description (Revelation 19:20). Those who dwell on the earth, the inhabitants of the earth who have fallen into the deceptive words and practices of the beast and his prophet, will be enthralled by the beast. They will be astonished at the sight of the beast because they do not accept the truth (2 Thessalonians 2:9-12).

Wisdom, much like the exhortation given about the beast from the earth, is needed to discern and consider what information John is being given (Revelation 13:18). The seven heads are seven mountains on which the woman sits. (Remember, mountains represent kingdoms or empires.) The woman's origins are Babylon, from the tower of Babel. She will be carried by, and exist through, seven kingdoms that will have dominion over the known world. There are also seven kings, those who rule these kingdoms (Daniel 7:1-17). Five have fallen, one is, and one has not yet come, and when that one comes it will only be for a short amount of time. This is a description of the known world empires that have oppressed and persecuted the covenant people of God for the purposes of the dragon. These kingdoms are from the perspective of the Bible in its narrative of God's redemptive plan, and of Satan's attempts to thwart that plan. The prophet Daniel saw four of those kingdoms from his perspective of the coming of Messiah (Daniel 2 and 7). The five that have fallen are Egypt, Assyria, Babylon, Persia, and Greece. The one that currently is would be the Roman Empire. There is one yet to come, still future, that will exist only for a short amount of time (Revelation 12:12; 17:10; 20:3; 20:8). This last kingdom will be allowed to culminate during the 70th week of Daniel, and peak during the half-an-hour that heaven is silent (Daniel 9:27; Revelation 8:1).

The beast who was, and is not, is an eighth, and is going to destruction. The eighth day is that which brings, or, makes a covenant. Infants were circumcised on the eighth day to be included into the covenant people of the Old Testament (Genesis 17:12;

29:35; Luke 2:21; Philippians 3:5). The Feast of Tabernacles, which was the seventh feast of the year, portrayed God dwelling with His people. This feast has eight days (Leviticus 23:36; John 7:37). David, of whom God made the kingly, Davidic covenant, was the eighth son of Jesse (1 Samuel 17:12). Noah, the eighth person on the ark, was the one with whom God made a covenant after the flood (Genesis 9:8-17; 2 Peter 2:5). Eight days are mentioned in other significant contexts also (Luke 9:28; John 20:26).

The significance of this personage being the eighth, is that he also makes a covenant (Daniel 9:27; see also 2 Thessalonians 2:2-9). In Daniel chapter 9, the prophet is given a 70-week prophecy that brings to a close the decrees of God. Many interpreters of that particular text make the reference to a covenant made with the Jews, or Israel. It is the assertion of this author that the covenant is made with the world, *the many.* The verse does not use the term Jew, Israel, or Daniel's people, in reference to this covenant made by the one who will come, and then be destroyed.

The tens horns will ultimately receive power with the beast. Up until now, the kingdoms of world history have been uniquely led by individual kingdoms and their rulers who have had isolated authority. The last kingdom will be led by a composite of rulers, who will then give their allegiance to a world savior who will be the counterfeit of Jesus Christ (2 Thessalonians 2:3-4). He will come proclaiming that he is the one that all have been waiting for. They, the composite of global rulers, will be of one mind and give their sovereignty and individual authority to the beast. The system of false worship moves from working through each of the heads of the beast in turn, to working globally through the ten horns.

John then hears the explanation of the many waters. This explanation takes us back to the beginning of the vision. The harlot sits on the beast. Therefore, the beast, and the many waters, consist of many people. People in opposition to God. The beast that rises out of the sea is a particular kingdom that consists of many people (Revelation 13:1). The source of the beast is the sea, which also consists of many people. It is also the voice of many people within the sea who have maintained the testimony of Jesus (Revelation 1:15; 14:2; 19:6).

The ten horns will hate and turn against the harlot. She represents many, many different and diverse and false forms of religions (Revelation 17:5). She is the mother of harlots. The ten kings will strip her of her garb, her many different means of idolatry, and consume her. They will only consume the harlot. She does not disappear. The ten kings completely appropriate who she is in her diversity, into one single manifestation of false worship and religion. The people of the world take their allegiance and power of the various world religions and give it to the final beast. There will be unanimity within a city-state, and between nations. This is in line with the beast from the earth who causes an image to be made of the first beast. Then the inhabitants of the earth will worship the first beast (Revelation 13:11-17). This worship will be required by everyone, without exception, and is why those who do not worship the image will be killed. What each head did on its own will be done on a global scale (Daniel 3:4). Up until this point in the future, the harlot has only been a "means to an end" for the plans of Satan. He not only wants to destroy God's people, but also create a kingdom which brings him worship (Isaiah 14:13-14). It is sobering to realize that God gives people what they want if they do not humble themselves before Him as Creator. He has our best interests in His heart and plans. But there are many instances where God "gives them over," to whatever people continually pursue outside of His purposes (Romans 1:24-26). This is a judicial sentence on the part of a just God. God hardened Pharaoh's heart only after Pharaoh hardened his own heart. If people pursue anything but Him, it will be costly (2 Thessalonians 2:11-12).

The last explanation of the woman relates that she is the great city which rules and has dominion over the kings of the earth. The term, the great city, is used many times in the book of Revelation. The great city is always in opposition to God and His people (Revelation 11:8; 14:8; 16:19; 17:5; 18:10-21). The great city, the harlot Babylon, is in contrast to the city of God. The New and Holy Jerusalem is the bride of Christ. In the next section will be seen the extent and the depth in which the harlot Babylon has controlled the world. Be encouraged! Worship the true God!!

Diagram #5

TIME OF SEPARATION

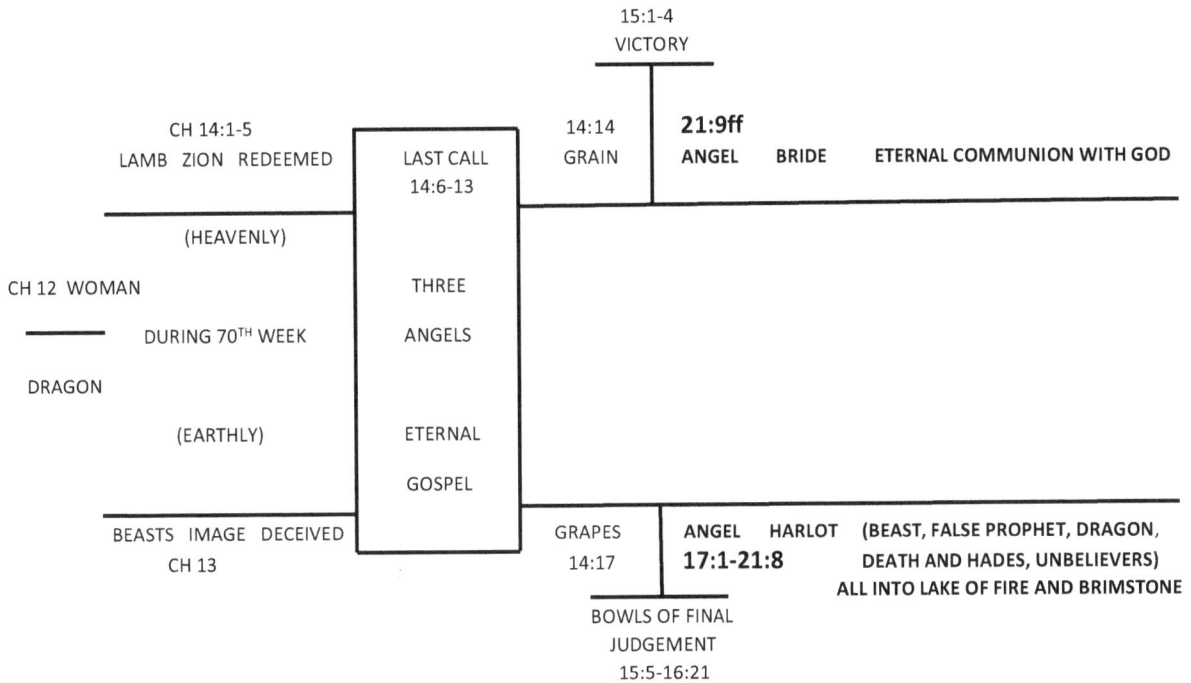

As we look at the diagram above, it is prudent to consider the contrasts we find between Revelation 17:1-21:8 and Revelation 21:9-22:5. Revelation 17:1 starts with an angel showing the great prostitute. John is carried away in the Spirit to a wilderness setting. The following verses show the judgements of the beast, the false prophet, the dragon, and death and Hades, all being cast into the lake of fire. All of our interpretations must fit this context. Revelation 21:9 starts with an angel showing the Bride, the wife of the Lamb. John is carried away in the Spirit to a mountain setting. The following verses narrate the rewards and status of the Bride of the Lamb, and her eternal communion with God.

20

The Business of the Harlot
Revelation 18:1-19:10

18:1-8 John, after being shown the origins and the history of the harlot, and after being given the description of the beast in his relation and association to the harlot, is now being shown the judgement and downfall of the system that they have maintained. John sees another angel of great authority coming down from heaven. The whole earth falls under the authority of his revelation. The angel cries with might and intensity, declaring the fall of Babylon the Great. Babylon is fallen, is fallen! Given in double statement, proclaims the certainty of the fall of the great city. There are many times in the book of Revelation that an allusion to an Old Testament reference portrays the transition from a particular historical event in the past, to a cosmic, universal event of future judgement (Isaiah 21:9; Jeremiah 50-51; Revelation 14:8). (Familiarity with Isaiah 13-14, 21, and Jeremiah 50-51 are important to this narrative.) In Revelation 14, verse 8, the same scenario, which is just before the bowls of wrath, is recapitulated here in describing the eternal judgements that will occur against the harlot.

The system that the harlot has put in place has become a habitat and living place for many kinds of unclean creatures and behaviors that are an affront to the commands and person of God. The nations, or peoples of the earth, have been influenced and have been willingly involved to the point of being taken in by the harlot. The nations have rejected the devotion and activities of true worship commanded by the true God. The rulers of the earth, those who provide leadership, have committed these acts of idolatry and rejection along with the harlot. The harlot has made herself wealthy and rich, and the kings of the earth have become rich through her activities of idolatry.

There is a sobering call to the elect to come out of her (Isaiah 52:11; Jeremiah 51:45; 2 Corinthians 6:17). This is a real-time, relevant plea from the book of Revelation. This call applies to us today. We are children of the day, not the night (1 Thessalonians 5:4-5). Be separate from the harlot's activities. The elect people of God are not to be involved in the system the harlot has designed and implemented. We cannot let ourselves be deceived. Spiritual discernment, based on the truths of God's word must be exercised (Hebrews 5:12-14). The believers are in the world, but not of the world (John 17:15). This is a hard posture to hold. It is not a static position that we have or not have. It is a life of a growing, consistent, sanctification toward God and away from the system of the world. We must come to the growing realization that this life is not all there is. We deny ourselves for the glory of God and for a witness and testimony to others (1 Corinthians 10:13). The harlot has taken everything that God has given to us as a gift and made them the end-game objects of worship and self-sufficiency. The harlot convinces and deceives the world that this life is all there is, and that there is no measure of accountability to a creator God to whom all must answer.

To be involved in the sins of the harlot, is to receive the judgement of the harlot. God is a just God. Her sins having reached to heaven is a statement of the fullness of her violations. They have grown to the point that God must act in judgement (Genesis 18:21; 19:13; Revelation 16:19). The harlot is to receive the same in judgement. Judgement will be rendered to her in multiplied fullness of the overflowing of wrath. It is equal to the measure that she is guilty against God and His saints (Revelation 17:6). The measure of her luxury and wealth, false worship and opposition to God, will be the measure that she will suffer torment. The harlot has a haughty attitude of self-sufficiency. That is the heart of any deception (Isaiah 47). She is in contrast to the bride, the wife of the Lamb (2 Corinthians 11:2; Revelation 14:4-5). Her final judgement will come all at once, suddenly, in the day God has ordained. Much of the language of judgement is written as if it has already occurred. This is the certainty that God is indeed sovereign over the affairs of man (Job 12:16-25). In this prophecy the whole world is affected, not just one particular empire or city.

The Participants with the Harlot

18:9-20 The willing participants who have been committing spiritual fornication and who have made a living from the harlot, will grieve and be stunned at her end. The grieving will be with open sobbing and despair. Their whole existence consisted of an adherence to, and the behavior of, the harlot and her existence. The kings of the earth will try to pull away from the harlot, because of their fear of her torment. In one hour, in an abrupt season, her judgement will come.

Those who had made merchandise of the harlot's business will mourn at the loss of their opportunity and position. The world has made merchandise an end in itself, rather than fulfilling the role of stewards. Their merchandise was directly related to the deceptions of the harlot. The list that John is given shows just how encompassing and decadent the business of the harlot had become. From the merchandise used in life, to the grasping and merchandising of the very souls of individual people. These were used in the deceptive practices of the harlot. The list was not only physical in its nature, but reached into the unseen, eternal spirit of the people involved. The inhabitants of the earth who have bought into the business of the harlot will be left empty souled. What they were deceived into trusting will be found to have no eternal value. The deceptive, temporary satisfaction that the harlot brought will be found to be fleeting at best.

Those who made merchandise of the system of the harlot will again place themselves at a distance to try to disassociate themselves with her judgement. They will be astonished at the suddenness and finality of her judgement. The use of shipmasters, sailors, and traders on the sea, begs us to remember of what the sea is a symbol (Daniel 7:2-3; Revelation 4:6; 13:1; 15:2; 21:1). The analogy lends completeness in that those who make merchandise of the mass of humanity, the sea, would be symbolized in nautical terms. In the world of John's time, the seas were the main means of commerce and travel between kingdoms. The merchants express a deep, intense, mourning and grief. In the West, grieving for the most part, and much of the time, is silent, reserved, and internal. It is often passive-aggressive. In the context of the East, of which Revelation's original readers would have been, grieving was open, heard, and expressed with volume. A third time in this section alone, the astonishment at the fall of the harlot is expressed. This adds to the testimony of the text and of the finality and completeness of the fall of Babylon (18:10, 16, 19).

John hears a call for heaven, the holy prophets, and the holy apostles to rejoice over the fall of the harlot. The reason for the rejoicing is that God has avenged and vindicated them (Revelation 6:9-11; 17:6; 19:2). It must be remembered that the harlot, the system of Babylon, was active in her opposition to God and His people from the earliest beginnings of the tower of Babel. There will be many, from all ages, who will be part of the call to rejoice.

The End of The Harlot

18:21-24 John sees a mighty angel who takes up a great millstone and casts it into the sea. The millstone is symbolic of grinding, destructive judgement. (Jeremiah 51:61-64; Matthew 18:6). The analogy is that the judgement of Babylon, the great harlot, likewise is meted out. The sounds of joy and rejoicing will not be heard again in the great city. The creativity of the artisans and the sounds of preparation and substance of life, will not be found any more. The light of any kind of revelation and illumination of any kind, will not be seen any more. The language and testimony of those who testify of the hope of the world will not be heard any more. Instead, the deceptive words of the harlot's demonic origins that influenced the works of her great leaders and kings, will be exposed as the reason for her downfall. And the harlot will be held responsible for the blood of all those who have been killed by her.

The Testimony of The Harlot's Fall

19:1-5 Because of the judgement of the great harlot, John hears the voices of multitudes in heaven. Their response to the final judgement of the harlot gives praise to God, and to God alone. Salvation, glory, honor, and power are ascribed to God. The declaration is that God is just, and that He is righteous in all He does. God is completely and fully right in His actions toward the harlot. She has had a system of false worship and allegiance since the beginning, and has opposed and killed any who worshipped the true God. God vindicates His faithful servants (Revelation 6:9-11; 17:6 18:24). Again, there is praise to God, and a testimony to the eternality of the judgement. Where there is smoke, there is fire. Fire is symbolic of judgement. The twenty-four elders and the four living creatures, and those who have been waiting the longest, proclaim: So be it! Then the elders and the living creatures give praise to God. Then a voice from the throne commands all who fear and are His servants, to give God praise. This voice is that of Jesus, who is God seated on the throne (Revelation 3:21).

The Wife of the Lamb Exalted

19:6-10 John continues the vision. He hears the voice of a great multitude, the sound of many waters as the sound of mighty thunderings. This great multitude speaks as the many voices throughout time who have proclaimed God and His Messiah. They speak as one, and the sound is as many waters. They have spoken the words of God, as it were: His thunderings. Praise God, for He is all-powerful. Gladness and rejoicing have come. The harlot has been removed. The marriage of the Lamb has come. The bride, the wife, the church, the body of Christ has made herself ready (2 Peter 3:11-12). She is complete. Believers are to long for, look for, and love the appearing of Jesus. The bride is given the garments that portray an existence full of righteous works. Not because she is deserving of her position because of her works, but she is clothed in works which she has accomplished because of her position. We are saved for good works, not because of them (Ephesians 2:9-10).

The voice tells John to write of the blessedness of those called to the marriage supper of the Lamb. This is in contrast to the supper of God, which is judgement (Revelation 19:17). The blessedness of the participants is verified by God Himself (Genesis 15).

As is the case so often in the book of Revelation, the angels who bring the messages need to be seen in association with the sender of the messages that they bring. We do not generally give the same seriousness and respect to the messenger that we would give to the one, or One, sending the message (Mark 12:1-12). (In antiquity, how the messenger is treated is equal to treating the one sending the message.) Believers, equally, have a great responsibility in being the messengers and ambassadors of God (2 Corinthians 5:18-19). The angels are usually aligned so closely to the One who sends the message, that John, and many interpreters as well, confuse the issue by trying to identify the message and the messenger with the One sending the message. John confuses the angel with the One sending the message. He falls in worship and is corrected by the angel. The angel declares that he is a fellow servant of John's, and all those who hold the testimony of Jesus (Revelation 1:9). Worship God alone! This is the message of the whole Bible! The testimony of Jesus, the Messiah, is behind all prophecy (John 5:31-47; Romans 1:16). Be encouraged! Maranatha!!

21

Jesus Comes
Revelation 19:11-21:8

In chapter 17, we were given the origins and history of the harlot and the beast. In chapter 18 we were shown the business of the harlot, and the extent of the harlot's influence. As we moved forward, we read of the judgement of the harlot as if it has already happened. To the readers and hearers of the book of Revelation, these sure words concerning the judgement of the great harlot would have been a great encouragement to overcome, persevere, and endure.

The language used communicates nothing short of the certainty of judgement and the end of the career and activities of the harlot. Included in this judgement is her responsibility for the deception and persecution of the saints throughout the history of the world. The suddenness and completeness of her doom is portrayed in the phrase, "in one hour" (Revelation 18:10, 17, 19). To the suddenness of the "one hour" we can associate the "thief in the night" idea from other parts of Scripture (1 Thessalonians 5:2-4; 2 Peter 3:10; Revelation 3:3; 16:15). To those who

are perishing, this time will be sudden and unexpected. To those who are in Christ, this event will not be a surprise (1 Thessalonians 5:4-10). The intense grief of those who participated in her business is shown by the words: Alas, alas! (Revelation 18:9, 16, 19).

To these thoughts echo the words and call to the saints to separate themselves from the harlot and all her ways (Revelation 18:4). There is finality to the fall of Babylon. There is a description of the vengeance that God will inflict upon the harlot for her treatment of the saints (Revelation 19:2). In contrast to the harlot, the bride of the Lamb has made herself ready (Revelation 19:7).

The continuation of this section (Revelation 19:11-21:8), will see the coming of Jesus in all His glory and authority. We will see the defeat and judgement of the component members involved with the work of the harlot. Each of these members will be cast in to the lake of fire burning with brimstone (Revelation 19:20, 20:10, 14, 15). Jesus' coming will be the trigger, and He is the agent of judgement.

Faithful and True

19:11-16 John sees heaven opened. He is given the privilege of seeing the second coming of Jesus Christ and His return from heaven. It is written as if it has already happened, so sure is the certainty of this event. He is seen as riding a white horse, the horse of victory and leadership. True to Jesus' promise, He is called Faithful and True (Matthew 24:27-29; Revelation 1:8; 3:14). His ways, His judgements, and His wars, are made with complete knowledge, and therefore, with justice (Revelation 2:16). Jesus sees all and judges rightly. He has many facets and dynamics of His authority. With the meaning of a name is included reputation, character, and attributes. To know someone's name was to have a knowledge or control over them, or insight into that person in some intimate way. That no one but He Himself knows His name, means that He is one of a kind. He has no rival, does not share His authority or personality, and His identity is uniquely His. A name is identity and reputation (Revelation 2:17; 3:12). He is seen as robed in His priestly work of dealing with the sins of mankind (Hebrews 9:11-15). His name is the Word of God, the full explanation and message of God (John 1:1-2; Hebrews 1:1-3; Colossians 1:15).

The armies of heaven who return with Him share His rule, dominion, and authority. Those who are with Jesus are the saints returning with Him, clothed in their righteous works (Jude 14-15; Revelation 2:26-27; 3:5; 3:20-21; 19:8). With His very words, and by His words alone, He defeats His enemies and takes His place as ruler of the new heavens and the new earth (Revelation 1:16). The promised Messiah was prophesied to rule the nations (Psalm 2:8-9; 110:1-3; Hebrews 1:8-13; Revelation 2:26-27; 12:5). He alone treads the winepress of the wrath of God (Revelation 14:14-20). He has a name on his robe and on his thigh, the name: King of Kings, and Lord of Lords (Revelation 17:14). The robe identifies the person and their work, much like a uniform and insignias. The thigh was a Greek and Hebrew metaphor for the foundation and basis and the strength of a person (Genesis 24:2-9; 32:25-32). His name is His strength. Swearing by the thigh was equal to promising at the expense of your posterity.

The Supper of God

19:17-21 Then John sees an angel standing, having a direct revelation from God. The angel directs all the birds in the heights of heaven to prepare for the great supper of God and the great destruction of the enemies of God. Birds, vultures, and eagles were seen as carrion in the judgement pictures. Wherever these birds would gather signified great destruction (Job 39:27-30; Hosea 8:1; Matthew 24:27-28; Luke 17:34-37). The extent of the supper will be diverse and complete.

John sees the beast, and all who had given allegiance and loyalty to it gathered together. They gathered to make war against the One sitting on the white horse. Those gathered are all who had participated in any form of false worship. This same gathering is noted in other places in the book of Revelation, from several differing perspectives (Revelation 16:16; 17:14; 19:11-16; 20:7-9). The beast's kingdom, and the beast's false prophet, by whom the inhabitants of the earth are deceived, are captured and thrown alive into the lake of fire burning with brimstone. And the rest, the kings and their armies, are killed by the word of the One who is seated on the white horse (2 Thessalonians 2:8). The birds are filled with the destruction.

The Destruction of Satan

The Holy Spirit, in chapters 12-16, has given us the history, struggle, conflict, and separation of the two groups of people. From the time of Christ's first

coming until the final judgements of the seven bowls of wrath (Revelation chapters 12-16). In the same way, Revelation 20:1-10, in a specific way, will give us the history of Satan and his activities from the time of Christ's first coming until Satan's destruction. (This passage will not contradict the prophetic narrative of the little horn of Daniel 7.) There is no way of completely outlining all the differing views that are expounded from these verses. This author's explanation will be completely at the mercy of the text and the context. The context will be drawn from the structure of the book. There are some prevailing interpretations and scenarios that have details with little basis or reference points with other parts of Scripture. Again, to have multiple subsets of believers existing at concurrent times does not fit with the principles that the Scriptures allow for all eternity-bound saints.[1] Considering that this book is the Word of God, and the warnings given at the end of the book, it seems wise and prudent to accept and work with an eschatological interpretation that promotes little, or no speculation.

Remember, this particular group of verses is given by one of the angels who had the seven bowls of God's wrath (Revelation 17:1-21:8). The second and contrasting view will be given by another angel who had the seven bowls of God's wrath (Revelation 21:9-22:5). These two angels dictate the literary structure of this part of the book of Revelation. This will be part of the section that narrates the judgement of the participants of the harlot. The participants are: the beast and false prophet (already given), Satan, death and hades, and the unbelievers. All are cast into the lake of fire burning with brimstone (See below: Diagram #5, Page 173).

20:1-3 John sees an angel having a key to the bottomless pit. The angel also has a great chain for binding. This angel has the authority over the pit and anything that is put there. He took hold of the dragon, that is, Satan, (first so described in chapter 12), binds him and casts him into the bottomless pit. This is a recapitulation of Revelation 12:9). (If the binding is the same event of 12:7ff, then the reigning (20:4) also involves the overcomers sharing in the victory of Jesus.) The event of Satan "being cast (20:3)," has the same Greek root word for what was predicted by Jesus (Mark 3:27; Luke 10:18; John 12:31). The bottomless pit is the abode of Satan, the demons, and those evil spiritual beings who are held for final judgement (Luke 8:31; Jude 6; Revelation 9:11; 11:7; 17:8). The angel binds and sets a *restriction* on Satan for the period of 1000 years. Jesus uses the same word for bind when speaking of one of His purposes when initiating His kingdom (Matthew 12:29). The binding involves shutting him up and setting a seal over him. The seal is similar in many ways, to any seal that cannot be annulled by the one being sealed. This event is another description of what occurs in chapter 12, verses 7-12. He is bound, to restrict him from *deceiving* the nations into battle.

We need to study the text. Try as we might, we must not to come to it with any pre-existing interpretations. First, the seal is controlled by someone besides Satan. Second, the restriction is given as a specific kind of activity (Revelation 20:3 and 20:7). Third, the binding is not necessarily related to any of the many evils and horrors that mankind finds evident on the earth. Many passages of Scripture are very clear that Satan is active in many other ways (John 10:10; 2 Corinthians 11:14; Ephesians 2:2; 1 Peter 5:8; 1 John 5:19). Satan's goal all along has been to annihilate the covenant people of God. In the past, he has been working through the kingdoms of history. Presently, Satan can only work in pockets and restricted locales (and he has his minions in all places). Satan is waiting, but he is still in the position of subjugating only *parts* of the world (See Revelation 12:17, standing on the sand of the sea). Eventually Satan will be allowed to use a global world system to globally persecute believers. Fourth, the 1000 years is symbolic. As with all the numbers in the book of Revelation, it is difficult to have a consistently literalistic interpretation of the numbers that will be coherent.

One-thousand is a number of fullness. Ten is the number for man in his activity and existence (Revelation 2:10). In apocalyptic literature, 1000 is symbolic for the fullness, entirety, and the volume of the existence of mankind. God keeps His covenants of mercy to *all* those generations who love and keep His commandments, to a thousand generations (Deuteronomy 7:9). This means that His words are for *all* generations (1 Chronicles 16:15; Psalm 105:8). Before God we could not answer rightly even once in a thousand times, in *all* our attempts (Job 9:3). He owns the cattle on a thousand hills, that is, on *all* of the hills (Psalm 50:1). One day

in His courts is better than *all* the days anywhere else (Psalm 84:10). God sees *all* the days of mankind on the earth as if they have passed already (Psalm 90:4). There are, and always will be, scoffers who say that this book of Revelation is not relevant, not truthful, and has no bearing on the history that *we* make. We are reminded that concerning God's plan for the reversal of all things, and the renewing of creation, that He has sovereignty. The whole existence of mankind is seen by Him as already passed, and every single day that we experience is but one of many that from His omniscient, longsuffering perspective, is part of His planned whole (Isaiah 46:10; Psalm 139:16). Just as *all* the days of man are as a day past to the Lord; to the Lord, like a day past, is His knowledge of *all* the days of man that will yet be (2 Peter 3:8). (When Hitler declared that the Third Reich would last a thousand years, he was not giving it a final day. He was declaring that it would last forever, for the duration of mankind.) After the 1000 years are finished, Satan will be released for a little while. This "little while" is mentioned, or alluded to, several places in the book of Revelation (Revelation 8:1; 12:12; 17:10).

20:4-6 John sees thrones, and the ones sitting on the thrones. The ones sitting on the thrones were there by authority. These thrones are places of authority given by God (Revelation 3:21; 4-5). Judgement was made on behalf of them, and for who they represent. Then John sees the souls of those who had died because of their witness of Jesus and for word of God. These are not bodies, but souls existing between death and the final resurrection. (Revelation 6:9-11). (These souls are not glorified.) These souls have not given into the deception of false worship that results in their becoming marked by the beast. They reign for the same amount of time that Satan is bound from deceiving the nations. This reigning is similar to that which Christ asserts because of His victory over the cross and death (1 Corinthians 15:25; 2 Timothy 2:12; Hebrews 1:13; Revelation 2:26-27; 12:7-11). When believers endure to the end, they become co-heirs in the authority that Christ has won for them (Romans 8:17; 15:20).

We must remember that this is written in symbolism. There are souls under the altar (Revelation 6:9-11). The souls under the altar have not received any type of physical body for eternal existence. The souls are told to wait, as Jesus is waiting until His enemies are made a footstool (Hebrews 1:13; 10:13-14). Part of this dynamic is still future for Him and for believers (Romans 16:20; 1 Corinthians 15:25; Revelation 22:12). We are co-heirs with Him (Romans 8:17). We are His brethren (Hebrews 2:11; 13). When we are born again, we receive new life. Our spirits are quickened. The overcomers are told that they will be seated on Jesus' throne with Him (Revelation 3:21). We were placed with Him when we first believed (Ephesians 1:13-14; 1:20; 2:6). This is a throne of authority with Jesus, the last Adam, who has won back the seat of dominion lost at the Fall (Acts 7:55-56). This is also equal to the "time of refreshing," *until* the "restoration" of all things (Acts 3:19-21). Believers *are (present tense)* a royal priesthood (1 Peter 2:9; Revelation 1:6; 5:10).

One major discussion is the meaning of the first resurrection of the souls who "lived and reigned" with Christ for the 1000 years. (While Satan is bound.) Jesus declared that He is the God of the living (the same Greek word meaning for "lived," see Matthew 22:29-33). The phrase "resurrection of the dead" is used to describe Abraham, Isaac, and Jacob, as being of the living (though we cannot assume that it means they had been glorified). Believers are to be before God as being alive, as from the spiritually dead, in our Christian life (Romans 6:11-13). We have passed from death to life (John 5:24; 1 John 3:14). Unbelieving Israelites receive life from the dead when they accept Jesus as Messiah while still living a physical life (Romans 11:15). We are seated in the heavens in Christ Jesus, while alive physically, and made alive in Christ. We are not dead in trespasses and sin any more (Ephesians 2:1-5; Colossians 2:13). There is a "now and not yet" to our having life. The *hour now is,* when those who are dead will hear the son of God and will have life (John 5:25). There is yet *an hour that is coming* when the same who have received life, will hear His voice again, and come forth from the graves to the resurrection of life eternal (John 5:29). These souls also reign with Him in the same dynamic of His "now and not yet" reign (Acts 2:34-35; 3:20-21; 1 Corinthians 15:25-26; Hebrews 1:13; 2:8). This understanding should make the believer stand in awe and worship God for what our guarantee and inheritance consists, and because of the love and sacrifice of Jesus our Lord. We, even now, share in this reality of our salvation (2 Peter 1:2-4). Jesus said that He had overcome the world, and He declared that before His crucifixion (John 16:33)!

The first part of verse 5 is like a parenthetical insertion to describe the ones who do not have this position of reigning with Christ. The unbelievers will not stand in their positions until the judgement occurs (Revelation 20:11-14). The first resurrection is for those who follow the Lamb and who do not receive the mark of the beast. They have faithfulness to Christ and to the commandments of God. Blessed are those who have part in the first resurrection. Those who are transformed, faithful, and walk according to the Spirit have passed from death into newness of life, while still living a physical life now (John 5:24). The second death has no power over those who overcome (Revelation 2:11).

A first resurrection assumes a second resurrection. The second resurrection will occur when all believers receive their glorified bodies. That there is a second death, assumes a first death. The first resurrection for believers is a spiritual one, and the second is a physical resurrection (1 Corinthians 15; 1 John 3:2). The first death for unbelievers is a physical one, and the second death is the spiritual, eternal one (Revelation 20:14). Why mention the exemption from a second death if believers have been physically raised?[2] They have not been physically raised and glorified. Those who experience the first resurrection will be priests of God and of Christ (Revelation 1:6; 5:10). To see the 1000 years in any other way asserts multiple subsets of believers, and, violates the understanding of Scripture in relation to the unity and oneness of the body of Christ.

20:7-10 John is told that after the 1000 years is ended, Satan will be released to *deceive the nations* that are in the four corners of the earth (Revelation 11:7a; 12:17; and 13:7 note the same event). This is the beginning of the short time (Revelation 12:12; 20:3). This is also in reference to the last world kingdom that Satan will develop to oppose God and persecute God's people (Revelation 9:1-2; Revelation 13; 2 Thessalonians 2). The nations are given the titles of Gog and Magog. This is an allusion to the Old Testament prophecy of a significant battle in which the rulers of the nations would oppose the work of God in redemption (Ezekiel 38-39). (See

comparison below, Page 174). This, like many allusions to the Old Testament, takes what happened in a particular sense, and expands it to represent a universal and cosmic event. Gog and Magog represented the Gentile, non-believing peoples of the world who were in opposition to God's people and His plan. Gog has as its root meaning the idea of that which is gathered.[3,4] Magog is the process of being exalted out from that which is gathered. Then, Gog and Magog are peoples who are gathered, and lifting themselves up, come up against God and His Christ for battle.

This battle description is a recapitulation of what has been mentioned before (Revelation 16:16; 19:19). The phrase: "to gather them together for battle," is used in both cases. We must see this as the same event from a different perspective. The nations are from the four corners of the earth, or, from the whole earth (Revelation 7:1; 9:15). The sands of the sea are symbolic of a great number of people (Genesis 32:12; 2 Samuel 17:11; Hosea 1:10; Romans 9:27; Revelation 13:1). The nations surround the camp of the saints, the beloved city. Those who are members of the beloved city belong to the city of the saints, the New Jerusalem. They are also in the four corners of the earth, or the breadth of the earth (Hebrews 12:22; Revelation 21:2). The Devil is granted a short time in which he will overcome the saints (Daniel 7:21; Revelation 13:7, 15). Judgement from God comes from heaven and consumes them (Daniel 7:22; 2 Thessalonians 2:8). The Devil, or Satan, symbolized by the Dragon, is cast into the lake of fire burning with brimstone. He is in the same place as the beast and false prophet. They are tormented day and night, and forever and ever. This is Satan's final and eternal judgement.

Some millennial views insist that there will be a literal 1,000 year reign of Christ, with another final uprising at the end of that 1,000 year period. How does this view fit into the prophecy of Daniel? Do the saints possess the kingdom during the 1,000 years and then lose it? How many distinct groups of people must there be during the 1,000 years? More importantly, does Christ reign, and then deal with an uprising against His personal, physical presence a second time? No! This part of Scripture is a recapitulation of other passages of the book of Revelation.

The Great White Throne

20:11-15 John then sees a great white throne on which is seated the One in whom the earth and the heavens have fled away. There was no place to dwell for those who oppose God. John sees the dead, both small and great, standing in judgement before the great white throne. Those standing represent the unbelieving dead who have been raised for judgement. Books of deeds and works were opened. These books are representative of the works and deeds done by the ones standing before the great white throne (Luke 12:47-48). The Book of Life is opened. The dead are judged according to the books containing their works. The sea, representing the mass of humanity who lived and worshipped opposing God and His purposes, gave up all the dead it contained. Death and Hades gave up the dead that they possessed. All of the dead were present. Death and Hades were no more (1 Corinthians 15:26). Death and Hades were cast in to the lake of fire, the second and eternal death. If anyone standing before the throne did not have their name found in the Lamb's Book of Life, they were thrown into the lake of fire. The eternal punishment of Satan and his hosts was never meant for humans, but when they choose to follow him, they suffer his fate (Matthew 25:41). In contrast, the overcomers will always have their names found in the Book of Life (Revelation 3:5).

The New Heaven and New Earth

21:1-8 After all that opposed God is judged, John sees a new heaven and a new earth. The first heaven and earth came to an end. There was no more sea. No more world system in opposition to the will and purposes of God (Revelation 4:6; 13:1; 15:1). John then sees the holy city, the New Jerusalem, coming down out of heaven (Revelation 3:12; 19:7; 21:2; 21:10). Here, she comes to her new home. This is one of the elements of interpretation that will add to the confusion if we do not understand the structure of the book of Revelation. The bride is seen three different times. Does she come down from heaven once, seen from three different perspectives, or does she come three times? This author asserts that she comes only once. Here, it is to give contrast to the fall of the harlot, Babylon. In chapter 19, verse 7, she is portrayed as coming into her own inheritance because of the King of Kings and Lord of Lords. In chapters 21:9-22:5, the angel devotes the whole section to the description and status of the bride. The husband-wife and groom-bride metaphors are part of the relationship language used in many parts of Scripture (Isaiah 62:1-5; Ezekiel 47:21-23; Ephesians 5:25-27; 2 Corinthians 11:2; Revelation 3:12).

The New Jerusalem is a picture of the community of the redeemed from all ages (Galatians 4:21-31; Hebrews 11:10; 12:22-24; Revelation 3:12). There was fellowship and intimacy in the garden of Eden. This fellowship and intimacy will be restored. John hears a loud voice saying that the dwelling place of God is with men. Jerusalem will be His people and God Himself will be with them and be their God. There will be no more tears, death, sorrow, or crying. These will all be ended and gone. He who sits on the throne declares that all will made new and superior to the old that has ended (Matthew 9:17; 2 Corinthians 5:17; Hebrews 8:13). These words are declared to be true and faithful. John hears this after his vision of the bride (similar to Revelation 22:6a) These promises are based on what Christ has accomplished.

John hears a voice from the throne who identifies Himself as God (Revelation 1:8-11). The One on the throne declares that He is the Alpha and Omega (Isaiah 41:4; 44:6; 48:12; Revelation 1:8; 22:13) In Revelation 22:13 this title is claimed by Jesus Christ, revealing His deity and identity as God. The same dynamic is true of Beginning and the End (Revelation 21:6; 22:13). The fountain of the water of life is freely given to those who thirst and accept it (Isaiah 55:1; John 7:37-38). The description now comes down to the individual, personal promise of being in a one-on-one relationship with God. The overcomers of the world system of the dragon and the beast, who follow the Lamb wherever He goes, shall be the recipients of eternal joy and blessings. But those who habitually practice immorality, fear of the world, and violate the purposes of God, shall find their place in the judgement of eternal death (Revelation 20:14). The unbelievers have been separated and judged. In the next section, the Bride of Christ takes the stage of eternity.

Be encouraged! Righteousness will rule!!

Diagram #5
TIME OF SEPARATION

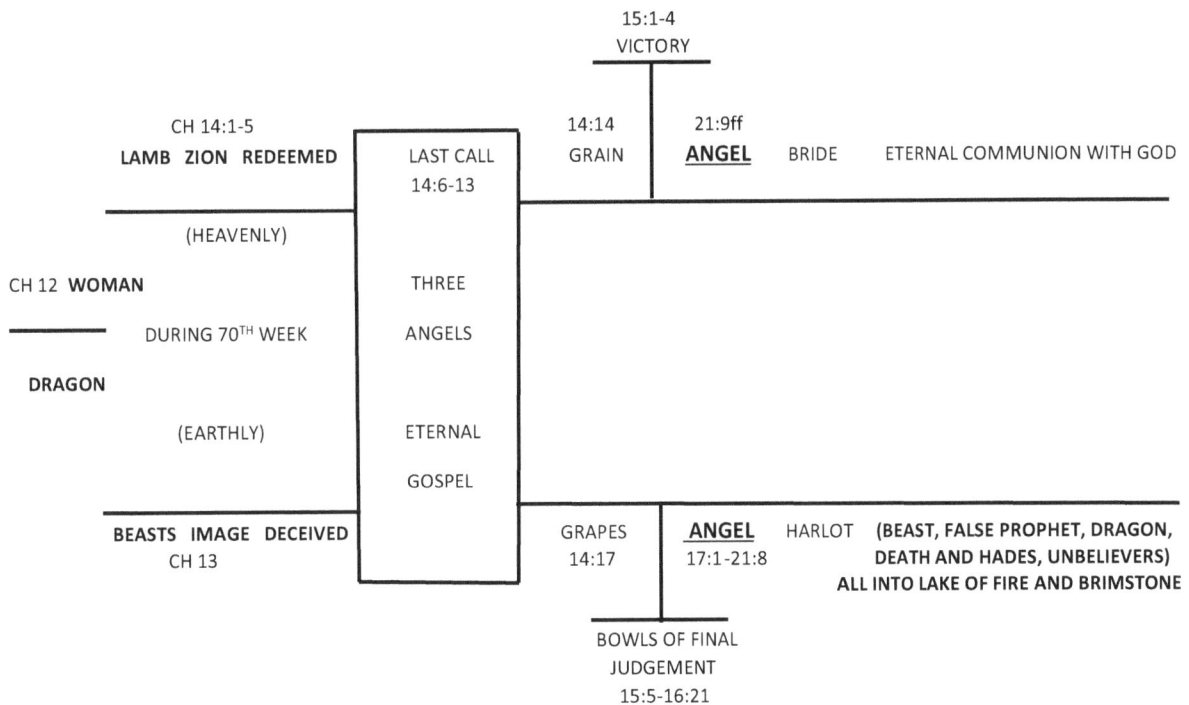

15:1-4
VICTORY

CH 14:1-5 | 14:14 | 21:9ff
LAMB ZION REDEEMED | LAST CALL 14:6-13 | GRAIN | **ANGEL** | BRIDE | ETERNAL COMMUNION WITH GOD

(HEAVENLY)

CH 12 **WOMAN** | THREE ANGELS
DURING 70TH WEEK

DRAGON

(EARTHLY) | ETERNAL GOSPEL

BEASTS IMAGE DECEIVED CH 13 | GRAPES 14:17 | **ANGEL** 17:1-21:8 | HARLOT | (BEAST, FALSE PROPHET, DRAGON, DEATH AND HADES, UNBELIEVERS) ALL INTO LAKE OF FIRE AND BRIMSTONE

BOWLS OF FINAL JUDGEMENT 15:5-16:21

Revelation 20 Compared To Ezekiel 36-48

Ezekiel 36-37:14
New Heart and Spirit
(Eze. 36:26-27; Jer. 31:31-34;
Isaiah 44:3; John 3:5; Acts 2;
2 Cor. 6:16; Eph. 5:26)

(Beginning of 1000 years.
Rev. 20:1-3; Rev. 12:7-12
Satan Bound)

(20:1-3)
Satan Bound   Matt. 12:29; Rev. 12:7-11
Bottomless Pit   Rev. 9:11; 11:7; 17:8
Deceive no more until   Rev. 13:11

(20:4-6)

Thrones   Rev. 4-5; Rev. 3:21
Souls   Rev. 6:9-11
Lived/reigned w/Christ. Rev. 2:26-27; 12:7-11
First resurrection.   Rev. 2:11; 20:6
Priests of God and Christ.   Rev. 1:6; 5:10
He who overcomes.
        Rev. 2:7; 2:11; 2:21; 2:26; 3:5; 3:21

Ezekiel 37:15-28
One Shepherd -Messiah
(Hebrews 1:13; 10:11-13
Psalm 110:1
Matt. 21:43; Luke 19:42;
John 10:16 - One Shepherd)
(During the 1000 years.)

(20:7-10)

Satan Released   Rev. 9:1-2; 2 Thessalonians 2
Short time   Rev. 12:11; Rev. 13
Deceives the nations.
    Four corners of the earth. Rev. 16:13-14
    Gog and Magog. (Eze. 38-39)

Ezekiel 38
(End of the 1000 years.
Beginning of the short
  time. (Rev. 20:7-9a)
Nations gathered.)
Gog and Magog.

Gather for battle.   Rev. 16:16; Rev. 19:19
Sands of the sea.   Rev. 13:1a
Saints/city   Rev. 13:7,15; 16:6
Fire

Ezekiel 39
(End of short time.
Rev. 20:9b-10)
Judgements.

Final judgement.   Rev. 16:17-21
    Rest of the dead.   Rev. 20:5a; 20:11-15
    Second death.   Rev. 20:14
    (21:1-22:10)
New Jerusalem

Ezekiel 40-48

22

The Bride, the Lamb's Wife
Revelation 21:9-22:15

The structure of the book defines this section that contains the description of the bride of Christ. One of the angels who had the seven bowls introduced the section about the judgement and destruction of the harlot (Revelation 17:1-21:8). Likewise, one of the angels who had the seven bowls will be the guide giving the description and consummation of the bride, the Lamb's wife (Revelation 21:9-22:5). It will be important to observe the similarities in the visions of the two women (see below, Text Comparisons of Harlot and Bride, Page 182). Again, the very first verse declares that this book of prophecy was given in signified, apocalyptic language (Revelation 1:1). Symbols will be used to describe the reality and characteristics of the bride. It is important to state: there is only one bride of Christ, encompassing all the saints of all history. The interpretation that develops several groups of saints, operating during different dispensations, results in the incorrect conclusion of having more than one bride.[1]

21:9-21 John is taken by one of the angels who had the seven bowls of God's wrath to see the bride, the Lamb's wife. These verses will describe a woman who is in distinct contrast to the harlot shown in the previous section. The covenant people of God are described by many metaphors, a vineyard, a flock, a mountain, a temple, and a body, just to name a few. Another of these metaphors is of a woman, or wife (Isaiah 62:1-5; Ephesians 5:25-27; 2 Corinthians 11:2; Revelation 3:12). John is carried away in the Spirit, to a great and high mountain. This is in contrast to the harlot, who was seen in the wilderness (Revelation 17:3). A mountain is a place of status, of protection, of prominence, of significance, and a kingdom (Daniel 2:35, 44-45). John sees the holy city, Jerusalem, descending out of heaven (Revelation 19:7; 21:2). The bride, the Lamb's wife and the holy city, the new Jerusalem, are one and the same. She has the glory of God. John is not seeing literal brick and mortar buildings and walls associated with physical structures in a geographic location. He is seeing the body of Christ, the completed, glorified, unified, community of the covenant people of God from every age.[2] We are given, in symbolic language, an intended explanation of the nature of God's design for a new existence.[3] The bride's light, or revelation, what she reflects, was like a jasper stone. This stone was on the high priest's breastplate. It is also the color that surrounds the throne of God (Revelation 4:3). Jasper represents something of the glory of God, and is used to describe the holy city's foundation and walls (Revelation 21:18-19). The jasper was clear as crystal, being without condemnation or judgement (compare Revelation 4:6 with 15:2).

There was a great and high wall. Walls were used to promote unity, give protection, provide security, and set limits and boundaries. There are twelve gates, with twelve angels at the gates. There are names on the gates, which are the twelve tribes of the children of Israel. This is one of the many places that the Biblical image of Israel must be understood. Israel was the name given to Jacob as a precursor to the name of God's people. Set apart for His purposes, they were to give and show light to the nations.

Gates are means of entrance into a community. The entrance into the holy city is by the gates into Israel, that is, entrance into the covenant people of God. The particular nation of Israel was never a strict physical lineage from Abraham, Isaac, or Jacob. There were many who were considered part of the commonwealth of Israel from Gentile nations and not physical descendants of Abraham, such as Rahab, Caleb, Ruth, etc. (Ephesians 2:11-13). There are many who were before Abraham who are considered as being included into the people of faith, and mentioned in the great cloud of witnesses of Hebrews (Hebrews 11-12:2). Being a child of Abraham, and of his faith, is defined as those who have the faith of Abraham (Romans 3-4; Galatians 3:28-29). In matters of faith, the spiritual has always taken precedence over the physical (Deuteronomy 10:12-16; 30:6; Philippians 3:3). This is true in the New Testament as well as the Old Testament. Having three gates on each side with the names of the twelve tribes, is reminiscent of the wilderness set-up of the camp of the Hebrews (Numbers 2:1-34).

The wall of the city had twelve foundations. The foundations have the names of the twelve apostles of the Lamb. Here is where a literal vision of a physical city is lacking. We must see this symbolic imagery as giving the readers and hearers of this book a description of the characteristics of the city, and not a visual that can be drawn. First, the foundations of a city are normally laid first. In the vision given to us, the apostles of the Lamb of the New Testament are the foundation. The foundation gives support to the walls. The Lamb, as the cornerstone, gives alignment to the whole structure (1 Peter 2:4-10). The twelve tribes from the Old Testament, named as the walls with the gates are shown as being placed upon the foundation. The foundations of this Jerusalem come *after* the walls historically. (Jesus was the reality of the shadows, even though the shadows came first.) This shows the unity of the twelve tribes *and* the twelve apostles as the covenant people of God from the Old *and* the New Testaments (Ephesians 2:11-3:7). (There were actually more than twelve tribes. And, which twelve apostles do you choose to use?) It is not the tribes or the apostles that is the leading thought in this passage, but the idea that God's administration is always associated with the number 12. Here, the administration is given in terms of God and the Lamb, who are One and the same. The disciples knew this administration when they cast lots to replace Judas (Acts 1:15-26).

The one speaking to John had a gold measuring instrument. Gold represents something of the greatest value. What is measured will be claimed as having great value. The city was laid out as square, and then is described as a cubed shaped. It is equal in length, width, and height. The holy of holies, the earthly place where God dwelt among His people, was also a cube shape (1 Kings 6:19-20). The wall was 144 cubits. One-forty-four is the testimonial witness number of the administration of God (Revelation 7:4-8). It was given in the measuring context of men, but it has a spiritual meaning (Revelation 1:20).

The construction of the wall, and what a wall represents, was consistent with the glory of God Himself. It was of jasper, and of great value and without blemish. The foundations of the wall, having the names of the apostles, are represented by having the twelve stones that were most likely associated with the twelve tribes. These were on the breastplate of the high priest (Exodus 28:17-21; 39:8-14). The first foundation stone, jasper, is associated with the throne and glory of God (Revelation 4:3). The stones were an instrument that reflected colors by light. God is light. The stones represent the administration of God in and through His people, who are called to reflect His manifold glory.

The twelve gates were twelve pearls. Gates are the entry point into a city. A pearl was a rare and valuable item of jewelry often used to adorn a woman (1 Timothy 2:9). A pearl was used as a metaphor for the Gospel of God, and not to be cast before those who would not acknowledge its value (Matthew 7:6). Here, it is associated with entrance into the kingdom of God, and of a great value that few people will find (Matthew 13:45-46). The street of the city was pure gold. The street is the broad public plaza or commons where business, fellowship, and activity occurred (Nehemiah 8:1; Proverbs 1:20; Psalm 144:14; Ezekiel 16:24-31; Daniel 9:25). Pure gold is without dross or impurity.

21:22-27 John did not see a temple in the city. The tabernacle and the temple were where God dwelt, and, was the mediating location where God and His people met for fellowship. There was no need of a temple or mediating place of worship. God and the Lamb are the temple and the dwelling where everything exists (1 Corinthians 15:24-28). Intimate fellowship is directly with the Lord. There was no longer need of the sun or the moon as the agents of God's

revelation and means of guidance. The glory of God was the illumination of the city, the bride. The Lamb is the light, as God is light (1 John 1:5).

During the Old Testament economy, the dwelling place of God was the place prescribed for worship and service. It was given as a particular place, and activities were observed in a particular manner (Deuteronomy 12:1-14). The temple and the tabernacle were not only a place. They also gave the means and direction by which the people were to approach God. The New Testament brought a dynamic change in how God would deal with His people (John 4:21-24). This was because of the work of Jesus on the Cross. The place and means of worship would change. The indwelling of the Holy Spirit would be new and different (John 20:22; 7:37-39). Therefore, the identity of the temple would be radically different (1 Corinthians 3:16-17; 6:19). Jesus fulfills the role of the Old Testament temple and becomes the New Testament temple Himself.

The city had no need of the sun or moon to give light. The sun and moon were agents of God's light and the revelation that He provided (Revelation 12:1-2). God Himself is there, and His is a personal revelation.

The Lamb is the means by which we see and know God. By Him everything we know and see is determined (Isaiah 60:19; John 8:12). The renewed people of the nations of the earth, who have received the salvation of God through Christ, will be part of the worshipping community of God (Isaiah 60:3-5). The gates will not need to be shut, for there will be no evil, or danger, or thief that will be present (Isaiah 60:11; 1 John 1:5). The believers of all nations shall bring their glory and praise of God into the city.

22:1-6a There is a source of eternal life that comes from God and from the Lamb (John 7:38). The river flows from the ruling authority of God *and* the Lamb. The tree of life is in the midst of the street and on both sides of the river. This is a reversal of the limitations set on mankind as a result of the Fall (Genesis 2:9; 3:24). In the Garden of Eden, the tree of life provided eternal life. The Garden of Eden was a probationary place that eventually would have grown to cover the whole known earth (Genesis 2:8; 3:23-24). This is finally achieved in the new heaven and earth. This restored tree of life is in the middle and midst of everything that occurs in the city. The tree of life is nourished by the eternal life flowing from God and the

Lamb. The imagery and symbolism of the tree in the middle and on both sides of the river of life is spatial, and difficult to see in a literalistic way. The reality we are to grasp is that of the complete testimony of what God will infuse into the new creation, as His gift of eternal life. The tree provides complete and continual production of God's administrative work in eternal life. There will not be a season where God does not provide eternal life.

The Greek word translated "healing" in most versions, is also translated "household" in other places (Matthew 24:45; Luke 12:42). This has the idea of a group, or household of servants. Leaves are symbolic of works and service. Adam and Eve *covered themselves* with leaves, of which God exchanged for His conditions of *coverings for sin* (Genesis 3:7, 21). The olive tree was cursed, being full of leaves and having no fruit (Mark 11:13). Therefore, the work of the tree of life was for the household of God's servants who come from all nations. It also refers to God's ongoing and eternal service *towards* the nations.

There shall be no more curse. The new heaven and new earth will be a reversal of the curse. There shall be no more separation. The throne of God and of the Lamb will be present in the community of His people. The kingdom of God that was prophesied by the prophets and apostles will be a reality (Ezekiel 48:35; Daniel 7:27; 1 Peter 2:9; Revelation 1:6). The servants, the redeemed of God, will see Him as He is (1 John 3:1-2). We shall see His face. There will be no separation, and no mediating measures to the relationship (Genesis 3:8a; Exodus 33:11a; 1 Corinthians 13:12). His name will be on their foreheads (Revelation 3:12; 7:3). There will be no allegiance, thoughts, or loyalty to any other but the Lord. We will be his prized, personal possession (Psalm 17:8; Revelation 3:12).

There will be no ignorance of God. We will know as we are known (1 Corinthians 13:12). Relationship with God and the Lamb will be personal and present. There will be no need of any mediating means of revelation (Isaiah 2:3; Jeremiah 31:34). The servants of God will also reign (Daniel 7:18; 2 Timothy 2:12; Revelation 3:21). We reign because we are co-heirs with Christ (Romans 8:16-17). After seeing the vision of the bride, the wife of the Lamb, John is told the words given to him are faithful and true (see the similarity with Revelation 21:5).

22:6b-15 Jesus calls Himself the one who is faithful and true (Revelation 3:14). His words are good because of who He really is. The Lord of the holy prophets confirms what the angel has delivered to His servants. The message delivered is to shortly take place, for the time is at hand (Revelation 22:10). Behold, take note, I am coming suddenly (Revelation 2:5, 16; 3:11; 22:12, 20). Blessed is he who maintains the sacred occupation of keeping the words contained in the prophecy of this book (Revelation 1:3). The book of Revelation is a prophetic book. There is a switch from one speaker to another. This may be a case of one speaker interpreting the vision with assistance from another speaker (see Daniel 8:16).

John declares that he personally saw and heard the visions of the book. When John falls at the feet of the one delivering the message, he is chastised again for confusing the messenger with the one who sent the message (see Revelation 19:10). The context is again in the light of the statement that: these are the true sayings of God. The angel instructs John, and the reader, that the worship of God is the only true and acceptable worship. This section has a striking resemblance to the exaltation language used at the destruction of Babylon (see Revelation 19:9-10).

John is told to not seal the words of the prophecy of this book. This is in contrast to Daniel, who is told to seal up the book. The prophecy of Daniel was for many days yet into the future, for the time of the end (Daniel 12:8-9). The prophecy of Revelation is relevant for the time of those reading and hearing the book. It includes our current time up to the end. The last days will make the division between believers and unbelievers irreversible. Daniel saw this as future, John sees it in the present (Cf. Daniel 12:10; Revelation 13:9-10). Since prophecy has been completed with the book of Revelation, how a person responds now will determine their eternity. He who has an ear, let him hear.

Again, John is told that Jesus is coming suddenly. This is the second of three times that this is stated (Revelation 22:7; 22:20). Jesus will bring with Him the rewards He will give at His second coming (Matthew 16:27). Jesus is the complete explanation of God, His word, and His final and full revelation (Hebrews 1:1). In Revelation 22:13 the title Alpha and Omega is claimed by Jesus Christ, revealing His deity and equality with God (see Isaiah 41:4; 44:6; 48:12; Revelation 1:8; 21:5-6). Jesus is the consummate judge of all that will be eternal.

Blessed are those who are obedient to the fulfilled commandments of God in Christ Jesus. They are forgiven by His blood and they are given access to the tree of life. They have entered into and belong to the community of God's people. Those who do not cease from that which God finds abhorrent will be left eternally outside the camp. May our lives continually be a loving testimony and witness of Christ before those who need to see their sin and their need for forgiveness. We have the answer (1 Peter 3:10-15). Be encouraged! The Lord will return!!

Text Comparisons for the Harlot and the Bride

Revelation 17:1-2

Angel of the seven bowls
Harlot

Revelation 17:3-18:24

In the Spirit
Into a wilderness
A woman
Babylon

Revelation 19:9-10

Blessed is the one who keeps
the testimony of Jesus
John worships angel
Angel is fellow servant
Worship God

Revelation 19:11-16

Christ comes (in one hour)

Revelation 19:17-20:15

Beast, false prophet, Satan,
and unbelievers judged.

Revelation 21:6-8

Alpha and Omega
Water of Life
Those outside separated

Revelation 21:9

Angel of the seven bowls
Bride/ Lamb's wife

Revelation 21:10-22:5

In the Spirit
To a mountain
A bride
Jerusalem

Revelation 22:6-11

Blessed is the one who keeps
the prophecy of this book
John worships angel
Angel is fellow servant
Worship God

Revelation 22:12a

I come quickly

Revelation 22:12b

Rewards are with Jesus

Revelation 22:13-15

Alpha and Omega
Tree of Life
Those outside separated

23

The Epilogue
Revelation 22:16-21

As the prologue of the book sets out the means and purpose of the book, so the epilogue will set out the boundaries and the warnings. The expositor and interpreter of the book of Revelation is wise to understand and keep both ends of the book in mind.

22:16-21 Jesus Himself authorizes and validates the message of the book of Revelation. It is from His angel to the churches (See Revelation 1:1-11). He is the root and offspring of David (Matthew 22:41-46; 2 Timothy 2:8; Revelation 5:5). Jesus is the Bright and Morning Star, the messenger and revealer (Numbers 24:17). He is the One who will shatter the darkness and bring in the new day (2 Peter 1:19; Revelation 2:28). This begins as we accept and believe the prophecy of Jesus' coming again, and is to be fulfilled at His appearing. This is testified to by the Holy Spirit, the bride of Christ (the personification of the church), and all who look for, long for, and love His appearing (Isaiah 55:1-9; John 14:15-18; 16:7-11; 2 Timothy 4:8). They say: "Come!!"

There is a sober warning to anyone who adds to, or subtracts from, the prophecy of this book. We are not to neglect any part or add to any part. One of the current dangers by many well-intentioned expositors, is taking a part or piece of the prophecy and developing an elaborate end-time scenario around it that does not fit back into the context of the book. This is true for any part of Scripture (Deuteronomy 4:2; 12:32). Some of this will have eternal significance. To ignore any part of His call to purity and endurance will also have eternal significance.[1] The whole counsel of God must be our source and standard for any interpretation (Acts 20:27; 2 Timothy 4:3-4). What we know correctly now, will have significance for our experience and responsibility in eternity.

The third time, Jesus declares that He will come suddenly, abruptly, and quickly. While it is today, we must live every day spiritually and practically in light of the return of Jesus (Hebrews 3:13, 15; 4:7). We are commanded to live in communion with the Savior until He comes again (1 Corinthians 11:26). We must not become distracted by the world, into palliative and surrogate gospels and activities (John 8:21). Seek Him and His righteousness while He may be found (Deuteronomy 4:29; Isaiah 55:6; Matthew 6:33; 2 Corinthians 6:2).

John declares: So be it, Come! The unmerited favor of the Lord Jesus Christ be with all the saints. Amen!

Appendix A

The Four Living Creatures

The appendices that follow address various topics for discussion that are crucial for the understanding and interpretation of the book of Revelation.

This appendix is primarily a discussion of the similarities between the four living creatures of Revelation 4, and the four living creatures of Ezekiel 1 and 10. There are enough similarities that the conclusion can be made that the living creatures are indeed the same creatures seen in both passages. The differences can be explained by the context of each book, and by the posture and position of the creatures in each particular passage. The two narratives are more alike than they are different. There are other places in the Scriptures where the creatures are located, and the clues for these similarities are found in the Ezekiel passages. In both narratives, the living creatures are always described in unity, and are unified in their activity.

In the book of Revelation, we are given a scene which represents a composite picture of the living creatures in relationship to the throne of God (Revelation 4-5). They have an intimate position in the midst of, and encircling the throne. They also have a posture and role of separation. In the book of Ezekiel, the four living creatures are between that which is created and the firmament. There they also have a posture and role of separation. There is mention of a firmament above the creatures, with a throne and a voice that comes from above the firmament, with someone on the throne (Ezekiel 1:22-28). The voice, as one of authority, is described as the glory of God. The One on the throne then give commands to Ezekiel. In the books of Revelation and Ezekiel, the four living creatures are always working and functioning together as a group. Take the time to compare the two texts.

In the book of Ezekiel, the four living creatures are called "cherubim" (Ezekiel 10:2-20). This name gives us the clue to the task and the consistent posture of these creatures. In the Genesis account of the Fall, the Lord places cherubim at the entrance of the garden to guard the way to the tree of life (Genesis 3:24). This is a duty and position of separation because of the judgement placed on Adam and Eve. In the construction of the ark of the covenant there are two cherubim placed at each end of the ark with their wings covering, or guarding, the mercy seat (1 Samuel 4:4; 2 Samuel 6:2; 1 Chronicles 13:6). The mercy seat is described as the place where the Lord "dwells between the cherubim." This is described by the Psalmists in terms like "He who dwells between the cherubim" (Psalm 80:1; 99:1). The throne of God is carried on the cherubim (1 Chronicles 28:18; Psalm 18:10). The picture here is that of God riding in a chariot, which was generally reserved for royalty. The cherubim were included in the decorations and vessels of Solomon's temple, and with the temple described in Ezekiel (1 Kings 6:23-35; 7:29, 36; 2 Chronicles 3:11-12; 5:7-8; Ezekiel 41:18-25). It should be noted that the particular locations and places in which the cherubim were presented and displayed, they are always placed to represent separation and guardianship. Satan is also portrayed as the covering cherub (Ezekiel 28:14-16). He once had great responsibility.

The cherubim are always associated with where God has chosen as His dwelling place. They are always shown in close proximity to the throne of God. They are present in heaven, the temple, the ark of the covenant, and with the temple furniture. These are all used to show the pattern for approaching God. Their songs and their praise in Revelation always declare God's holiness and separateness (Revelation 4:8). The cherubim are part of the ongoing narrative of the book of Revelation up to chapter 19, verse 4. They are part of the worship and celebration of the judgement of Babylon the Great. It is important to note they are not part of the scene of the new heaven and new earth of chapters 21 and 22. They are no longer needed to provide separation. The relationship between God and His creation has been restored.

There are many reasons for the differences of descriptions of the four living creatures between John and Ezekiel. They are two different prophets seeing the living creatures at different times in the life of God's people. If the creatures are performing similar tasks in general, then they could have different descriptions of their characteristics specific to their location. John sees them in heaven. Ezekiel sees them on earth at the temple and in the process of leaving. The living creatures are described in more general terms in heaven by John. In Ezekiel, their position was as a result of God's judgement on the nation of Israel's iniquity. In Ezekiel, they are moving with God as His glory leaves the temple and the city. The whirlwind in Ezekiel is used as a description of general judgement, as are the wheels used to represent specific judgement.

In Ezekiel, the description is given as though they are as a single creature with combined features (Ezekiel 1:10-11). In Revelation, John describes them as separate (Revelation 4:7). It is important that whatever they are doing, it is performed as a group. Ezekiel sees them as having four wings, and John sees them with six wings. This difference could represent where, or how, they are ministering. The differences could represent what they needed to perform their task in relation to the different locations that the context reveals. We should be careful to not limit what God can do with His angelic creatures.

In the book of Revelation, the use of numbers gives us information. They may not have an ordinal use. The number four is always related to the earth, or to that which has been separated. The four living creatures have an association with God's creation. There are not just four of them. In fact, they may be many in number. The four living creatures are only described by four distinct characteristics. Notice, the four descriptions are not given in the same format. The first is *like* a lion. The second is *like* a calf. The third had *the face like* a man. The fourth was *like a flying* eagle. These descriptions give us characteristics, not a visual we can draw. Like a lion informs us of their powerful position and equally powerful function. The calf is the offspring of a bull, which had the distinction of being representative of majesty and superiority (Deuteronomy 33:17). It is a characteristic of work. This living creature characteristic is assuredly portraying prominence, but because it is shown as a calf, it is a derived prominence. Neither of these first two creatures need be confused with the One who is on the throne. The creatures are created beings serving as they were created to do. The third living creature has the *face like* a man. The face was seen as the most prominent part of the body, and is presented toward, or in front of, as in standing before or against another individual (Psalm 34:16). The idea here is that this living creature characteristic presents an "in your face" position toward the ones it is to keep at a distance: the fallen creation. It is representing that which is separated, from that which it needs separated from. The fourth living creature is presented as a large bird in flight, that is, the wings are spread. Whenever wings are used as a metaphor or an anthropomorphism, the concept is that of representing the extending activity of the one who performs or provides it. Under His wings I am safely abiding (Psalm 91:4). His wings carry the Israelites out of Egypt (Exodus 19:4). Wings are a picture of the complete extent and reach of safety and power (Matthew 23:37). They are never portrayed as just existing on the side of a bird. The wings of the fourth living creature are active in their duty. They are covering, spread out in a posture of complete and guaranteed enclosure. Wings that are touching is portrayed on the mercy seat of the ark of the covenant.

In a different capacity, all four living creatures in Ezekiel had the *likeness* of a man. This means that they have the same capacity as man, as being a *representative steward* of God. Man was created in God's image and His *likeness* to steward His creation. Their feet are described in the same way as the risen Christ in Revelation (Revelation 1:15). The living creatures in Ezekiel had the hands of a man under their wings on all four sides, and the wings touched one another.

Man's hands represent his works. The four living creatures' primary task was to keep separate the works of man from the throne. The works of man are under the restrictive authority of the living creature's wings. The wings touched, leaving no gap for access. The coals of fire represent their purity. The torches represent the Spirit of God that is their power. The living creatures themselves are always active. Their movement, their spirit, and their wheels, always move in synchronized motion.

An additional subject that adds to the interpretation of the four living creatures is the understanding and contrast of the angelic creatures called "seraphim" (Isaiah 6:2). They are not the same kind of creatures. Seraphim are another of God's angelic creatures who also have a specific task. They are seen as above the throne of God. Contrast this to the cherubim who are around and in the midst of the throne. They are above the throne to represent that *God* is between them and His creation. They may be the creatures called "destroying angels" in other parts of the Bible. Could they be the four angels held at bay from destroying the earth-dwellers in the book of Revelation? (Revelation 7:2; 9:14).

The Hebrew word for seraphim is also translated as "fiery serpents" in the wilderness wanderings (Numbers 21:6-8; Deuteronomy 8:15). They are also used for the final judgement of nations (Isaiah 14:29; 30:6; see Revelation 9:13-19). Moses was instructed to make a bronze serpent that the people had to look upon to be saved (Numbers 21:9). They had to look upon the very thing that was causing them their death. The Israelites later made an idol of that serpent, which was eventually destroyed in the days of Hezekiah (2 Kings 18:4). Jesus stated that He must be lifted up, as the serpent in the wilderness was lifted up, pointing to the way in which we must look in order to be saved. (John 3:14-15). The means of death became the means to life. These seraphim are not to be confused with the cherubim of Revelation and Ezekiel.

Appendix B

The Olivet Discourse

One cannot study the book of Revelation without noting the strong connections with the Olivet Discourse. The Olivet Discourse is so-called, because Jesus gave it while teaching the disciples on the Mount of Olives. The teaching and encouragements that Jesus gave were in response to the observations and questions made by the disciples concerning the grandeur of the temple structures and His going away. The subject of Jesus' going away led the disciples to inquire about His return, and the subsequent implications of His return and the establishing of His eternal kingdom.

While Jesus mentioned His second coming and the Day of the Lord in various places in the Gospels, the Olivet Discourse is the most intensive discussion in one setting. The Discourse is found in the synoptic gospels (Matthew 24; Mark 13; Luke 21). The context of this discourse is also framed by the events before, and after, the somewhat private discussion that Jesus has with His disciples. Just before, Jesus had come into major conflict with the religious leaders of His day (Matthew 22:41-

23:39; Mark 12:35-44; Luke 20:1-21:4). It is after the time on the Mount of Olives that Jesus soon would experience His passion. It was also about this time that Jesus would begin to restrict His redemptive contact with the religious leaders (John 11:54). This is extremely important, as it gives context to the fact that Jesus would soon give very judicial statements to the ethnic nation of Israel for their unbelief in Who He claimed to be (Matthew 21:43; 23:37-38; Mark 11:12-14; Luke 19:41-44; 20:13-16; John 1:11).

In placing the three narratives of the Olivet Discourse side by side, we can discover a harmonization of the information that Jesus gave (see below, Page 196). Just like the book of Revelation, there is an aspect of recapitulation used in the narrative. Either Jesus states His return in three different ways, or, He returns three different times (IE. Matthew 24:27, 30, 39). The way in which we read this will be of the utmost importance. We need to place the three narratives of the Olivet Discourses beside each other for comparison. Then we can compare what the three Olivet Discourse narratives contain alongside our structure and interpretation of the book of

Revelation. Revelation will not contradict what Jesus has said. The book of Revelation and the Olivet Discourse will not contradict what Daniel the prophet had been given. Jesus said as much (Matthew 24:15; Mark 13:14).

At the beginning of the Olivet Discourse, the disciples are asking questions. They had made an observation about the temple. Jesus remarks that the temple will be torn down. The number of questions they ask could be seen as two, or possibly three. What will be the outcome of the tearing down of the temple? What will be the signs of His coming back, and, what will be the signs of the end of the age? At issue here is what details concern the temple, and, is the second coming *and* the end of the age the same event?

I will give headings to each section. The Scripture references will be given. Then, I will give commentary to each section and how they tie together.

THE QUESTIONS – Matthew 24:1-3; Mark 13:1-4; Luke 21:5-7.

There are at least two questions that are asked by the disciples. Tell us, when will these things be? And what will be the sign of your coming, *and* of the end of the age? When will these things be? What they are asking about is in response to Jesus' statement: "I say to you, not one stone shall be left here upon another that shall not be thrown down." The second set of questions is interesting in light of the statement that Jesus made concerning the stones being thrown down. The fact that they are good students of the Old Testament prompted the second question. They knew the destruction of the Temple was a precursor to His coming back and of a new kingdom (Daniel 9:26). What they did not understand was the timespan that could occur between the sixty-ninth and seventieth week of Daniel's 70-week prophecy. This timespan between the last two weeks, an interval period or postponement, was because of the rejection of Jesus as the King of the Jews (Acts 1:6-8; 2:34-39; 3:19-21). Jesus answers both questions in what seems to be a back and forth, present and future, format.

THE WAITING TIME – Matthew 24:4-8; Mark 13:5-8; Luke 21:8-11.

These characteristics of the events to occur are exactly what the first four seals represent in the book of Revelation (Revelation 6:1-8). There would be a plethora of false teaching that either takes away from the person of Jesus Christ, or, presents a counterfeit for the unwary who fall into deception. There follows from this, a time of Satan's restricted reign, and the disunity and strife among the peoples of the earth. This in turn leads to the lack of real peace, wars, famines, and death in all its dynamics.

A CALL TO PERSONAL ENDURANCE – Matthew 24:9-14; Mark 13:9-13; Luke 21:12-19.

This is equal to the fifth seal of Revelation (Revelation 6:9-11). This persecution is general to the followers of Christ, and, is given in a specific sense to each and every believer. It will occur until the Lord returns. This is testified to within the book of Revelation concerning the saints who did not lose the testimony of Jesus (Revelation 12:17). Notice that the account of Luke states: "But before all these things". This takes us back to the beginning of the events of the previous verses. Persecution will occur until all the ones who will be martyred has occurred. Then Jesus will come and repay the unbelieving world for their hatred of the saints.

THE DESTRUCTION OF THE TEMPLE – Matthew 24:15-28; Mark 13:14-23; Luke 21:20-24.

Jesus starts by calling to their attention the Abomination of Desolation of which Daniel the prophet spoke (Daniel 11:31; 12:11). The Abomination of Desolation, or, the Abomination that makes Desolate, was an event of terrible proportion that occurred as a result of the civil war between the Ptolemies and the Seleucids. In this war, Antiochus Epiphanies temporarily ceased the practice of Judaism in his attempt to completely Hellenize the region. It did not help that he was terribly irate at losing, in a very big way, the war that he was waging in the South. This was countered by a guerilla army led by the Maccabees. This victory by the Maccabees over Antiochus came to be celebrated by the Holiday of Hanukkah.

Jesus is telling the disciples that there will be a desolation like unto what the prophet Daniel spoke. He then gives instruction as to the means of safety that must be observed to escape the devastation. These same instructions are given in Luke and prefaced by calling the Abomination of Desolation "a surrounding of armies against Jerusalem." We know from history that this was the destruction of the city of Jerusalem in A.D 70 by the Roman legions. Jerusalem has changed hands many times. But more significantly, the Temple has not been used for worship since that time by the Jews. It has been desolated. It is quite unlikely that any consistent use of the sacrificial system has been in play since the tearing of the veil at the death of Jesus (Matthew 27:51; Hebrews 10:19-21).

The counterfeits of Satan will continue after the Abomination that causes Desolation. Compare Matthew 24, verses 23-24, with verse 5. Matthew 24, verses 27 - 28, are about the coming of Jesus, but are given as a contrast to the deceptions given in Matthew 24, verses 23 -26. In Luke 21, verse 24b, Jesus talks of the city being trampled by Gentiles, that is, the nations. This occurs concurrently with the times of the Gentiles, and until the times of the Gentiles be fulfilled. The times of the Gentiles is the time of this current dispensation. As Paul puts it (Ephesians 1;10; 3:1-6), when the "fullness of the Gentiles" are being included into the covenant people of God (Romans 11:17, 25-26; see Hosea 1:10). This is the time of gathering all into one flock (John 10:16).

JUDAISM LOSES IT PLACE AS THE AGENT OF GODS REVELATION –
Matthew 24:29; Mark 13:24-25; Luke 21:25-26.

The physical universe, and all its parts, are at one time or another used by Scripture to represent some reality greater and more significant than themselves. The sun, moon, and stars, as agents of light, are used as far back as Genesis to represent the particular, ethnic people of God (Genesis 37:9). These agents of light are then used as symbols to communicate the condition and status of ethnic Israel as God's means of His revelation to the world. What happens to them is given in symbolic language (Isaiah 13:9-10; Joel 2:10, 31; 3:15; Acts 2:20; Revelation 12:1). Notice in Peter's Pentecostal address, that there will be universal evangelism of the Gospel *after* the activities of the sun, moon, and stars (see Acts 2:20-21). Also, the tribulation that Israel will experience during the destruction of the temple, will *precede* the activity of the sun, moon, and stars. (The word for tribulation used here is the same as used other places for the idea of great pressure. The structure of the language is different in Revelation chapter 7, verse 14, where the great tribulation is mentioned as: *The tribulation the great*). The sun, moon, and stars losing their light and positions, is symbolizing the change of God's means of revelation in the world.

JESUS SECOND COMING – Matthew 24:30-31; Mark 13:26-27; Luke 21:27.

These verses describe the true coming of Jesus in contrast to the false comings described in the above verses. The characteristics of Jesus second coming given in these verses, along with all of Scripture, must all agree without contradiction with any interpretation of Jesus' coming. If all the Scripture that is given about His second coming is brought to the table, many of the incorrect conclusions, divisions, and inconsistencies within the church would disappear.

SPECIFIC SIGNS FOR THE ABOMINATION OF DESOLATION – Matthew 24:32-35; Mark 13:28-31; Luke 21:28-33.

Jesus moves back to the Abomination of Desolation. There are signs to be observed. They, the current generation, are to be like the people of Issachar (1 Chronicles 12:32). As Jesus answers the two major questions of the Disciples, He moves from the present, to the future, and back to the present. The key to this section is found in Mark 13, verses 23, 29, and 30. The phrase "these *things*" gives definition to who "this generation" must be. This generation will experience the fall of the temple and the destruction of Jerusalem. Jesus teaches to watch the fig tree, and all the trees (Luke), as examples of the events to unfold. The events are sure, because His word is sure. We are to believe the Word of God *as* the Word of God.

BACK TO THAT DAY – Matthew 24:36-44; Mark 13:32-33; Luke 21:34-36.

Jesus moves back to "that day." But of that day, the day of His future coming, *no one knows*. The days of Noah were instructive about how God judged and purified the world at the time of the Flood. It is also noteworthy that God preserved Noah through the time of testing and purifying of the world, not removing him from it (See Revelation 3:10). The "sureness" of judgement was known to Noah as it approached. The people outside the Ark were caught unaware. Jesus states that a time of separation will occur under similar circumstances. There will be a great separating of the saved from the wicked (Matthew 24:31; 1 Thessalonians 4:13-5:1-10; 2 Thessalonians 2:1-12).

BEING WATCHFUL AS WE WAIT – Matthew 24:45-51; Mark 13:34-37.

Being watchful is more than just being aware that Jesus will come again. We are to be people who live lives that reflect the hope that we have been given in Him (Hebrews 10:24-25; 2 Peter 3:12). We can even hasten the day (2 Peter 3:12). Matthew 25 gives us the be-attitudes of the kingdom nature we are to exhibit. We are to always be ready, always be expanding the kingdom of God, and always be involved in practical ministry to each other and the world around us. There are many places that the "we" are told that Jesus' coming, and the Day of the Lord, will come as a thief in the night (1 Thessalonians 5:2; 2 Peter 3:10; Revelation 3:3; 16:15). But we are also told that the Day should not overtake us as a thief (1 Thessalonians 5:4-11).

Revelation Chapter 6

1st seal

Bow (arrows-Eph. 6)   crown of overcomer
White horse – (contrast with Ch.19) **Conquest**,
            Rider is conqueror vs. coming to serve
Given a crown
Rev. 12:12, 17   Satan is prince of the power of the
air, world in the lap of the evil one
Wars and conflict – James – pride
1 John 2 - antichrists –like Nimrod

2nd seal

War
take peace vs. Romans 5:1
given a sword
sword –short in length, close combat, personal,
(see John 18:10 –Peter)

3rd seal

Bread by weight – Ezek. 4:16; Lev 26:26
Scales – uneven balances
Oil and wine – unharmed New Covenant advance
Disobedience = **Famine** in OT

4th seal

Sword – long, far reaching (Jesus mouth, Mary heart)
Death – one to one ratio, universal, sure
Hades or Sheol
Fourth – of the earth, complete
Beasts – ungodly teachers and leaders

5th seal

Souls under the altar – were a sacrifice
White robes – righteousness and victory
Rest – Jesus said I will give you rest
Imprecatory Psalms ask for vindication
Slain – past and future   **Martyrdom**
Until Jesus returns

6th seal

Change in the Landscape of Heaven
Sun, moon, stars   **(Genesis 37:9-11)**
Joel 2:10; **2:31**; 3:15   **Matt. 24:29   Mark 13:24**
Luke 21:25   Acts 2:20; 3:17-26
Rev. 6:12-14; 12:1; 21:23; 22:5   (Romans 9:4-5)

All Judgement Given to The Lamb
Mountains and rocks   **Luke 23:30-31**
Islands moved   Hosea 10:8
Men hid themselves   (see Isaiah 2:19-21)
Wrath of the Lamb upon unbelievers

Matthew 24, Mark 13, Luke 21

Matt. 24:4-5   Mark 13:5-6   Luke 21:8

Matt. 24:6   wars and rumors of wars
            (but end is not yet)
      Mark 13:7 (7b the end is not yet)
         Luke 21:9-10 (will not come immediately,
                              not next)

Matt. 24:7b   famines, pestilences, and earthquakes

Matt. 24:8 (beginnings of birth pangs)
      Mark 13:8   (v8b the beginnings of sorrows)
         Luke 21:11

Matt. 24:9-13 (24:14)   Mark 13:9-13
      Luke 21:12-19 (note: v12 before all this)
Matt.24:15-22   desolation   (Daniel 11:31)
   (Matt. 24:23-28)   false hopes proclaimed –
                  (v26-27 is contrast))
      Mark 13:14-20   (v21-23 false hopes)
      Luke 21:20-24 (Gentiles – see Romans 11:19-27)

Matt. 24:29
   Mark 13:24-25
      Luke 21:25a
   (24:32-35) a lesson from natural signs

Second Coming
Matt. 24:30-31   Mark 13:26-27   Luke 21:25b-28
         Mark 13:28-31; Luke 21:29-33)
Matt. 24:36-44; Mark 13:32-37; Luke 21:34-36

Appendix C

The History and Judgements of Satan

The book of Revelation cannot be fully appreciated and understood without knowing the major themes that run throughout the whole of Scripture. One of those themes involves the origins, history, activity, and judgements of Satan. To know the nature of Satan's origin, the historical contexts in which he operates, the focus of his activities, and the judgements associated with his doom, gives the believer encouragement and confidence to persevere, overcome, and endure.

Knowing why Satan tempted Adam and Eve adds significance and meaning to our being created in the image and likeness of God. Satan is powerful, but he is only given everything that he has. Everything Satan does, God uses for His own purposes (Romans 8:28). As heinous as Satan is, he can go no further than God allows him to go (Job 1-2). God is not the primary enemy of Satan. Mankind is the primary enemy of Satan. It was the creation of mankind that prompted the action and pride of Satan to remove Adam from the position of steward of God. That stewardship and dominion included

ruling over Satan himself (Hebrews 1:13-14).

The book of Genesis is indeed a book of beginnings. It is a record of the foundations of the created order, of faith, and of redemption. It is the part of the Scriptures that gives us the origins of everything that we need to know. In Genesis we find the beginnings of all that we deal with and need to understand up to this very day. To read quickly through the accounts that are contained in the first 12 chapters of Genesis, without ever seriously reflecting on the content, is to miss what God has revealed to us as our origin, our purpose, our morality, and our destiny. What God had originally created as very good, was soon to become, by the choices of mankind, disobedient, corrupt, and fallen.

One of the many beginnings that the Genesis narrative describes, is the Fall of mankind. Included with this historical record of the Fall of Man is the serpent, the tool that Satan used to corrupt the purposes of God. From the Genesis account we know *who* was involved in the Fall. We know *when* the first couple was deceived. We know *how* they were deceived. We know *what* Satan used to deceive them. The question of *why* Satan deceived them is of the utmost importance, and gives us a fuller explanation concerning his activities throughout the Biblical narratives.

All of the angels were created, either before, or during creation (Genesis 1:31-2:1). The heavens and the earth, and *all* the hosts of them, were finished. And God declared that it was very good. The angels are said to have sung praises to God during the events of creation (Job 38:4-7). Therefore, Satan is a created being (Ezekiel 28:15). The Bible informs us that all things were created by Jesus, and for Jesus (Colossians 1:16). We also know from Scripture that Satan was created, as in his original state, very beautiful. Satan had a covering, or a protective capacity (Ezekiel 28:11-15a). Satan was originally created as the model for perfection, with wisdom and a specific purpose and giftedness by God. It is quite possible that Satan (not his original name), could very well have been God's right-hand man, as it were. Satan was in the role of God's personal agent of security. His role gave him access to God in a particular way that no other angel may have had.

The Scriptures tell us that Satan was in the garden of Eden, the paradise of God (Ezekiel 28:13a). Satan was perfect in his ways *until* iniquity, or sinfulness, was found in him (Ezekiel 18:15b). Note that Satan was in Eden in his perfection *until* iniquity was found in him (Ezekiel 28:13a). It was in his access to the garden of Eden that Satan fell into his sinfulness (Genesis 3:1ff). It was his temptation of Adam and Eve that caused his fall from his position as the anointed cherub who covers.

If all the angels sang at creation, then Satan was created before Adam and Eve came onto the scene. Adam and Eve, being created in the image and likeness of God, were given stewardship and dominion over the creation of God. That was something that Satan could not let continue (Genesis 1:26-38; 3:8). Satan was being displaced by what, he would perceive, was a temporarily inferior creature (Hebrews 2:5-12). By tempting Adam and Eve to disobey God, Satan was able to assume the dominion that had been given to Adam (Isaiah 14:12-16; Ezekiel 28:15b-19). When and why Satan fell adds gravity and significance to our being created in God's image and likeness, and of our being given dominion. Angels can physically appear as humans, but are not created in the image and likeness of God.

Instead of Adam now having the right-hand position as steward of God, Satan became the one who was present with Adam's dominion. Satan uses that position to accuse mankind before God (Job 1:6-12; 2:1; Zechariah 3:1-2). The right-hand position as an accuser was a formal, and judicial position in the courts of the day. In the Old Testament economy, Satan still had access to God because there was no one in the position vacated by Adam. This was because of Adam's sin. Satan had still lost his position as anointed cherub (Genesis 3:14), but assumes the role of accuser to keep man from returning to the role for which man was created. The first mention of the Gospel is right after the temptation of the man and the woman. God declares that the seed of the woman will crush the serpent's head (Genesis 3:15). Because we will reign and rule with Jesus, Satan will also be crushed under our feet (Romans 15:20). He is always trying to corrupt the plan of salvation.

Satan has attempted, many times, to corrupt, destroy, kill, and end the plan of God's redemption. God's plan was to bring forth a Messiah, an Anointed One, in whom the world would be saved. Satan's attempts were on a large scale, as in corrupting the majority of humans before the flood (Genesis 6:1ff). His attempts included trying to kill the deliverer Moses when he was born (Exodus 1:15-18). He led Cain to kill righteous Abel in jealousy (Genesis 4:1-15). He nearly wiped out the kingly line of David. (Only Joash survived (2 Kings 11:13)). He led the covenant people into idolatry several times. He tried to kill Jesus as an infant. He had Jesus betrayed and crucified.

During the earthly ministry of Jesus, Satan comes to Jesus as the accuser saying: "If you are the Son of God" (Luke 4:3). Jesus is tempted into distrusting the word of God. He is then tempted to distrust the care of God. Jesus is ultimately tempted to receive the nations the easy way, thus bypassing the cross. It is interesting that Jesus never argues that Satan did not have the capacity to make that promise. At that time, the kingdoms of the world *were* under Satan's dominion (1 John 5:19). If Satan's temptations would have succeeded, he would have made the last Adam subservient to him, thus keeping his position and retaining dominion of the earth. He then would have kept all of mankind under his reign of death.

Satan's greatest attempt was the crucifixion and death of Jesus. Without the resurrection, we would have no hope (1 Corinthians 15:12-19).

Jesus, during His earthly ministry, makes judicial statements concerning the future of Satan (John 12:31; 13:27; 14:30; 16:11; 17:15). We know from the Old Testament prophets that Satan was cast out of his position as covering cherub. Yet Jesus declares that Satan *will be cast out* (John 12:31). This was something yet to happen. The position that Jesus is talking about, is Satan's position of accuser of the brethren. This took place at the crucifixion, resurrection, and ascension of Jesus.

In the book of Revelation, we have this event briefly narrated. It is the reversal of this right-hand situation and the return of a man having dominion. It is the man Christ Jesus, the last Adam, who secures the role of being at the right hand of God (Revelation 12:1-5). Jesus comes to redeem mankind from his sin by dying on the cross, and then ascending to the right hand of God as the last Adam (Acts 7:55-56; 1 Corinthians 15:45).

The event of the exaltation of Christ displaces Satan as accuser (Revelation 12:10). We now have Jesus as our advocate (Hebrews 7:25) at the right hand of God the Father (Hebrews 1:3; 8:1; 10:12; 12:2). The exaltation of Christ changes reality in other ways as well. Before the cross, Michael, the warrior angel who fights for God's people (Daniel 10:12-14, 21), could only declare God's eventual judgement against Satan (Jude 9). Because of the cross, Michael is given the authority to displace Satan in a war within the spiritual realm. This war casts Satan to the earth until the final judgement (Revelation 12:7-13). There are battles still being fought, but the war is won.

Currently, Satan is confined to the realm of the earth. In the Old Testament, Satan did everything he could to keep the Messiah from being born and following the Father's will. Jesus is tested, or tempted, by Satan to receive by his hands what God will give Him (Luke 4:5-7). Now, from the beginning of the New Testament until today, he is against the followers of Christ. He does not have the authority to do anything he wants. He can only do what God allows him to do (James 4:7). He is full of wrath (Revelation 12:12). Satan is intent on destroying as many lives as he can (John 10:10a; 1 Peter 5:8) and dragging them all into an eternity separated from God (Matthew 25:41). He is prince of the demonic realm (Ephesians 2:2; 6:12). He is a deceiver (2 Corinthians 10:4-5; 11:14).

It is important to remember that Satan is very intelligent and resourceful. He pre-empts and counterfeits the plans of God in many cases. He uses many things that God has created for good to his own evil ends. He is the originator of all that violates God's purposes (John 8:44).

Satan will be allowed to gather the nations of the earth in one final attempt to thwart the eternal plans of God (Revelation 16:14; 20:3, 7-10). His final judgement will be eternal torment in the lake of fire burning with brimstone (Matthew 25:41; Revelation 20:10).

There are four phases to the story of Satan. First, his creation as a perfect being. Second, his fall from his position of authority before God. Third, his casting out of heaven as accuser (and the Son of Man then being seated at the right hand of God). Last, his final defeat and eternal judgement at the second coming of Jesus (2 Thessalonians 2:8).

The future for those who hold a faith in Christ, is a future which has already been won by our Lord and Savior Jesus Christ (1 Corinthians 6:3, Ephesians 1:20-21, 2:6, Revelation 3:21). Why Satan tempted the first humans in the first place, and the Love which led God to redeem us back to Himself, increases significantly our value as God's pinnacle of creation. We are created and designed to have dominion and stewardship. His plan of salvation to send His Son in the likeness of human flesh (Philippians 2:7), to take away sin and death, is of eternal significance. It is only then that we can even begin to fully understand Jesus as the last Adam (1 Corinthians 15:45). We can then understand the full implications of the new heavens and the new earth (Isaiah 65:17; 66:22; Romans 8:19-22; 2 Peter 3:15; Revelation 21-22). Our physical bodies will be glorified as His now is (Ephesians 4, I Corinthians 15; 1 John 3:2). Our dominion will be restored as God's stewards (Revelation 2:26-27). The current creation groans (Romans 8:22). The new creation has already been inaugurated. Those who overcome will be seated on Jesus' throne with him, as He overcame and sat down on His Father's throne (Revelation 3:21). And Satan will no longer be in the picture.

Timeline: History of Satan

In Eternity Past	At Creation	At the Fall	The Flood	As Accuser	The Time of Christ	As Adversary	In Eternity Future
|	|	|	|	|	|	|	|
Ezekiel 28:15a	Genesis 3:1-15			Job 1:6-12	Rev. 12:1-5	2 Cor. 10:4-5	1 Cor. 6:3
Colossians 1:16	Isaiah 14:12-16			Zech. 3:1-2	Rev. 12:7-13	Eph. 6:12	Matt. 25:41
	Ezek. 28:15b-19			Luke 4:3ff	Luke 10:18	Eph. 2:2	Rev. 20:7-10
				Jude 9	John 12:31	James 4:7	
						1 Peter 5:8	

	|		|	
	Job 38:4-7		Genesis 6:1	
	Genesis 1:31-2:1		2 Peter 2:4	

Appendix D

The Return and The Rapture

The coming of Jesus is that which should characterize every believers' daily perspective, in their current situation and in their hope for the future. It is both Biblical and spiritual to maintain a mindset and alertness about the return of Jesus. Believers are to long for, look for, and love His appearing. The return of Jesus is mentioned many times and in many contexts in the Scriptures. In the New Testament, the second coming is referenced more times than His first coming. We are to be increasing in our responsibility towards one-another as we anticipate the Day approaching (Daniel 12:3; Philippians 2:14-16; Hebrews 10:24-25). Those who do not have a hope for the future, struggle to find purpose in the present.

There are so many views concerning the "rapture" of the saints. Why bring another treatise to bear on a topic that has such a divisive reputation? Precisely *because* there are so many views. Precisely *because* there has developed an apathetic approach to it, even from the perspective of the church. Precisely *because* there is a negligence on the part of the church to defend the hope that we have.

Precisely *because* the enemy can remove our passion by removing our hope. There can be only one answer to the question of the rapture of the church. This attempt is, at the very least, an attempt to contribute something, small or great, that might trigger the movement to a consensus. It concerns the testimony of Scripture and the whole counsel of God. The rapture is a matter of apologetics, both inside and outside the church. It is a matter of being Biblical and Spiritual.

We need to have a correct theology infinitely more than an accurate chronology.[1] Many of the contemporary discussions pursue the timing and placement of the rapture of the church without giving due attention to the theology that the whole Bible brings to bear on the subject. As we move through the various Scriptures that address the second coming of Jesus, our conclusions need to be tested and conformed to them. In days gone by, the church met in councils to decide issues of the faith. They hammered away at the issues until a conclusion was reached for the good of the whole church. When we realize the cost and commitment that it took, considering the eras that these individuals lived in, the time and effort needed to accomplish their goals was enormous. With the current communications technology at our disposal, how can the church be so divided and wholly divergent in this regard.

It is said, "we need to agree to disagree." I would add, "for now." Why does so much of the needed discussion on this topic not happen. The neglect of many to have humility before the Word of God has created an apathy on the part of others to pursue a solution to that which "causes division" (Isaiah 66:2b). The Bible does not have a problem with division for the right reasons (Luke 12:49-53). Those who are on the outside of Christianity see the results of this negligence and partisanship, and are turned off from the church. The Gospel proclamation has suffered. Loyalty to a particular group, a leader, a teacher, or a denomination, should not be the issue. Loyalty should be to the Word of God.

Being objective is a task of deliberate work. Most people who are emotionally attached to a personality, position, or a tradition will find it exceptionally hard to see differently even though parts Scripture may not align with their views. This issue needs

to be decided by the Word of God (Luke 16:29-31). The opposition to our knowing the truth is not without a source. It is the work of the evil one. Keeping the church divided, is keeping the church ineffective.

Is the rapture a primary issue? Not for some. But it is still a faith issue from the Word of God. If the deity of Jesus is one of many issues that characterize correct orthodoxy, then, the coming Jesus is one of the main issues that promotes correct orthopraxy. We have been given information that is for our encouragement and preparation. Jesus held the people of His day responsible for His first coming (Luke 19:41-44). Likewise, we are being negligent as a church. We, the leaders and teachers of our day, have a responsibility to lead His people to the truth (Acts 20:27-31). Indeed, the shepherds of the church have an obligation to teach the truth of this issue, to the shame of those who do not submit themselves to the whole of Scripture (Titus 1:9).

One can hear of a "doctrine of the imminent return of Christ." Where are the Scriptures that convey that the next eschatological event (without anything else to precede it) is the rapture? There has been an exclusion of the whole counsel of God? When did imminent return start as a doctrine? Did Peter believe in the imminent return of Jesus to rapture him? Even before the prophecy was fulfilled of how Peter would die (John 21:18-19)? Did the disciples hold the imminent return of Jesus to rapture them, even before the fulfilled prophecy of 70 A.D?

Apocalyptic movies and literature are big business, and huge profits are earned on over-dramatizations and sensationalism that does not align with Scripture.[2] Many false claims have been made that promote a false sense of security, and many will find themselves unprepared for the trials that will certainly come. The church is to continue the testimony of Jesus, even in, and especially in, times of trial. The purpose of the rapture is to show the glory, sovereignty, power, care, and promises of God.

1 Thessalonians 4:17

This verse of Scripture has as its primary focus the comfort and encouragement toward its readers. The major concern is the resurrection of those who have already died in the Lord Jesus. The larger context is 1 Thessalonians 4:13, through 1 Thessalonians 5:11. The certainty of the return of Jesus is without debate.

The Thessalonians were in the midst of persecution and many of their fellow believers had died from various causes. The encouragement that Paul gives to the Thessalonians, by the word of the Lord, is that those who have died will come with Jesus when He returns. Indeed, they will precede those who are still alive. The Lord Himself will return from heaven with a shout, with the voice of an archangel, and with the trumpet of God. This return of Jesus will be sudden, as a thief in the night (1 Thessalonians 5:2). The return of Jesus will not be silent (there is a shout, a voice, and a trumpet). It will catch those living in darkness by surprise, but not the believers who are watching, who are sober and alert (1 Thessalonians 5:4-8).

In context, the dead in Christ will rise first, then, those believers who are still alive will join the resurrected believers who have been called out of their graves just ahead of them. Both will meet the Lord in the air and be with Him forever. The order is: return, resurrection, rapture, and reunion for eternity.[3] All other forms or inference must follow this order.

The word "rapture' is a transliteration from the Latin word, *"rapio."* The Greek word *"harpazo,"* used here, is translated "caught up" in most English translations. It means to take something forcefully (Kittle), with a force suddenly exercised (Vines). The word is often used to describe stealing with force. The Greek word *harpazo*, is used many other times in the New Testament. Each time this force is used, it is without any effort by that which is being taken. Philip is *caught away* from the Ethiopian eunuch (Acts 8:38). Paul is *caught up* to the third heaven (2 Corinthians 12:2-4). The Man-child is *caught up* to the throne of God (Revelation 12:5). In the passage discussed above, the believers, both the dead and those still alive, are *caught up* together to be with the Lord at His coming.

The particular purpose for this catching away is to remove believers before the events of the wrath of God. The wrath of God is associated with the day of the Lord. We are not appointed to wrath (1 Thessalonians 5:9). At issue here is what constitutes the wrath of God? All unbelievers are under the settled and abiding wrath of God by the very fact of not being in Christ (Ephesians 2:3). The day of the Lord will conclude time as we know it, with an eruption of wrath that will result in eternal judgement. Believers are not appointed to this wrath.

As far as the book of Revelation is concerned, the only part that is called the wrath of God are the seven bowls. This brings up a major issue. The *tribulation* is what the unbelieving world system, energized by Satan, perpetrates on the people of God as oppression, persecution, and death. *Wrath,* in contrast, is what God has against the sinful, unbelieving world system that will end in eternal punishment. Tribulation and wrath are not used interchangeably. We *are not* appointed to wrath. We *will have* tribulation (John 16:33; Acts 14:22; 1 Thessalonians 3:4; Revelation 1:9). Tribulation purifies the believer in their faith, while the same events will confirm the unbeliever in their unbelief.

What does 1 Thessalonians 4:17 have in common with other passages of Scripture concerning the return of Jesus? The trumpet (1 Thessalonians 4:16)! Jesus declares that when He returns, He will gather His elect from the whole earth with the *sound of a trumpet* (Matthew 24:30-31). Paul states that at the resurrection, not all shall be asleep. We shall be changed. Suddenly, in a moment, *at the last trumpet* the dead will be raised incorruptible, *and*, we shall be changed (1 Corinthians 15:51-52). This passage also mentions that this is a mystery (verse 51). In the book of Revelation, just before the *seventh trumpet, the last trumpet*, there is a mystery that will be finished (Revelation 10:7). Notice that it occurs when the angel is *about* to sound. This is important, as the seventh trumpet contains the seven bowls, which are the wrath of God (Revelation 15:1).

We are terribly amiss if we do not think the book of Revelation, with its focus and purpose on the final wrap-up of the decrees of God, does not contain in its narratives, a direct symbolic reference to the rapture of the saints. There are interpretations that insist that the rapture occurs between chapters 3 and 4. If this is true, and John represents the church, then he must represent the church throughout the book of Revelation. There are times after chapter 5 where John is on earth seeing visions of activities in heaven (as in Revelation 10:1).

There is inference to the rapture, or the exodus of the saints, from the 144,000 (the church militant) to the innumerable number of the church triumphant (Revelation 7). The two witnesses are called the two lampstands. Lampstands represent the church. They are called up (Revelation 11). The first of the two harvests is performed by the Son of Man (Revelation 14; Matthew 24:30-31). These are not three separate events. It is one event described three different ways.

Since God is perfect in wisdom and clear in His explanations, there can be no inconsistencies or contradictions in our interpretations. If we come to the book of Revelation with a subjective set of lenses, we will never see the whole truth. Some interpretations of the book of Revelation have the church being taken out between chapters 3 and 4. Others between chapters 5 and 6. There are, however, saints mentioned in other places after these chapters. Any saints that are in the midst of the seventieth week, of any ethnicity, are not going to hear or read the Word of God and conclude that they are experiencing the wrath of God. That would mean that the promise of 1 Thessalonians 5:9 did not apply to them! The book of Revelation is a symbolic book, so the event of the "catching up" will be symbolically represented (Revelation 1:1).

The timing of the Lord's return, and as such, the timing of the rapture, is indeed unknown. It cannot be known. It will not be known (Matthew 24:36; Acts 1:7). It is sudden, causes separation, and the timing is secret (Matthew 24:40-44). It is like a thief, but it is not silent (2 Peter 3:10). The unbelievers will not be ready, but we are called to be ready and looking up (Luke 21:28; Acts 1:11; Revelation 1:7). The rapture, the catching away of believers before the final judgements, will be an historical, complete, cosmic, decisive, and dramatic, one-time event (Matthew 24:31). It will include all believers.

The following table contains many passages (and my observations) that address the second coming of Jesus (see the end of Appendix D, Page 209-210). They are not exhaustive, but a sincere, thorough study will be greatly beneficial, immensely rewarding, and will especially be an aid in discernment. All human conclusions as to the return of Jesus can be wrong, but they cannot all be right. Scripture does not align with views that have multiple raptures, multiple comings, or multiple subsets of believers experiencing different realities concurrently. There is only one bride of Christ!

The biggest trigger for error concerning the rapture is the misunderstanding of chapter 20 of Revelation. It is often not understood within its context and the structure of the book as a whole (see Revelation 20 discussion). There are no survivors of God's wrath to populate another dispensation. Just as chapter 12 gives the origins and history before the narrative of the beasts, so chapter 20 contains the origins and history concerning the narrative of Satan's final judgement. Any view of the return of Jesus must satisfy all the Scriptural passages.

To be sure, we cannot be dogmatic where Scripture is silent (Revelation 22:18-19). But can we defend and hold as valid, convictions where alignment with Scripture is not possible? The enemy has sown a cynicism and neglect of the book of Revelation. There is division, and outright rejection of the book itself. The world is moving towards a judgement. There is a futility abounding in some worldviews that there is no cause and effect, no cosmic order, and no cosmic plan. The book of Revelation contains the encouragement that believers need to be able to overcome, persevere, and endure. It could be, that we will not fully want to understand the contents of the book of Revelation, until we fully realize how much we need it.

Revelation Ch. 14 - The Harvest

The following list of Bible passages are associated with the Second Coming of Jesus. Considering the different views that are held, what elements does each passage contain? Does the passage contain, or infer, the Second Coming? What does the passage reveal about the Second Coming of Jesus? Who does it affect? Where does it apply? Taking all the characteristics of these passages into consideration, how many times does Jesus return? Is there an order of events that all the Scripture passages suggest? Would there be any time-spans to consider if more than one return is needed? When do believers receive their glorified bodies?

Dan. 9:27

A prince will confirm a covenant. Broken in the middle. Spreading of abominations. Consummation - Desolator destroyed

Dan. 12:1-3

A time of trouble. People will be delivered. Written in the Book. Dead raised – to Life or judgement.
The wise will lead others to righteousness

Matt. 13:24-30, 36-43; 28:20

Kingdom of Heaven. Sower, field, sons of the King, sons of the Devil, Harvest at the end of the age.

Matt. 16:27

Son of Man - Angels - Rewards

Matt. 24:36-44

No one knows. Noah's flood. The day Noah entered the ark. Business as usual. One taken, one left. Unknown hour, unexpected by whom?

Matt. 25:31-46

Son of Man in glory -Angels with Him. Throne. All nations gathered. Separate the sheep from the goats. To punishment or Eternal life.

Luke 17:26-37

Noah - the day he entered. Lot – the day he left. Business as usual. Until the day/On the day. In that night - One taken, one left

Luke 21:25-28, 34-36

Signs. See the Son of Man - Look up. Lest the Day come upon you unexpectedly. Will come as a snare to all who dwell on the earth

Acts 1:9-11

While they *watched*. Received Him out of their *sight*. While they *looked*.

Stand *gazing* up. Will so come in like manner as you *saw* Him go.

1 Cor. 15:51-52

Mystery - Not all will sleep, but all be changed. In a moment. Twinkling of an eye. At the last trumpet. Dead raised, we shall be changed.

1 Thess. 4:15-17

Word of the Lord. Those alive will not proceed those asleep. Lord Himself ascends with a shout. Voice of an archangel. Trumpet of God. Dead in Christ rise first. Those alive caught up together with them (the dead). Meet the Lord in the air. Always with the Lord – comfort one another.

1 Thess. 5:1-11

Day of the Lord – thief in the night. "They" say – Peace and Safety - destruction, shall not escape. But "you" – not in darkness that this Day should overtake you. Light and day vs. night and darkness. You are not asleep. Watch and be sober. Those who sleep, and drunk at night. We are not appointed to wrath.

2 Thess. 2:1-8

Coming of Christ, gathered together. Not troubled. Falling away comes first. Man of lawlessness revealed before the day, claiming deity. Restrainer

taken out of the way. Works of Satan. Deception. They do not receive truth. Lawless one destroyed. God sends them delusion, to believe the lie, and are condemned.

2 Peter 3:1-13

Reminder – scoffers – the promise of His coming. Ancient world perished by flood, currently preserved for fire. God is patient – day as 1000 years, 1000 years as a day. Day of the Lord as a thief in the night. Noise, heat, burned up, dissolved. Holy conduct hastens the day. New heavens and new earth.

Rev. 1:7

Every eye will see Him, even those who rejected Him will mourn.

Rev. 10:5-7

Angel declares – time will be no longer. In the days of the sounding of the seventh angel's trumpet. When he is about to sound. Mystery of God would be finished. As declared to the prophets. (Rom. 11:25; 16:25-26; 1 Cor. 15:51-52; Eph. 1:9-10; 2:11-22; 3:1-3; 2 Thess. 2:7).

Rev. 22:12

He comes quickly, suddenly. Rewards of every person are with Him.

Appendix E

Israel

The identity and existence of Israel is one of the major subjects of the Bible that must be discussed in order to understand the book of Revelation. Dispensationalism has a more literal reading of the Old and New Testaments. The dispensationalist suggests that there are segments of God's plan as it pertains to different groups of people during different eras. The other end of the interpretive spectrum insists that the promises made in the Old Testament are transferred to a new and different group of elect people, displacing the previous group. This is often referred to as replacement theology. Replacement theology and covenant theology are not the same. Replacement theology could be seen as a form of anti-Semitism. In Jesus' judicial statements against the religious leaders of His day, He could possibly be accused of the same. He was not replacing Israel.

Election is the same in the Old Testament as it is in the New Testament. We must be careful not to identify a group of people as elect who do not come under the Biblical criteria for the elect. Election is God's prerogative. It is not hereditary. It is a sovereign act of God. God is the Savior and He never changes. Israel is elect, but not all Israel (Romans 9:6; 11:7). God's New Testament people are also called the elect (1 Peter 2:9; see Isaiah 43:20). *This appendix will be full of questions that must be satisfactorily answered.*

Does a literal reading of the Old Testament answer the question: Who is Israel? Is it based on being a descendant of Abraham (see following diagram, Page 212)? What about Ishmael, Esau, and the sons of Keturah? Is it based on the name, Israel? The northern kingdom, in all its errors, *was* called Israel. Is it included just because of the name? What about the southern kingdom being called Judah during the divided monarchy? Is it excluded because of a name? The narratives in the Bible suggest there were migrations of the faithful from all the northern tribes entering Judah before 722 B.C. The covenant with Abraham included all the nations being blessed (Genesis 12:3b; Galatians 3:8). As with the covenants with Isaac and Jacob (Genesis 26:4; 28:14). The truly faithful are known only to God and are invisible to us (Deuteronomy 10:12-17; Romans 4:11).

PHYSICAL DESCENDANTS OF ABRAHAM
(Abraham and Nahor – sons of Terah)

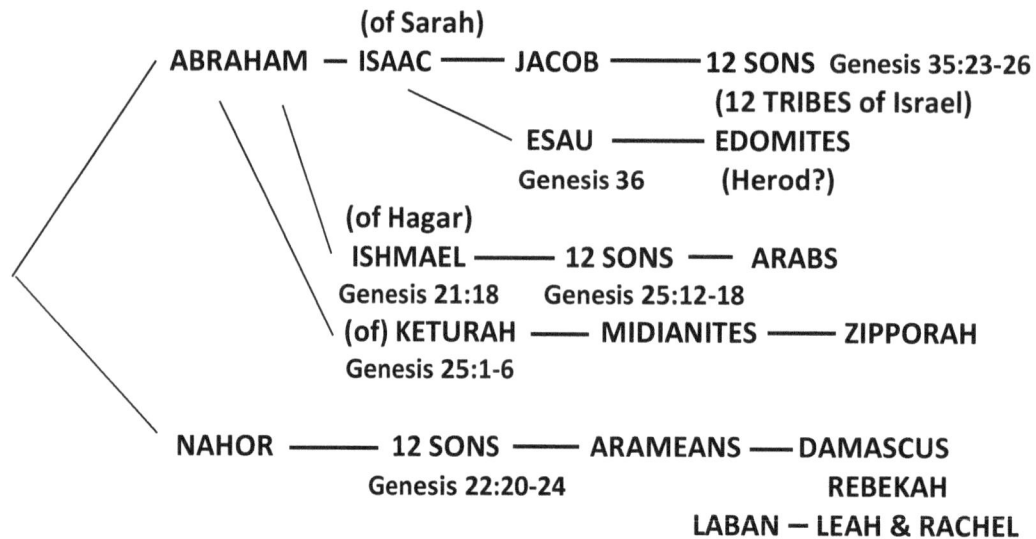

(of Sarah)
ABRAHAM — ISAAC —— JACOB ——— 12 SONS Genesis 35:23-26
                                    (12 TRIBES of Israel)
                        ESAU ——— EDOMITES
                     Genesis 36   (Herod?)
        (of Hagar)
        ISHMAEL ——— 12 SONS —— ARABS
     Genesis 21:18   Genesis 25:12-18
        (of) KETURAH —— MIDIANITES ——— ZIPPORAH
        Genesis 25:1-6

NAHOR ——— 12 SONS —— ARAMEANS — DAMASCUS
          Genesis 22:20-24   REBEKAH
                              LABAN — LEAH & RACHEL

Sons of Jacob – (Leah) – Reuben, Levi, Simeon, Judah, Issachar, Zebulun
  - (Rachel)- Joseph, Benjamin
  - (Bilhah, Rachel's maidservant) – Dan, Naphtali
  - (Zilpah, Leah's maidservant) – Gad, Asher

Sons of Joseph (of Asenath) – Manasseh, Ephraim   (Jacob adopts them as his own)
              Genesis 46:20   Genesis 48:5-6
                                                        (Become two of the twelve tribes)

If the argument is made according to the land promises, which land promises do we focus upon? If one takes all the land promises given to Abraham and his descendants, there must be something about them that is greater than the specifics given. There is not a consistent literal interpretation of the land promises that can be made (compare Genesis 15:18:21 and Genesis 17:8; Ezekiel 37:21-25). Did the land promises mean something more? Did Abraham or his descendants fully inherit the physical land? Did Abraham understand it in a greater dimension (Hebrews 11:8-10)? Did Jesus fulfill the land and peace promises as He did the ceremonial and sacrificial requirements? Were the literal fulfillments, in terms of actual physical boundaries, conditional for the people (Deuteronomy 28:63; Acts 2:36)? What does everlasting mean in each context of the land promises? Was the land a symbol of something greater?

How do they relate to the new heaven and the new earth?

This author does not intend to question that God gave promises to His people. Only that the complete picture be understood as to what they entail, and for how long. To be too literal is to invite a tangent that was never intended. To maintain calling a person or a group "chosen," just because they are called Jews, or to *always* directly associate Jews as being chosen just by being Jewish, goes against the contents of Scripture. There were Jews of Jesus' day who would not have been called "chosen" by Him (John 8:39-44). Similarly, in our day, being on the membership role of a church or religious institution, just because it is called a church, does not always provide security as being part of the elect.

There are dynamics of Israel in the Old Testament that need to be discussed in order to get a clearer understanding of just who the elect covenant people of God were, and still are. There are also questions about the Old Testament terminology used in the New Testament as applied to the church.

Sometimes it is wise to look objectively at both extremes and search for some answer that is in the center. Other times it may be advantageous to look for something that may have been missed altogether. Certainly, we must be allowed to respectfully ask questions where the obvious may be overlooked. Are there characteristics of God's election that are true to both Testaments?

Is it in God's perfect and ordered nature to have multiple subsets of elect and chosen people? Is there only one group of covenant people, consisting of the militant and the triumphant? How do we get into error by being too literalistic, or too spiritual? Are we humble enough that God can allow us to see the veracity of the whole subject? Are we able, with our predispositions to hold with one view only, to let our understanding be molded by a continual searching of the whole counsel of God? Can we stay in that tension between holding a strong conviction, and studying to show ourselves approved? Can we allow ourselves to come out from behind a definition or a system that the Bible does not give?

The truth of this matter must be understood both theologically and historically. Theological in the sense that we know God has sovereignly ordered it. Historical in the sense that He is seen working within the historical narratives given in the Bible. Since God is perfect in wisdom, and clear in His communication, there can be no inconsistencies in our interpretation. It is only our understanding that needs to remain humble and malleable. This author would like to suggest a dynamic, and maybe a solution. The idea of "the Remnant pattern."

First, we need to define our terms. The term Israel first appears when Jacob's name is changed (Genesis 32:28; 35:9-15). This name change was made by God Himself. God changed Jacob's name, not his family ancestry, and not his ethnicity. The name change was a continuation of the plan of God to bring forth a Redeemer and redemption through a people. The name change was part of the covenant process. The name Israel means to strive with God, or, ruling with God.[1] Did God make covenants with a national, geo-political nation of people, or a covenant-keeping, spiritually-minded community of people? There *were* those who *continually* rejected the theocracy God was establishing.

Israel is the name given to the covenant community of God. It was

not an ethnic designation. Israel is more inclusive than just Jews. Jew is a term that is often used too broadly. (Note: Israel is a sacral term that is used for the totality of God's elect people. It is the name of the people chosen by God).[2] The term Israel, as the elect, is also exclusive. Many are called, but few are chosen (Matthew 20:16; 22:14; 2 Peter 1:10). There are many times that interpreters use the term Jew when discussing Israel. Jew is used of people who practice a specific religious confession, irrespective of their national allegiance or residence. It can also define an inhabitant of the province of Judah. The terms Israel and Jew are not always interchangeable in Scripture. We need to be careful when we do the same. Is Abraham a Jew? How?

As the term appears in the Bible, Israel as the name to describe a specific, particular, ethnic group of people is only one use of the term. We are too narrow if we intend to limit it to an ethnic use only. Israel as a title, establishes the status of God's elect. The term Jew is established by ceremonial practice, or land of residence or ancestry.

We know from Scripture that to be part of the elect is to be of the faith of

Abraham (Galatians 3:5-9). Abraham's faith is the focus of the inclusion. The just will live by Faith (Habakkuk 2:4; Romans 1:17; Galatians 3:11; Hebrews 10:38). Abraham was the grandfather of Jacob, through Isaac. Isaac was the child of promise. Do we see Abraham as belonging to the people of faith, called Israel, even though the name Israel was given to his grandson? There are some who forget when the name change occurred.[3] If Abraham is part of Israel, then we must admit that there is a broader dynamic to the term Israel. Just as Abraham's faith justified him before the giving of the Law, so Abraham's faith came before the naming of the community of faith called Israel. Is Abraham part of Israel? How?

Being a part of Israel is not always about being a physical descendant of Abraham. There were many physical descendants of Abraham who were not part of the covenant people of God. Ishmael had twelve sons who were to become twelve tribes (Genesis 25:12-18). Abraham married Keturah, of whom the Midianites came (Genesis 25:1-6). Isaac had a second son, Esau, of whom the Edomites were descendants (Genesis 36). The Jewish leaders of Jesus' day could claim to be physical descendants of Abraham, but they were not of the faith of Abraham (John 8:37-44). Ethnicity, or physical heritage, is not the requirement for being part of Abrahams family by faith. Ethnicity is not the requirement for being part of Israel, the people of faith, and the faith of Abraham.

There is a case for ethnic Israel as a particular nation in the Old Testament. But even within the particular nation there is a distinction between the group as a whole, and the ones within that group who hear God's personal call of faith in their life. In the Old Testament, there are two Hebrew words translated assembly, or congregation. The Hebrew words are *edah* and *quhal*. You could be part of the *edah*, but not part of the *quhal*. You could be part of the larger group, but not part of the smaller, distinct, group of the spiritually faithful. It is the word *quhal* that is often translated church (*ecclesia*) in the LXX. The Greek word for church, (*ecclesia*), is a neutral term for a specific group called out of another group. Thus, in the Old Testament, there were situations where a specific group of people were called out of the larger group because of a specific call of God.

Jesus said that He was going to build His church, the called-out ones (*ecclesia*), from both the Jews *and* the Gentiles. (Note: no one is ever called out of Israel.) His calling would be based on the confession of His Messiahship, of which both Jews and Gentiles would need to confess (Galatians 3:28-29). There may also be a too broad an emphasis on the word church. There are other instances where the Greek word *ecclesia* is used to convey other groups of "called out ones" (Acts 7:38; 19:32). That is why Jesus uses the possessive "my" church. This is what the Apostle Paul is addressing when he says that not all Israel is Israel (Romans 9:6-8). Jesus, when addressing Nathaniel, declares that Nathaniel is indeed (truly) an Israelite, with no deceit (John 1:47). Not all the children of ethnic Israel (Jacob) are the ones who, by faith, answer the call of God. Not all are looking for and will put their trust in the real Child of promise, the Messiah (John 8:33-40). The same idea is meant when Paul uses the phrase "Israel of God" in Galatians (Galatians 6:15-16). This phrase assumes there is an Israel that is "not of God."

This is true for the churches of Revelation as well as the churches of today (Revelation 2-3). When the seven churches are seen as a group, there are only two that have nothing negative said about them. When you look at the individual churches, you come away with the impression that there is definitely a minority of the faithful within each. It is the difference between what is seen by Man, and what is known by God (1 Samuel 16:7; 2 Timothy 2:19).

Being a part of the particular nation of Israel was never about being a direct descendant of Abraham, Isaac, or Jacob. There are many times that the Old Testament narrative mentions the difference between the native born, and the stranger among you (Exodus 12:19, 49; Leviticus 16:29; 18:26; 19:33-34; 24:16-22; 25:23; Numbers 9:14; 15:14-30; Deuteronomy 1:16; 10:12-22; Joshua 20:9; Ezekiel 47:21-23). The strangers, or aliens among you, were those who had attached themselves to the nation of Israel because of their faith in the One true God. These strangers, or sojourners, were required to follow all the civil, moral, and ceremonial laws as if they had belonged to the nation from the beginning. In the Old Testament administration that God ordained, a person not of Hebrew descent who attached themselves to the system of religious worship and belief of Israel, became a member of that people group. Did they become a legitimate member of the covenant community? Yes! With all the covenants, services, and the blessings. Then, if the fulfillment of Israel's faith was belief in Messiah Jesus, then becoming a Christian is entering into the covenant membership of Israel, by being in Christ (Messiah) Jesus (Galatians 3:29; 4:28; Ephesians 1:10; 2:11-13).

The native born, physical descendants of Abraham, were to treat the strangers among them as if they were their own relatives by birth. The gentiles, God-fearers, and "aliens among you," became inheritors of the promises given to the nation as a whole. Some notable people who were part of Israel but not descendants of Abraham were, Caleb, Tamar, Ruth, Uriah, Rahab, and the Rechabites (for the Rechabites, see Jeremiah 35:2-19). These are just a few cases of the many people who were part of the constituted nation of Israel.

The term Israel is used of the United Kingdom under David during the monarchy. When the kingdom was divided after the death of Solomon, the northern kingdom took the name of Israel. The southern kingdom took the name of Judah, after their largest tribe. The northern kingdom was often called Ephraim, after their largest tribe (as in Hosea, also see discussion of Revelation 7). The northern kingdom never had a king who followed God. The northern kingdom of Israel was overtaken and re-peopled by the Assyrians. The southern kingdom of Judah was taken captive into Babylon for 70 years. When the people returned from Babylon, they were called by the name Israel. This was used until the fall of Jerusalem in A.D. 70. Even the use of the name Israel as a national name did not reflect its intended meaning. It is true, in large part, even today.

This brings us to the Remnant pattern. Think of the remnant as a minority. (Most often they were.) As we look across the historical narrative of Scripture there is something that God does again and again. He leaves, or purges, or trims away by judgement, the many who choose to not follow His commands and precepts, and gives favor to the few who do. From the many, He chooses by design a faithful remnant to continue His purposes. (In fact, God only needs one person to continue His plans and keep His promises: as with Moses (see

218 | P a g e

Exodus 32:10) and Joash (2 Kings 11:1-3))

At the beginning of creation God had told Adam and Eve to go forth and multiply and subdue the Earth. The first murder occurs, and God uses Seth to continue the line of faith. The world becomes corrupt, and God chooses Noah, a man who has favor in the sight of God, to survive the Flood. Out of the Chaldees, God chooses Abram to follow Him by faith. Of all of Abraham's descendants, God chooses to do a miracle and bring forth a child of promise, Isaac. Of Isaac's two sons, God chooses the younger, Jacob, to continue His plan. Jacob produces the 12 sons who will become the 12 tribes of Israel (Genesis 35:23-26).

The 12 tribes find themselves captive in Egypt until the time of Moses. During the wilderness wanderings, there is pruning and testing. Most of the people who were taken out of Egypt die in the wilderness except for two, Joshua and Caleb. They were great men of great faith. During the times of the kings, God chooses David and proclaims a royal dynasty that will endure for eternity. After many years of sin and warning the people of Israel are taken into captivity, with only a remnant who would return to the land (see Ezra and Nehemiah). Many who

had built homes and businesses in Babylon chose to stay in Babylon.

During the time of Christ, the nation had grown again to a large population. At that time, we also find included those called God-fearers and proselytes (Acts 2:5-11). Again, most of the nation comes under judgement for rejecting the Messiah Jesus (John 1:11-13). It is at this point that Jesus issues some very judicial statements concerning the consequences for their rejection (Matthew 8:11-12; 21:43-45; 23:37-39; Luke 19:41-44). Some of the condemnation given by Jesus was initiated by their own words: "We have no king but Cesar" (John 19:15). We will not have this man rule over us (Luke 19:14). "His (Jesus) blood be on our heads, and on our children" (Matthew 27:25). Paul may have been speaking of the siege of Jerusalem in his reference to the wrath of God (1 Thessalonians 2:14-16).

Once again, God uses a minority, a remnant, to continue His plan and purpose. That remnant this time, is known as the disciples. A remnant of the particular people of God becomes the Spirit-filled body of Christ (The Messiah). God has constantly and consistently narrowed the covenant people of God to those who have faith in Him, and in Jesus as Savior and

Messiah. He is still doing just that. The covenant people of God are always those who "had ears and could hear." This phrase is used in the four Gospels, and also used in the letters to the seven churches (Matthew 13; Revelation 2-3).

Why does it seem strange to see the early believers as that continuing remnant pattern? There is progressive realization, restoration, and increase, of a minority people of faith that God continues to work with and work through. Where *do* the disciples fit in? They are definitely Jewish, and yet are the foundation of the New Testament church. The first century church was foundationally populated by converts from Judaism. When did the church go from Jewish converts to Gentile converts? The church has always been about Gentiles being grafted into an olive tree, of being brought near from being "far off," of another sheepfold, and added to the commonwealth of Israel. Do Jews converted today leave Israel? No. But they leave Judaism and are "called out."

Dispensationalism models that set aside one group of elect people for another, separate group of elect people does not allow for the obvious overlap of people groups like the early disciples. Who will be taken when Jesus returns? Believing Jews *and* believing Gentiles. Who will be left to endure the wrath of God? Unbelieving Jews *and* unbelieving Gentiles. Holding dispensationalism too strongly will limit the ability to see the big picture. To create sub-sets of covenant people goes against the Scriptural commands to seek unity and oneness. There is no Jew or Greek, no slave or free, no distinction of people who are in Christ. God is all and in all.

What do you do with all the saints and people of faith before the time of Jacob? Hebrews chapter 11 declares that we are part of the unity that is observed by the great cloud of witnesses. Hebrews chapter 11 cannot be broken up, and it is not given in a dispensational mode. This faith community is from the time of Creation to the present. It includes those who would receive and read the book of Hebrews. It is not complete without us (Hebrews 11:40). How do we define the commonwealth of Israel if it does not include all those who have gone before Christ? This commonwealth also includes all who were once far off and have been brought near and are now in Christ (Ephesians 2:11-13). Again, Paul talks of the people of Israel, his brethren, in terms of the fathers and the promises. Some of those fathers and promises were before the name change of Jacob (Romans 9:1-5). The criteria for being included into the covenant people of God is the same for the Old Testament and the New Testament. It is circumcision of the heart (Deuteronomy 10:16; 30:6; Romans 2:29). The faith of Abraham (Genesis 15:6; Galatians 3:5-9). It is the prescribed pattern and way of approaching God, whether it be the Tabernacle, the Temple, or Jesus Christ (Deuteronomy 12:5-7; John 14;6; Hebrews 8:1-6). From external to internal. Gentiles, those not from the physical descent of the Patriarchs are included into Israel in both Testaments. Paul, using an illustration from the Old Testament, asserts this unity when he talks about "our fathers" in the wilderness (1 Corinthians 10:1-13, see Numbers 10-13). Paul is including his believing Gentile audience as having the "our fathers" in the wilderness.

What is the problem with *all* the people of faith in Yahweh inheriting *all* the promises of that faith? Israel was challenged to become a nation of priests (Exodus 19:5-6). This was not for their benefit, as an end in itself. They were to be the priests to the nations, for the benefit of the nations, to bring them to God. They refused out of fear (Exodus 20:18-21). This gives greater emphasis to the way Peter uses it of the church (1 Peter 2:9-10). Jesus chastised them for not keeping the temple as a house for the nations (Isaiah 56:7; Mark 11:17). The spiritual people of Israel are not set aside. The people who walked in unbelief have set themselves aside (Acts 13:46). God is only doing what He has always done in using a minority of the faithful in continuing to build the community of faith. The faithful, in Christ, are added to the covenant community. The unbelievers are cut off.

We find a whole new dynamic when the New Testament when we remember that the word "Christ" is the Greek translation of the Hebrew word "Messiah." To be in Christ is to be in The Messiah. When we read the New Testament, knowing that we are in The Messiah will have a strong implication for being included in the covenant people of God, namely Israel. This inclusion is by faith alone, in the Messiah alone.

The Old Testament did not see the church as we usually perceive it. It is not separate and distinct from the Old Testament faithful. But it did see the

Gentiles coming to faith, being included, and being brought near. The earliest members of the church were made up of those who practiced Judaism. The first gentiles became believers in Messiah by accident, without the Apostles having really planned it (Acts 11:19-21). (Cornelius was a God-fearer (Acts 10:1-3).) The Jerusalem council was not convened to decide what to do with Jewish believers coming to faith in a gentile church, but, gentile believers coming to faith in a Jewish Messiah and His church. The restrictions were in order that the Jewish believers would not be offended (Acts 15:19-20). In the Old and New Testaments, it was always a case of gentiles being added into the covenant community. The church is the "called out ones." Called out of the world? Eventually. At first, they were the *called-out ones* from the ethnic nation of Israel. The New Testament story is not about the Old Testament Messianic community being displaced by a different community. It is about God taking a faithful remnant and adding to it through Jesus (John 1:11-12). When Jesus spoke of building His church, He was stating that He would bring together those called out of the Jews and the Gentiles, not a distinct new group devoid of a remnant of Jews who would believe.

The wild branches, the non-Jewish believers, are grafted into the olive tree (Romans 11:17-18). The ones cut off, Jewish by faith, can be grafted back into the tree (Romans 11:23-24), but only after professing faith in the Messiah. The two, gentiles and Jews, become one new man (Ephesians 2:14-22). The two flocks will become one flock, with one Shepherd (John 10:14-16). What is the olive tree called? What is the new man called? What is the one flock called? It is the covenant community of Jewish and Gentile believers, members together of one body, who have put their hope and trust in Jesus (Ephesians 4:4-6) They follow the commandments of God and hold the Testimony of Jesus (Revelation 1:2, 9; 6:9; 12:11, 17; 19:10). The Temple of God now consists of both Jews and Gentiles who are one in Christ (2 Corinthians 6:14-18; Ephesians 2:17-22; 1 Peter 2:5-10; all with Old Testament references). Jesus prayed for this (John 17:17-23). The book of Hebrews states the unity of the complete faith community (Hebrews 11:39-40).

When Paul speaks that all Israel will be saved, he is not speaking of the physical descendants of Abraham in a strict sense (Romans 11:26a). He is talking about all who will be of the covenant community of faith. The context does not allow for just the physical descendants of Abraham, Isaac, and Jacob. Paul had just written about the unbelief of his brethren. He addresses the wild branches, the Gentiles, as being grafted into the olive tree, Israel. He makes much of the humility that is needed to understand that it is because of unbelief that the cultivated branches, the ethnic Israelites, have been cut off. It is unbelief that can also cut *them* off, and that the cultivated branches can be grafted back into the tree if they believe. The tree is the common denominator. It represents the covenant people of God. The olive tree represents Israel. The true, believing Israel.

Paul speaks of a mystery (Romans 11:25). This is the same mystery that he writes about in other places (Ephesians 3:1-9). This mystery is the stewardship Paul has been given in bringing the Gospel to the Gentiles. The Gentiles have been brought near and included into the Commonwealth of Israel, the olive tree. Most Gentile churches need much humility in this regard. So, blindness has happened in part to Israel, that is, a portion of ethnic Israel is in unbelief. This blindness is until the fullness of the Gentiles has come in. Come into what? The olive tree, the one flock, the one new man, and the one body. The Gentiles, believing Gentiles only, are to come into the covenant community of the faithful. The covenant community has as its foundation the Apostles and Prophets of the early church, with Jesus Christ as the cornerstone (Ephesians 2:19-22). The Old Testament references that Paul uses at the beginning of this section in Romans 9-11, has as its context the idea of the Gentiles becoming part of the people of God and added to a remnant (Isaiah 10:22-23; Hosea 1:9-10). These become one. The ultimate restoration of Israel to God, the *all Israel*, includes Gentile believers. All Israel in the Old Testament also included non-ethnic members. Israel, like the church of the New Testament, is a divine institution. Israel was God's initiative. The church was Christ's initiative (Matthew 16:18).

There are metaphors that are common to the Old and New Testaments concerning the community of faith. You will find the bride and wife, with a husband and a bridegroom. You will find the vinedresser and the vine, the shepherd and the flock, the king and the kingdom, used of both Israel and the church. Both are ordained, established, sustained, and grown by God (John 6:44). Both are part of the process of God establishing a people for His very own. Both have external, internal, and invisible dynamics. The truly faithful are known only to God, and not by external attachment. They are known by spiritual union, which is invisible. The church is a continuation of the covenant that was given to Abraham, that all the peoples of the earth would be blessed (Genesis 12:3; Galatians 3:8-9). The Gentiles being added to the community of faith is fulfillment of that covenant. This addition was without the barrier of ethnic heritage (Ephesians 2:14).

This has great implications for understanding the narrative of the book of Revelation. The letters to the seven churches have as their teaching devices lessons from mistakes made by the Old Testament communities. They are given right from an Old Testament context. They are still very relevant for today. There is a strong sense that the faithful within the seven churches is a minority.

The majority of uses of the term Jews in the New Testament is in a negative context as it relates to the newly birthed church (Acts 13:44-47). This was true as well for their response to Jesus (John 8). In two of the churches it was a Jewish contingent that provided antagonism to the early believers (Revelation 2:9; 3:9). They, the Jews, will know that God loves the church (Deuteronomy 7:6-7; see also Isaiah 60:14).

The list of 12 tribes mentioned omits those tribes that led others into idol worship (Revelation 7). Idolatry is the major subject of warning in the book of Revelation. The two witnesses are based on real Old Testament people. It is the signs they use and not the actual people. The two witnesses act as a group, and, are called the two lampstands (Revelation 11:4). There are several times where saints are mentioned or strongly inferred. The saints in the midst of the events of Revelation will not read or hear the text of the book and conclude that they are experiencing the wrath of God. We, the saints, are not appointed unto wrath. God's word is true for all times, for all history, for all people. There is no place in the book of Revelation where the terms Israel and Jew can always be interchanged. There is no place in the book of Revelation where we can always assume, or add, the terms where they are not used in the text.

In the new heaven and the new earth, John sees the new Jerusalem, coming down out of heaven (Revelation 21-22). The New Jerusalem is described in combined Old and New Testament language, as a completed structure. Both tribes and apostles. The gates and entrances into the New Jerusalem are the twelve tribes of Israel (Revelation 21:12). The foundations of the city have the names of the twelve apostles of the Lamb (Revelation 21:14). The New Jerusalem is described as a combination of Old and New Testament people.

Understanding Revelation is *more* about correct theology than solving the details. We will never solve the details divorced from a correct theology. The details are important in making application. Revelation, as the capstone of God's complete revelation, makes much use of the whole counsel of God.

We cannot have a correct theological interpretation of the Scriptures without knowing the historical background and narratives. We cannot make sense of the historical narratives without a grasp of what God is doing in His big picture.

Appendix F

The Theology of Revelation

Theology is the study and knowledge of God. The book of Revelation contains much-needed input to add to our theology. The book of Revelation is the truth about God and the truth of God. And it is, by the book's own testimony, a truth worth dying for. We must know the theology that the book of Revelation contains, not just certain details of the last days.

It has been said that everyone has a theology. Some are good, and some are bad. Most people in the world have a theology that is based on deceptive religious counterfeits. (There are many things of God that Satan has pre-empted and counterfeited.) In the Christian context, it is probably best to maintain that we have, at best, an incomplete theology. Our theology will dictate our worldview and drive our behavior, or lack of right behavior. There is only one objective place that we can gain the knowledge that God intended us to have. That source is the Bible. In the current time of this writing, there is much concern over the increase of Biblical illiteracy and the lack of good theology. Many research groups have various data to confirm this. Too many

people are lethargic in their church attendance and their personal Bible study. Too many churches do not proclaim the truths of Scripture regularly. It is impossible to attain the knowledge that we need only from 30-45 minutes per week. Nonetheless, we are not released from the personal responsibility.

If one looks at the church calendar year the vast majority of resources, by percentage, are spent promoting, decorating, and celebrating the Christmas season. So, as a result, the unchurched, or nominal attenders, go away with a picture of Jesus as a baby in a manger. The book of Revelation touches on the Nativity with just an inference. The focus of Revelation is the ascension and exaltation of Christ. The early church met to celebrate the resurrection, exaltation, and certain return of Jesus in power and authority. The book of Revelation is all about the risen, glorified, authoritative Christ, who comes in judgement and eternal rule as *the* King. It is, after all, the Revelation of Jesus Christ as He is *now*.

At issue here is the increasing neglect of the Bible as the Word of God and, in particular, the need for the book of Revelation. Our theology is not, and never will be, complete without the contents of the book of Revelation. Theology must come first. The search and discovery of the details of Jesus' return cannot displace this priority. So much focus on the details of the book of Revelation are out of balance and cause division because a correct theology is missing. The details are important, but not at the expense of a good theology. The demons have a correct theology, but it does not help them (James 2:19). To be balanced, we must not consider theology to be the ultimate goal without the practical outworking of our faith. This balance is shown in the book of Revelation.

Jesus prayed that we would be sanctified by the truth, and that God's word is truth (John 17:14-17). We have a revealed truth. We have general revelation in creation. In the beginning, God said (Genesis 1). We then have special revelation. He has spoken to us through the prophets, and in these last days through His Son (Hebrews 1). We also have God's personal revelation in Jesus, the Word of God. We would not know this truth had God not given it to us. Our faith is not an invention thought up by man. It has always been God who initiated and sustained the relationships of faith (Genesis 12:1-3; Ephesians 1:13). Our trust in the history of that

revelation, from Genesis to Revelation, is what the Scriptures demand.

The book of Revelation is part of that truth. The Revelation is the only part of the cannon of Scripture that maintains and promises a blessing for reading and hearing it, both at the start and at the end. The Revelation was included from the beginning into the cannon of Scripture when other books were challenged. The Revelation completes the cannon of Scripture. The book of Revelation gives us some revelation that the rest of Scripture does not contain. The Revelation is like a capstone course that brings forward everything else we know from Scripture, ties them all together, and carries the narrative into eternity. The Revelation brings illumination to us about the mysteries of our faith. The book of Revelation brings the ultimate encouragement, or the ultimate warning, to each and every being in all of history. We must treat the book of Revelation with the same respect and humility that any other part of Scripture deserves (Isaiah 66:2; Revelation 22:18-19).

Showing verses and giving references is more than for the sake of statistics. It shows the consistency and uniformity of the scope of Scripture, especially for the message of the book of Revelation. What follows is not intended to be an attempt at systematizing a theology, but a treatise of information that we need to consider and test for good theology. Each of the following sections deals with areas of theology as it is contained in the book of Revelation. They are not exhaustive by any measure.

First and foremost, we must keep in mind that the book of Revelation was a letter. It was written to real people who had real issues. The book of Revelation was given by God, to the risen Christ Himself (Revelation 1:1-8). It is a letter written to the believers as a letter to be distributed to all the churches. The blessings and responsibilities to read and hear are explained to the reader (Revelation 1:3; 22:7). It was not written in the same way as other New Testament books are written, but that does not dismiss us from doing the work to understand it. In fact, it takes more work because we are not familiar with the keys for understanding apocalyptic literature.

The book of Revelation was also given in symbolism. This symbolism ties the Old Testament and New Testament together. It claims to be a prophecy given by God of what is and what will be. It claims a favor to those who keep the Word of God and have the testimony of Jesus (Revelation 1:9; 12:17; 19:10). It was given for us to understand.

The book of Revelation asserts God as the Creator of all that we can see and know (Revelation 4:11; 10:6). God as the Creator, has the authority to hold His created beings accountable for every thought, word, and deed that we have ever had, said, and done. God as the Creator, who created and sustains everything, has the right to conclude what He has decreed. This same truth is given by John and Paul (John 1:1-3; Colossians 1:15-17). In God's sovereignty as Creator, He chooses to inform us of His decrees (Amos 3:7; Revelation 1:1). God as Creator, preserves and protects (Revelation 7:2-3; 9:4). He is distinct, but not distant. God is involved in all that occurs throughout the book of Revelation (God's throne is mentioned over 30 times). God is sovereign ("it was given," is mentioned over 20 times).

The book of Revelation has an extremely high Christology and asserts the deity of Jesus Christ (John 10:31-33). There is no doubt about how the Jews received the statement,

"I and my Father are one" (John 10:30). Jesus as the Lamb, is given equal description, titles, and authority with God the Father (Compare Isaiah 41:4; 44:6, with Revelation 1:8, 17; 21:6; 22:13). John hears a voice from the throne who identifies Himself as God (Revelation 1:8-11). The One on the throne declares that He is the Alpha and Omega (Isaiah 41:4; 44:6; 48:12; Revelation 1:8; 22:13) In Revelation 22:13 this title is claimed by Jesus Christ, revealing His deity and identity as God. The Father and the Son are on the same throne (Revelation 3:21; 4:6). God and the Lamb are worshipped together as Savior (Isaiah 43:3, 11; Revelation 5:5-13; 7:9-10). God and the Lamb are associated together (Revelation 14:4; 21:22; 22:1-3).

When reading the book of Revelation, there are an infinite of number of instances where the One on the throne and the Lamb are working as One. Even the scene where the scroll is taken from the One on the throne conveys a picture of an equal authority (Revelation 5). The Lamb, the symbol of the sacrifice, is unique because He is the God-man. He is the transcendent One, fully God and fully man, and not of creation (Revelation 5:3). God and the Lamb are both seen as the Shepherd who lead their people to living water (Isaiah 55:1; Revelation 7:17).

The book of Revelation powerfully reminds us about the Person and work of the Holy Spirit. The Holy Spirit is often neglected in our pragmatic propensity to do things. Without the Holy Spirit, there is no power in the church (2 Timothy 3:5). One could spend an unending amount of time studying the work and dependence on the Holy Spirit as it pertains to the book of Revelation. The Holy Spirit mediates the activity of Christ, declares Christ's word, is involved with the prayers, inspires missionary witness, and speaks through the prophets. The Holy Spirit does, and is doing, exactly what Jesus stated He would do (John 16:8-11). The Holy Spirit is wholly involved in the book of Revelation, as a revelation about Jesus (John 16:14-15).

The book of Revelation completes our theology as it relates to the Gospel. The Gospel is much more than something we just accept to get salvation, as important as that is. We are saved, being saved, and will be saved. There is a past, present, and eternal dimension to our salvation. It started in the mind of God before the foundation of the world (Matthew

25:34; Revelation 13:8). It was given moments after the Fall (Genesis 3:15). The Gospel is carried and proclaimed throughout the narrative of the Bible and will continue to be the testimony of the saved until the end (John 5:39; 1 Corinthians 15:3; Revelation 19:10).

The book of Revelation defines many of the historical connections that are assumed in the rest of the Bible. Evil can be defined as "the violation of purpose."[1] Therefore, anything that is not ordained of God, and does not fulfill His intended purpose as given through Scripture, comes under the umbrella of evil, no matter how insignificant we may consider it. The foremost concept and root of evil is shown to be idolatry, an illicit spiritual relationship or union other than with God. This is why the Bible often uses the harlot and adultery metaphors to describe many nations, including Israel. For the believer, the sin and evil that is committed is covered by the sacrifice of Jesus. The judgement that we would incur for our sin is dealt with on the cross. Those who do not accept God's only way of salvation and forgiveness are left to answer for themselves to a God who has reached out to them. He has done all the work, and only asks us to believe Him. Mankind is continually seeking to

make their own way. The ultimate evil is turning from a loving God, who has provided the only way to assuage His perfect and holy standard. Mankind is continually seeking to provide for ourselves any means for preservation. This is called idolatry. Idolatry is any marginalization, displacement, or rejection of God of His rightful place as Creator and Lord. The book of Revelation shows us how far, and to what extent, mankind will go in this rejection (Revelation 16:9, 11, 21). Evil and its' source is unmasked, identified, and judged in the book of Revelation

At the foundation of this rejection is the lie that was birthed at the Fall. Satan, the arch enemy of man, to maintain his position has deceived and is deceiving the world into self-exaltation. The book of Revelation gives us the whole existence of Satan, from his sin of pride to his eternal demise. The book of Revelation also narrates for us his rule of the world from the time of his expulsion from heaven, until his being cast into the eternal punishment prepared for him and his demons (Matthew 25:41). The book of Revelation tells us of the extent of Satan's influence and activities (Revelation 12-13; 18:11-

13). Satan is exposed for who he has been, and who he currently is.

One of the many allusions to the Old Testament concerns the Exodus. The theme of the captivity, persecution, redemption, and the deliverance of God's people is the common message in the worship passages of the Revelation. The Exodus becomes a "type" from the Old Testament that is fulfilled in a global and cosmic "exodus" at the end times.

The book of Revelation speaks about tribulation without any apology. Tribulation is what the worldly system imposes on the followers of Jesus. Jesus said that in this world we would have tribulation (John 16:33). In that context, he also said that He had overcome the world. That was even before His crucifixion. Jesus said that the world hated Him, so the world will also hate those who follow Him. Paul was grateful to have shared in Christ's sufferings (Philippians 3:7-11). There are many interpretations that have certain subsets of believers who are not to endure the great tribulation. But there are saints within the narrative of the Revelation who do indeed experience the events that unfold (Revelation 1:9; 2:10; 6:11; 11:7; 12:17; 13:15; 16:6; 20:4). Our theology must include these saints

without compromising the whole of Scripture. The saints mentioned throughout the book of Revelation are still members of the elect. This must mean that they would have the same salvation, protection, provision, and purpose, that all saints are promised. These promises are valid for believers in the past, those in the present, as well as those in the future. There is a global persecution and tribulation of the saints portrayed in the book of Revelation. Persecution and tribulation are experienced in particular and pocketed locations in the world even today. In all cases, suffering for Jesus' is the path to victory (Revelation 12:11). Prophetic proclamation, followed by death and resurrection (Revelation 11:7-12).

We must be careful not to interpret the Revelation in our own limited context for our own comfort. Some interpretations maintain that believers are not appointed unto wrath, and therefore, will not be present for the great tribulation. If that is true, what about people who would be saved after the rapture? If the Holy Spirit is removed when the church is taken, what about those who believe and receive the Holy Spirit as a guarantee after the rapture?

The book of Revelation portrays to us the Day of the Lord, His judgement, and eternity. There is an eternality to God's judgements. Just as paradise will be the believers' eternal presence with God, hell will be the eternal separation from God for the unrepentant. Those who follow the Lamb will be with God, and He will be with them (Revelation 21:3-4). Those who rejected the Lamb, His sacrifice, and trusted in the work of their own hands (idolatry) and a salvation of their own making, will also experience an eternal existence (Revelation 14:9-11). This judgement will be based on what was known and rejected at the time of death (Luke 12:47-48; Hebrews 9:27). Judgement is based on the knowledge and responsibility given (Isaiah 14:12-15; Ezekiel 28:13-19). (That is why Satan cannot be redeemed.) Judgement will also be based on what evil the unbelievers have committed against the people of God (Hebrews 10:26-31; Revelation 16:5-6; 17:6; 19:2).

The judgements of God are based on His wrath against sin. We must reconcile the love of God with the justice of God. This is where the centrality of the Lamb is important. Throughout the book of Revelation, the Lamb is the symbol of God's dealing with sin. To reject God's provision of the Lamb as the payment for sin is to reject God Himself. For the Lamb is God Himself. To reject the Son is to reject the Father (Matthew 10:40; John 5:23). The Lamb is God in the flesh (2 John 1:7). The Lamb is the watershed for the payment of sin (Revelation 7:16-17). The Old Testament saints looked forward to the cross, and the New Testament proclaims and looks back to the cross. It is the Lamb who is worshipped with the One on the throne (Revelation 5:13). The Lamb is associated with the wrath of God (Revelation 7:17). It is the Lamb who treads the winepress of the wrath of God (Revelation 14:19-20; 19:15). There are some who see the judgements of God as harsh. This reveals a deficiency in knowing the holiness of God, and to what lengths He has gone to redeem His creation.

For the redeemed, the Lord God Almighty and the Lamb will be their eternal dwelling place and their eternal light. God will be all, and in all (1 Corinthians 15:28). The saints are made royalty (Revelation 1:6; 5:10). They will participate in the reign and rule of the Messiah (Daniel 7:27; Revelation 3:21; 22:5). This is the solution for the different translations of Daniel 7, verse 27. It is a shared rule. We will be like Him (1 John 3:2). We shall even rule over the angels (1 Corinthians 6:3).

Some of the best theology found in the book of Revelation comes to us from the hymns of praise throughout the narrative. The worship wars of today can learn a lot from the hymns that are in the book of Revelation. A study of the many songs and praises would yield a plethora of examples of what our praise, both individually and corporately, should include. Theology informs our worship. Theology focuses our worship.

The wise man declared that there is nothing new under the sun, that everything has been done before (Ecclesiastes 1:9-10). And we know that God never changes (Malachi 3:6). The book of Revelation seems to have a kind of typology when it comes to the many things it addresses. Sin and idolatry in the world today are the same sin and idolatry that has always been present. God deals with sin and idolatry the same way and with the same results. The sins that are addressed in a particular way in the Old Testaments, are dealt with in a cosmic way in the book of Revelation. So, we have Babylon, the particular

city in the Middle East. Babylon is prophesied about in Isaiah and Jeremiah. In the book of Revelation, Babylon is a symbol being used for the universal, historical, and contemporary world of rebellion being judged at the return of Christ. That is why it is so important to be familiar with how God the Spirit uses the hundreds of Old Testament allusions in the book of Revelation in a cosmic dimension. There will be no surprises. We in the West are not as familiar with symbolic communication and the language of apocalyptic literature. We must do the work to understand.

The book of Revelation reveals to us just how far the world has moved away from its Creator. It is more about not being deceived, than it is about preserving our lives. The theme of the defeat and judgement of those opposed to God, opposed to the Lamb, and who have continued to persecute His saints, is given as encouragement to the saints in whatever part of history they may find themselves.

May we study the book of Revelation to be equipped, mature, prepared, and sustained.

Notes

Introduction

1. Zacharias, Ravi. "Let My People Think Broadcasts." *RZIM*. RZIM.org, n.d. Web.

2. Lennox, John. *A Series on the Acts of the Apostles*. CD. RZIM. Norcross, GA. 2010.

Chapter 1

1. Sweet, J. P. M. *Revelation*. Philadelphia: Westminster, 1979. Print. Pg.70.

2. Beale, G. K. *The Book of Revelation: A Commentary on the Greek Text*. Grand Rapids, MI: William B. Eerdmans, 2013. Print. Pg. 52.

3. Beale, G. K. *The Book of Revelation: A Commentary on the Greek Text*. Grand Rapids, MI: William B. Eerdmans, 2013. Print. Pg. 51.

4. Mounce, Robert H. *The Book of Revelation*. Grand Rapids, Mich. Eerdmans, 1997. Print. Pg. 212.

Chapter 3

1. Walvoord, John F., Philip E. Rawley, and Mark Hitchcock. *Revelation*. Chicago: Moody, 2011. Print. Pgs. 16-18.

2. As with, Aune, David E., David A. Hubbard, Glenn W. Barker, and Bruce M. Metzger. *Word Biblical Commentary*. Nashville: Nelson, 1997. Print. Pg. 105.

3. Robertson, A. T. *Word Pictures in the New Testament: Volume VI, The General Epistles and The Revelation of John*. Vol. VI. Nashville, TN: Broadman, 1933. Print. Pg. 325.

Chapter 6

1. As with, Johnson, D. E. *Triumph of the lamb: A commentary on Revelation*. Phillipsburg, NJ: P & R Pub., 2001. Print. Pg. 63.

Chapter 7

1. Aune, David E., David A. Hubbard, Glenn W. Barker, and Bruce M. Metzger. *Word Biblical Commentary*. Nashville: Nelson, 1997. Print. Pg. 240.

Chapter 9

1. Jones, Floyd Nolen. *The Chronology of the Old Testament*. Green Forest, AR: Master, 2009. Print. Pgs. 224-254.

2. Flora, Jerry. *Adults Approach "The Revelation."* St. Petersburg, FL: Brethren House Ministries, 1985. Print. Pg. 25.

Chapter 11

1. As with Aune, David E., David A. Hubbard, Glenn W. Barker, and Bruce M. Metzger. *Word Biblical Commentary*. Nashville: Nelson, 1997. Print. Pg. 442.

2. As with Caird, G. B. *The Revelation of Saint John*. Peabody, MA: Hendrickson, 1999. Print. Pg. 95.

3. As with Smalley, Stephen S. *The Revelation to John: A Commentary on the Greek Text of the Apocalypse*. Downers Grove, IL: InterVarsity, 2005. Print. Pgs. 186-187.

4. Kittel, Gerhard, Bromiley, Geoffrey William, Ed. and Tr, and Gerhard Friedrich. *Theological Dictionary of the New Testament*. *10 Vols*. Grand Rapids, MI: Eerdmans, 2006. Print.

5. As with Beale, G. K., and D. A. Carson. "Revelation." *Commentary on the New Testament Use of the Old Testament*. Grand Rapids, Mich.: Baker Academic, 2009. 1081-1161. Print. Pgs. 1106-1107.

Chapter 12

1. Rosenberg, A. J. *Daniel; Ezra; Nehemiah: A New English Translation*. New York: Judaica, 1991. Print. Pgs. 109-110.

2. Aune, David E., David A. Hubbard, Glenn W. Barker, and Bruce M. Metzger. *Word Biblical Commentary*. Nashville: Nelson, 1997. Print. Pg. 510.

Chapter 14

1. Bauckham, Richard. *The Climax of Prophecy: Studies on the Book of Revelation*. London: T&T Clark, 2005. Print.

2. Aune, David E., David A. Hubbard, Glenn W. Barker, and Bruce M. Metzger. *Word Biblical Commentary*. Nashville: Nelson, 1997. Print. Pg. 620.

Chapter 15

1. Shaffer, Todd. "Don Carson's 26 Messages on Revelation." *Faith by Hearing*. TGC, 31 July 2012. Web. 18 July 2017.

Chapter 16

1. As with Hoeksema, Herman, and Homer C. Hoeksema. *Behold, He Cometh! An Exposition of the Book of Revelation*. Grandville, MI: Reformed Free Pub. Association, 2000. Print.

2. Shaffer, Todd. "Don Carson's 26 Messages on Revelation." *Faith by Hearing*. TGC, 31 July 2012. Web. 18 July 2017.

Chapter 19

1. Johnson, D. E. *Triumph of the lamb: A commentary on Revelation*. Phillipsburg, NJ: P & R Pub., 2001. Print. Pg. 246.

Chapter 21

1. Clouse, Robert G., et al. *The Meaning of the Millennium: Four Views*. InterVarsity Press, 1977. Pages 49-50.

2. As with Clouse, Robert G., et al. *The Meaning of the Millennium: Four Views*. InterVarsity Press, 1977. Pg. 171.

3. Weinrich, William C., and Thomas C. Oden. *Ancient Christian Commentary on Scripture: New Testament*. Vol. XII. Downers Grove, IL: InterVarsity, 2005. Print.

4. Augustine, and Marcus Dods. *The City of God*. Peabody, MA: Hendrickson, 2011. Print.

Chapter 22

1. Against Ironside, H. A. *Revelation: An Ironside Expository Commentary*. Grand Rapids: Kregel, 2004. Print. Pg. 184.

2. As with Hoeksema, Herman, and Homer C. Hoeksema. *Behold, He Cometh! An Exposition of the Book of Revelation*. Grandville, MI: Reformed Free Pub. Association, 2000. Print. PG. 696.

3. Smalley, Stephen S. *The Revelation to John: A Commentary on the Greek Text of the Apocalypse*. Downers Grove, IL: InterVarsity, 2005. Print.

Chapter 23

1. As with, Johnson, D. E. *Triumph of the lamb: A commentary on Revelation*. Phillipsburg, NJ: P & R Pub., 2001. Print. Pg. 330.

Appendix D

1. Begg, Alistair. "Truth for Life - The Bible-Teaching Ministry of Alistair Begg." *1 & 2 Thessalonians*. TruthforLife.org, 1995. Web.

2. Hoeksema, Herman, and Homer C. Hoeksema. *Behold, He Cometh! An Exposition of the Book of Revelation*. Grandville, MI: Reformed Free Pub. Association, 2000. Print. Back cover.

3. Begg, Alistair. *What is the Church?* CD. Truth for Life.org. Cleveland, Ohio. 2002.

Appendix E

1. Young, Robert. *Young's Analytical Concordance to the Bible*. Peabody, MA: Hendrickson, 2008. Print.

2. Kittel, Gerhard, Bromiley, Geoffrey William, Ed. and Tr., and Gerhard Friedrich. *Theological Dictionary of the New Testament. 10 Vols*. Grand Rapids, MI: Eerdmans, 2006. Print.

3. As does Tsarfati, Amir, and Rick Yohn. *Revealing Revelation*. Eugene, OR: Harvest House, 2022. Print.

Appendix F

1. Zacharias, Ravi. "Let My People Think Broadcasts." *RZIM*. RZIM.org, n.d. Web.

Charts/Diagrams/Comparisons/Text Tables

Bibliography of Study References

Augustine, and Marcus Dods. *The City of God*. Peabody, MA: Hendrickson, 2011. Print.

Brenton, Lancelot Charles Lee. *The Septuagint with Apocrypha: Greek and English*. Peabody, MA: Hendrickson, 2007. Print.

Comfort, Philip Wesley., and Walter A. Elwell. *Tyndale Bible Dictionary*. Wheaton, IL: Tyndale House, 2001. Print.

Goodrick, Edward W., and John R. Kohlenberger. *The NIV Exhaustive Concordance*. Grand Rapids, MI: Zondervan Pub. House, 1990. Print.

Green, Jay P. *The Interlinear Bible: Hebrew - Greek - English: with Strong's Concordance Numbers above Each Word*. 2nd Edition ed., Hendrickson Publishers, 2008.

Grenz, Stanley J., David Guretzki, and Cherith Fee. Nordling. *Pocket Dictionary of Theological Terms*. Downers Grove, IL: InterVarsity, 1999. Print.

Harris, R. Laird, Gleason Leonard Archer, and Bruce K. Waltke. *Theological Wordbook of the Old Testament*. Chicago: Moody, 1980. Print.

HCSB Study Bible, Holman Christian Standard Bible: God's Word for Life. Nashville, TN: Holman Bible., 2010. Print.

Josephus, Flavius, *The Complete Works of Flavius Josephus*. Translated by William Whiston. Nashville, TN: T. Nelson, 1998. Print.

Kittel, Gerhard, Bromiley, Geoffrey William, Ed. and Tr., and Gerhard Friedrich. *Theological Dictionary of the New Testament. 10 Vols*. Grand Rapids, MI: Eerdmans, 2006. Print.

MacArthur, John. *The MacArthur Study Bible: New King James Version*. Nashville: Word Bibles, 1997. Print.

Marshall, Alfred. *The New International Version Interlinear Greek-English New Testament: the Nestle Greek Text with a Literal English Translation by Alfred Marshall, and a Foreword by J.B. Phillips, Also a Marginal Text of the New International Version*. Zondervan, 1976.

NIV Study Bible: New International Version. Grand Rapids, MI: Zondervan, 1985. Print.

Sproul, R. C., and Keith A. Mathison. *The Reformation Study Bible: English Standard Version, Containing the Old and New Testaments*. Orlando, FL: Ligonier Ministries, 2005. Print.

Strong, James, John R. Kohlenberger, and James A. Swanson. *The Strongest Strong's Exhaustive Concordance of the Bible*. Grand Rapids, MI: Zondervan, 2001. Print.

Tenney, Merrill C. Editor. *The Zondervan Pictorial Encyclopedia of the Bible: 5 Vols*. Grand Rapids: Zondervan, 1976. Print.

The Ryrie Study Bible: New American Standard Translation with Introductions, Annotations, Outlines .... Chicago: Moody, 1978. Print.

Ussher, James. *The Annals of the World*. Larry Pierce, and Marion Pierce. Green Forest, AR: Master, 2007. Print.

Verbrugge, Verlyn D. *New International Dictionary of New Testament Theology: Abridged Edition*. Grand Rapids, MI: Zondervan, 2000. Print.

Vine, W. E., John R. Kohlenberger, and James A. Swanson. *The Expanded Vine's Expository Dictionary of New Testament Words*. Minneapolis, MN: Bethany House, 1984. Print.

Young, Robert. *Young's Analytical Concordance to the Bible*. Peabody, MA: Hendrickson, 2008. Print.

Zodhiates, Spiros, and James Strong. *The Hebrew-Greek Key Study Bible.* Grand Rapids, MI: Baker Book House, 1984. Print.

Bibliography of Reading References

Anderson, Robert. *The Coming Prince*. Grand Rapids, MI: Kregel Classics, 2008. Print.

Anderson, Robert. *The Lord from Heaven*. Grand Rapids, MI: Kregel Classics, 1978. Print.

Archer, Gleason L. *Three Views on the Rapture: Pre-, Mid-, or Post-Tribulation?* Grand Rapids, MI: Zondervan, 1996. Print.

Aune, David E., David A. Hubbard, Glenn W. Barker, and Bruce M. Metzger. *Word Biblical Commentary*. Nashville: Nelson, 1997. Print.

Barclay, William. *The Revelation of John*. Louisville, KY: Westminster John Knox, 2004. Print.

Bauckham, Richard. *The Climax of Prophecy: Studies on the Book of Revelation*. London: T&T Clark, 2005. Print.

Bauckham, Richard. *The Theology of the Book of Revelation*. Cambridge, United Kingdom: Cambridge UP, 2015. Print.

Beale, G. K. *The Book of Revelation: A Commentary on the Greek Text*. Grand Rapids, MI: William B. Eerdmans, 2013. Print.

Beale, G. K., and D. A. Carson. "Revelation." *Commentary on the New Testament Use of the Old Testament*. Grand Rapids, Mich.: Baker Academic, 2009. 1081-1161. Print.

Bewes, R. *The Lamb wins!: A guided tour through the Book of Revelation*. Fearn, Ross-shire: Christian Focus Publications, 2000. Print.

Branham, William Marion. *An Exposition of the Seven Church Ages*. Jeffersonville, IN: Voice of God Recordings, 2005. Print.

Bullinger, E. W. *Commentary on Revelation*. Grand Rapids, MI: Kregel Pubns., 1984. Print.

Bullinger, E. W. *Number in Scripture: Its Supernatural Design and Spiritual Significance*. Grand Rapids, MI: Kregel, 1988. Print.

Caird, G. B. *The Revelation of Saint John*. Peabody, MA: Hendrickson, 1999. Print.

Caird, G. B. *The Language and Imagery of the Bible*. Philadelphia: Westminster, 1980. Print.

Clouse, Robert G., et al. *The Meaning of the Millennium: Four Views*. InterVarsity Press, 1977.

Collins, Adela Yarbro. *The Apocalypse*. Collegeville, MN: The Liturgical Press, 1990. Print.

Darby, J. N. *Notes on the Book of the Revelation: To Assist Enquirers in Searching into That Book*. Lexington, KY: First Rate, 2017. Print.

Duck, Daymond R. *The Book of Revelation*. Nashville, TN: Nelson, 2006. Print.

Erickson, Millard J. *Christian Theology*. Grand Rapids, Mich: Baker Book House, 1985. Print.

Flora, Jerry. *Adults Approach "The Revelation."* St. Petersburg, FL: Brethren House Ministries, 1985. Print.

Fitch, Alger M. *Revelation*. Cincinnati, OH: Standard Publishing. Print.

Gregg, Steve. *Revelation, Four Views: A Parallel Commentary*. Nashville, TN: Nelson, 1997. Print.

Guthrie, Donald, J. A. Motyer, D. J. Wiseman, and Alan M. Stibbs. *The Eerdmans Bible Commentary*. Grand Rapids, MI: W.B. Eerdmans Pub., 1989. Print.

Guthrie, Donald. *New Testament Theology*. Leicester: Inter-Varsity, 1981. Print.

Hemer, Colin J. *The Letters to the Seven Churches of Asia in Their Local Setting*. Grand Rapids, Mich.: William B. Eerdmans, 2001. Print.

Hendriksen, W. *More than conquerors: An interpretation of the Book of Revelation*. Grand Rapids: Baker Books, 2015. Print.

Henry, Matthew, and Leslie F. Church. "New Testament." *Matthew Henry's Commentary in One Volume: Genesis to Revelation*. Grand Rapids, MI: Zondervan Pub. House, 1960. 1203-986. Print.

Hislop, Alexander. *The Two Babylons*. Neptune, NJ: Loizeaux Bros., 1959. Print.

Hitchcock, Mark. *The End: A Complete Overview of Bible Prophecy and the End of Days*. Carol Stream, IL: Tyndale House, 2012. Print.

Hitchcock, Mark. *Who Is the Antichrist?* Eugene, Or.: Harvest House, 2011. Print.

Hoeksema, Herman, and Homer C. Hoeksema. *Behold, He Cometh! An Exposition of the Book of Revelation*. Grandville, MI: Reformed Free Pub. Association, 2000. Print.

Hunt, Dave. *A Woman Rides the Beast: The Roman Catholic Church and the Last Days*. Eugene, OR: Harvest House, 1994. Print.

Ironside, H. A. *Revelation: An Ironside Expository Commentary*. Grand Rapids, MI: Kregel, 2004. Print.

Jeremiah, David. *Escape the Coming Night: Messages from the Book of Revelation. 4 Vol.* Turning Point Ministries. San Diego, CA. 1994.

Jeremiah, David. *The Book of Signs*. Nashville, TN: W Publishing, 2019. Print.

Johnson, D. E. *Triumph of the lamb: A commentary on Revelation*. Phillipsburg, NJ: P & R Pub., 2001. Print

Jones, Floyd Nolen. *The Chronology of the Old Testament*. Green Forest, AR: Master, 2009. Print.

Juster, Daniel C. *Revelation: The Passover Key: An Interpretation of the Book of Revelation*. Shippensburg, PA: Destiny Image, 1991. Print.

Kline, Meredith G. *God, Heaven and Har Magedon: A Covenantal Tale of Cosmos and Telos*. Eugene, OR: Wipf & Stock Publishers, 2006. Print.

Ladd, George Eldon. *A Commentary on the Revelation of John*. Grand Rapids, Mich.: William B. Eerdmans, 1972. Print.

Lee, Pilchan. *The New Jerusalem in the Book of Revelation*. Gulde-Druck: Tubingen, Germany, 2001. Print.

MacArthur, John. *Revelation: The Christian's Ultimate Victory*. Nashville: Thomas Nelson, 2007. Print.

McCutcheon, Lillie S. *The Symbols Speak: An Exposition of the Revelation*. Newton Falls, OH: n.p., 1964. Print.

McGee, J. Vernon (John Vernon). *Thru the Bible with J. Vernon McGee, Volume 5*. Nashville, TN: Thomas Nelson, 1983. 876-1080. Print.

Morris, Leon. *The Tyndale New Testament Commentaries*. Leicester: Inter-Varsity, 1987. Print.

Mounce, Robert H. *The Book of Revelation*. Grand Rapids, Mich. Eerdmans, 1997. Print.

Newton, Isaac, and Benjamin Smith. *Observations upon the Prophecies of Daniel, and the Apocalypse of St. John*. N.p.: ReadaClassic.com, 2010. Print.

Newton, Isaac, Larry Pierce, and Marion Pierce. *Newton Revised History of Ancient Kingdoms: A Complete Chronology*. Green Forest, AR: Master, 2009. Print.

Osborne, Grant R. *Revelation Verse by Verse*. Bellingham, WA: Lexham, 2016. Print.

Phillips, J. B. *The Book of Revelation - A New Translation of the Apocalypse*. New York, NY: MacMillan, 1957. Print.

Ramsay, and Mark W. Wilson. *The Letters to the Seven Churches*. Peabody, MA: Hendrickson, 1994. Print.

Rhodes, Ron. *The 8 Great Debates of Bible Prophecy*. Eugene Oregon: Harvest House, 2014. Print.

Riddlebarger, Kim. *A Case for Amillennialism: Understanding the End times*. Grand Rapids: Baker, 2013. Print.

Robertson, A. T. *Word Pictures in the New Testament: Volume VI, The General Epistles and The Revelation of John*. Vol. VI. Nashville, TN: Broadman, 1933. Print.

Rosenberg, A. J. *Daniel; Ezra; Nehemiah: A New English Translation*. New York: Judaica, 1991. Print.

Rosenthal, Marvin J. *The Pre-wrath Rapture of the Church*. Nashville: T. Nelson, 1990. Print.

Showers, Renald E. *The Coming Apocalypse: A Study of Replacement Theology vs. God's Faithfulness in the End-times*. Bellmawr, NJ: Friends of Israel Gospel Ministry, 2009. Print.

Smalley, Stephen S. *The Revelation to John: A Commentary on the Greek Text of the Apocalypse*. Downers Grove, IL: InterVarsity, 2005. Print.

Sproul, R. C. *The Last Days According to Jesus*. Grand Rapids, MI: Baker, 1998. Print.

Stevenson, Kenneth, Michael Glerup, and Thomas C. Oden. *Ancient Christian Commentary on Scripture: Old Testament*. Downers Grove, IL: Inter-Varsity, 2008. Print.

Stott, John R. W., Dale Larsen, and Sandy Larsen. *Revelation: The Triumph of Christ: 12 Studies with Commentary for Individuals or Groups*. Nottingham: Inter-Varsity, 2008. Print.

Sweet, J. P. M. *Revelation*. Philadelphia: Westminster, 1979. Print.

Swete, Henry Barclay. *Commentary on Revelation: The Greek Text with Introduction Notes and Indexes*. Grand Rapids, MI: Kregel, 1977. Print.

Tsarfati, Amir, and Rick Yohn. *Revealing Revelation*. Eugene, OR: Harvest House, 2022. Print.

Walvoord, John F., Philip E. Rawley, and Mark Hitchcock. *Revelation*. Chicago: Moody, 2011. Print.

Weinrich, William C., and Thomas C. Oden. *Ancient Christian Commentary on Scripture: New Testament*. Vol. XII. Downers Grove, IL: InterVarsity, 2005. Print.

Wesley, John. *Revelation Explanatory Notes & Commentary*. Lexington, KY: Hargreaves, 2017. Print.

Wiersbe, Warren W. *Be Victorious: In Christ, You Are an Overcomer*. Colorado Springs, CO: David C. Cook, 2008. Print.

Wiersbe, Warren W. *Revelation: In Christ, You Are an Overcomer*. Colorado Springs, CO: David C Cook, 2011. Print.

Wood, Shane J., Editor. *Dragons, John, and Every Grain of Sand: Essays on the Book of Revelation*. College Press Publishing Co., 2011. Print.

Wright, N. T., and Kristie Berglund. *Revelation: 22 Studies for Individuals and Groups*. Downers Grove, IL: IVP Connect, 2012. Print.

Bibliography of Audio/Visual Resources

Begg, Alistair. "Truth for Life - The Bible-Teaching Ministry of Alistair Begg." *1 & 2 Thessalonians*. TruthforLife.org, 1995. Web.

Begg, Alistair. *What is the Church?* CD. Truth for Life.org. Cleveland, Ohio. 2002.

Courson, John. *Revelation*. Searchlight Ministry. Mp3. Jacksonville, OR. 2004.

Davey, Stephen. *The Book of Revelation*. Mp3. Wisdom for the Heart.

Heitzig, Skip. *History's Last Chapter.* CD. Connections Communications. Albuquerque, NM. 1996.

Lennox, John. *A Series on the Acts of the Apostles*. CD. RZIM. Norcross, GA. 2010.

MacDonald, James. *Revelation*. CD. Walk in The Word. Elgin, IL. 2010.

Missler, Chuck. *The Book of Daniel: An Expository Commentary.* CD. Koinonia House. Coeur d'Alene, ID. 2004.

Missler, Chuck. *The Book of Revelation: An Expository Commentary.* CD. Koinonia House. Coeur d'Alene, ID. 2005.

Shaffer, Todd. "Don Carson's 26 Messages on Revelation." *Faith by Hearing*. TGC, 31 July 2012. Web. 18 July 2017.

Stone, Perry. *Breaking the Apocalypse Code*. Video. Voice of Evangelism. Cleveland, TN. 2012.

Swindoll, Charles R. *Revelation: Unveiling the End*. 3 Vols. CD. Insight for Living, Plano, TX., 2003.

Zacharias, Ravi. *"Let My People Think Broadcasts." RZIM*. RZIM.org, n.d. Web.

www.ingramcontent.com/pod-product-compliance
Lightning Source LLC
Chambersburg PA
CBHW081148090426
42736CB00017B/3226